Kabir Mohabbat and Leah McInnis: Delivering Osama:
The Story of America's Secret Envoy

First Draft Publishing/*Primary*

Kabir Mohabbat and Leah McInnis: Delivering Osama: The Story of America's Secret Envoy
Graeme Smith: Foreword

First published in English in Germany in 2020
by First Draft Publishing GmbH,

ISBN 978-3-944214-31-3 *(softcover)*
ISBN 978-3-944214-30-6 *(kindle)*
ISBN 978-3-944214-29-0 *(epub)*

Cover Photography: © Philip Poupin
www.philippoupin.fr
Typefaces: Heimat Mono *www.atlasfonts.com* & Arnhem
www.ourtype.be

First Draft Publishing GmbH, Berlin

www.firstdraft-publishing.com
info@firstdraft-publishing.com

To:
Kabir's Family
&
Mrs. Phyllis Oakley
& Don Woodward

And To:
Garland Deen "Mack" McInnis, Jr.

*"Once you crush the head of a snake,
the rest will die by itself."*

William Milam
United States Ambassador
to Pakistan

Table of Contents

Graeme Smith:
Foreword

American leaders started the war in Afghanistan with loud declarations that they would get Osama bin Laden and smash the Taliban regime that sheltered him. U.S. officials have been quieter about their covert negotiations with the Taliban before and after September 11, 2001, for help with killing or capturing the Al-Qaeda leader. With a sanguine perspective years later, any reasonable observer could see that negotiating for bin Laden—if successful—would have been less destructive than kicking off the longest war in American history, a conflict that today ranks as the deadliest war in the world. Nobody in the United States was feeling cool-headed at the time, however, and few had the stomach for bargaining with the simple mullahs who headed a pariah regime in one of the world's poorest countries. The ruins of New York towers were still smouldering when the U.S. halted negotiations and invaded.

Guessing the alternative paths of history is a fraught exercise, and it's impossible to prove that different choices would have had better results. If the Americans had cut a deal with the Taliban to get rid of the Al-Qaeda leader before 9/11, could they have averted the tragedy? If they reached agreement in the tense aftermath, could they have prevented thousands of subsequent tragedies in Afghanistan? There are no academically rigorous answers to such questions, but that does not ease the gnawing doubts.

Most of the players involved in the war have their own questions like this, about missed opportunities for steering away from disaster. Retired American generals will say that overwhelming numbers of U.S. troops should have been deployed earlier, or should not have been distracted by a parallel mission in Iraq. Retired American diplomats will say the post-invasion political order should have included the Taliban and other conservative Islamist factions, as a way of bolstering the legitimacy of the new authorities in Kabul. Such prominent commentators usually indicate regret about how the war was conducted, rather than rethinking why U.S. forces were necessary in the first place.

Perhaps fundamental questions about the origins of the war deserve greater attention. America invaded Afghanistan back in the days when the U.S. enjoyed a short-lived position as the sole dominant power in the world, flush with wealth after a long stretch of economic growth, easily capable of persuading allies to contribute tens of thousands of soldiers and billions of dollars to its campaigns. The idea of attacking a landlocked country on the other side of the planet, dismissing the government, and setting up a democracy modelled after Western systems seemed like a reasonable project. But the world has changed, even as the Afghan war grinds on, and it's now hard to imagine European governments showing the same enthusiasm for another U.S. adventure. China and Russian might not show as much patience next time the United States wants to set up large military bases on their doorsteps. American taxpayers who drive over potholes on their daily commutes are feeling more resistant to the idea of sending money to faraway lands to pay for roads, bridges, and other fundamentals of state-building.

Voices from the left and right of the political spectrum in Western countries are increasingly skeptical of endless wars. As U.S. power fades, there is growing demand for subtler solutions—not about how to win a war like the Afghan conflict, but how to avoid such a morass. Even if academics are loathe to play the parlour game of alternative histories, in other words, Western officials and policy experts will be taking a hard look at their governments' bruising experiences in Afghanistan and asking how things could have turned out differently.

Any serious effort to examine the failed diplomacy leading to war will require reading this quirky little memoir from Kabir Mohabbat. His text has been circulating for years as a kind of samizdat among veteran observers of Afghanistan, and his wild story has gained credibility among some of them. In these pages Mohabbat emerges as a gung-ho Texan businessman from a prominent Afghan family who is bad at writing, awful at turning a profit, and unreliable as a narrator—but indispensable as a witness to history.

Mohabbat dumps years of meeting notes, hotel receipts, and other evidence into the historical debates about whether there was a viable option of negotiating for bin Laden. In his telling, he served as an unofficial liaison between the Taliban and U.S. governments, trying to resolve the problem of bin Laden's presence in Afghanistan. Mohabbat says he wanted to improve bilateral relations between the two countries as a way of smoothing a path toward development of Afghan oil resources and making himself rich. His central argument is that the Taliban tried to give up the Al-Qaeda leader but the U.S. waffled and missed the chance to stop 9/11. After the attacks, he claims, the Americans failed to make a serious effort toward diplomacy.

It is unclear whether the protagonists of the Afghan drama took Mohabbat seriously. The official account in "The 9/11 Commission Report" makes only cursory references to his dialogue efforts. Still, Mohabbat appears to have enjoyed significant access to the Taliban at critical moments. On the morning after 9/11, he received a call from Mullah Akhtar Osmani, a senior Taliban figure, who put the phone on speaker mode so he could speak with the regime's leadership. The Taliban were dumbfounded by the attacks and skeptical that their Arab guests could have pulled it off.

They asked the Texan businessman to switch on CNN in his hotel room and translate into Pashto, because the mullahs shunned television and did not have access to international news. The Taliban were stunned that man-made objects such as the Twin Towers could have existed. The scale of the towers defied the imaginations of men who spent most of their lives in mud-walled village huts.

The Taliban became more worldly in the following years, as they survived an onslaught from the most powerful armies in human history. Year after year, they chipped away at the territory and legitimacy of the U.S.-backed government in Kabul. Western powers eventually realized they would not defeat the Taliban on the battlefield, and in 2018 the United States opened its first publicly acknowledged negotiations with the Taliban insurgents on the withdrawal of U.S. forces. As the peace talks progressed, it was striking how the conversations mirrored some of the discussions that Mohabbat witnessed two decades ago. Then as now, the U.S. was focused on threats from small bands of extremists. The Taliban continued to offer themselves as a bulwark against the dangers emanating from Afghanistan. The two sides continued to mistrust each other, struggling to bridge a gulf of misunderstanding. The negotiators encountered each other like emissaries from different worlds.

As of this writing, diplomacy continues.

Graeme Smith
October 2019

Preface

I, M. Kabir Mohabbat, acted as a secret diplomatic envoy from the United States Government to the government of the Taliban in Afghanistan. My first trip was in June 1999. My last trip began on September 3, 2001. The purpose of the trips eventually became to arrange for the delivery of Osama bin Laden into the hands of the United States using diplomatic channels. I was successful. Toward the end of February 2001, the Taliban put bin Laden under house arrest for the U.S. It was the job of the U.S. to go get him. The U.S. never acted. Why? After September 11, 2001, I helped negotiate the capitulation of the stubborn Afghan Government to U.S. demands.

This is a narrative of my attempts to secure Osama bin Laden for the U.S., but it is also an insider's look at the reclusive Taliban.

M.K.M.

Since the inception of this project, Kabir and I have done our best to recreate and to record, as accurately as possible, the events that occurred in countless meetings and communiqués among private individuals and government representatives in both Afghanistan and the United States over a period of years. Whenever possible, Kabir contacted others present at meetings to refresh his memory of events. He also relied upon photographic, video and written documentation during the writing of this work, so he could provide the reader with an accurate rendition of events.

For my part, I have attempted to interject my own voice as little as possible into Kabir's words and to render faithfully into writing the unfolding of Kabir's experiences as they were told to me. Because many of the conversations revealed in this book actually occurred in the Pashto and Farsi languages, and because English is not Kabir's native language, I have, out of necessity, exercised some linguistic editing to make the text and his story clearer. The substance and the meaning of Kabir's story, however, are his alone.

L.M.

Full size images of all original documents and pictures displayed in this book can be found here: https://www.firstdraft-publishing.com/osama

Chapter 1: My Sometime Career as a Mujahid

On September 16, 2001, I was present at the meeting of representatives of the United States and the United Emirate of Afghanistan (the Taliban) in Quetta, Pakistan. The meeting was about the world's most feared terrorist, Osama bin Laden. I wondered how I got entangled in the complex negotiations between the most powerful country in the world and the stubborn Taliban. At four o'clock in the morning when the difficult negotiations ground to a halt, I sat and marveled at how far events had taken me since I first stepped on to U.S. soil in 1974 as an eighteen year old university student. I wondered whether I had chosen this path or whether it was a God-given destiny.

I am a Pashtun, the largest ethnic group in Afghanistan. My family is from the Jaji Tribe in the province of Paktia near Afghanistan's border with Pakistan. I am descended from a long line of tribal chiefs. As a chief's son, participating in politics and in diplomacy were my birthright. Unfortunately, warfare was also part of my birthright. My country has been in a perpetual state of war for centuries.

My father, Allah Mir Khan, was chief of the Jaji Tribe in the 1920's. My family became known as "king makers" when my dad helped put General Mohammed Nader of the royal family on the throne in 1929. Within four years Nadar was assassinated and his son, Mohammad Zahir, became Shah. My family's position in the world rose with the star of Zahir. He ruled the country for forty years until he was overthrown by his cousin Mohammad Dauod in 1973. Then the communists invaded Afghanistan and all hell broke loose. But I get ahead of myself.

I was born in Kabul on October 10, 1956. Because of my father, we had political influence. While growing up in Kabul, our house near the Soviet Embassy was full of guests and government officials. As a boy it was often my duty to serve food and tea to our guests. I soon realized that it was easy for me to chat with everyone who entered our house, no matter how high ranking. For a young boy growing up protected by a loving mother and father and nine older siblings, transgressions were swiftly forgiven and forgotten. Life was good!

Because it was customary in my family to go to the U.S. for higher education, I was told to go. I fought against it, but my family won. My academic career began with English classes in St. Louis. I would later graduate from Southeastern Missouri State in December 1979, with a degree in Political Science.

As a favor to the king, my family became involved in diplomatic and educational contacts with the U.S. Naturally after the Soviets invaded Afghanistan in 1979, the U.S. offered us a place to live making it easy to become part of the U.S.'s resources when it sent aid to the mujahidin freedom fighters.

Even though I no longer lived in Afghanistan, years later when the U.S. realized that it needed a bridge to the Afghan Government of the Taliban, it was easy for me to volunteer and for U.S. officials to accept my help. I possessed knowledge of the U.S. and the Pashtun cultures (from which the Taliban arose), and had existing relationships with many American businessmen and government officials.

After King Zahir was deposed in 1973 by his cousin, the Soviet Union worked to tighten its political grip on Afghanistan. Without the steadying influence of the king at the head the government, Soviet policies ate away at destabilized Afghanistan as easily as termites feasting on a fallen log.

From India in May 1979, my brother Omar Mohabbat, a doctor in Kabul, called me at the university to explain that he had left Afghanistan for good. The Soviets had imprisoned him for ten days because of his position as the Deputy Administer of Education. Once imprisoned, Omar began plotting his escape from Afghanistan. Soon after his release, Omar asked for permission to leave Kabul to attend a medical conference in India. Soviet officials were confident that Omar would return because he left behind his wife, children and family, but he had no intention of returning.

Once out of Afghanistan, Omar set to work freeing the rest of the family. He explained over the phone that he had heard that over seventy members of the Mujaddedi's, another prominent family, had been killed by the Soviets. He didn't want our family to be among the missing and the dead. It was time for everyone to leave the country – by whatever means possible.

Omar made plans with our brother Sayad, a Colonel of the Afghan Army, for everyone's evacuation. Sayad divided the twenty-five members of our immediate family into two groups and negotiated with smugglers separately to take each group out of Afghanistan. All possessions were to be left behind in Kabul. Each person was allowed to take what he or she could carry on their backs over the mountains into Pakistan.

Dressed as nomads, one group made its way to the border town of Torkhum. The other group traveled to the town of Jaji in the Paktia Province and then went into Pakistan. Those traveling through Paktia encountered great hardships because there were no roads. They hiked through desolate mountains for five days and nights with little food, water or rest before reaching Pakistan.

During the forced march over the mountains, my brother Sayad was unable to help them. Before our family left Kabul, a Soviet Army death squad had begun searching for him. Warned about the danger, Sayad escaped to the rugged mountains of Afghanistan's eastern border with Pakistan.

When Soviets came to his house, his wife told the officers that he was in Mazar-e-Sharif on personal business. Sayad lived in mountain caves for weeks before it was safe to walk to the city of Peshawar.

The town of Peshawar in Pakistan's northwest frontier became my displaced family's new home. I wanted to join them, but my older brothers wouldn't allow it. They wanted me to finish at the university. Mid-December 1979, I graduated from Southeast Missouri State University with a degree in Political Science.

On December 27, the Soviets invaded Afghanistan to support the Soviet backed Democratic Republic of Afghanistan. When told that Afghanistan had been invaded by the Soviet Army, I knew that my plans to be a diplomat had ended and that eventually I must return to Afghanistan and become a mujahidin. I didn't know that it would take nine years for them to leave.

My brother Omar suggested that I visit Don Woodward, an old family friend living in Washington, D.C. Before leaving the U.S., Woodward, a career diplomat, acted as advisor to the American Embassy in Afghanistan during the early 1970's. I had not seen him for years. Interested in obtaining financial and material support for the mujahidin, Omar hoped Don would help.

Don guided me to the right people. He set up a meeting with Mrs. Hicks, the Director of the Afghanistan Desk at the U.S. State Department. I pleaded with her to ask U.S. authorities to help the Afghan freedom fighters. She said, "No." Officially, the U.S. did not want to create animosity between itself and the Soviets over Afghanistan. I had assumed that the U.S. would jump at the opportunity to fight its longtime Cold War nemeses by proxy.

Getting nowhere with Mrs. Hicks, Don suggested that I meet with Douglas Archer, the American Counselor General assigned to Peshawar, the city where my family now lived. He explained that Archer's current assignment with the

State Department was to assist the mujahidin leaders exiled in Peshawar.

Meeting Archer sounded promising. Once we met, I explained that I was from a large family of tribal fighters and that my brother Sayad had been a Colonel in the King Zabin's Afghan Army. Archer wanted a meeting in his compound in Peshawar with my brothers, any Army officers we could collect, and the chiefs of the local tribes as soon as he returned to Pakistan.

By late January 1980, ten of us stood in Counselor General Archer's compound in Peshawar. My brother Sayad, his friend Mohammad Gull of the Afghan Air Force, a few other Army officers, and some of the chiefs of the local tribes. We were surprised to learn that the U.S. Government supported many different groups of mujahidin chosen for major roles in fighting the Soviets.

The *Jabha-i-Najat Milli Afghanistan* party of Mr. Sibghatullah Mujaddedi and the *Mahaz-e-Milli* party of Mr. Pir Sayed Ahmad Gailani were the most moderate. Together they contained many career bureaucrats from the Afghan Government in office when the Soviets invaded. Eventually Gailani would be labeled the most moderate of all of the mujahidin leaders; some called his group the *Gucci mujahidin*. Related to the deposed King by marriage, Gailani had been educated in the West. His group advocated the return of King Zahir to Afghanistan. Because of this stance, Gailani's party would remain chronically unrecognized and underfunded by the nations willing to subsidize groups of Afghan freedom fighters. They would receive little help from Pakistan, the United States or Saudi Arabia.

These were just two of the groups formed to fight the Soviets. There were others. A party considered to be traditional or moderate was the *Harakat Inquilabi-Islami* party of Mr. Maulana Mohammed Nabi Mohammedi. It gathered support from moderate religious leaders. Mullah Omar would eventually become a member of this political party.

Groups supported by radical mullahs were the *Hizb-e-Islami* party founded by Mr. Younis Khalis and the radical *Jamiat-i-Islami* party of Mr. Burhanuddin Rabbani. The later party would eventually come to dominate much of northern Afghanistan. Rabbani's deputy, Ahmad Shah Massood, would prove to be the most successful tactician of the Soviet war. Rabbani's group would eventually come to be called the Northern Alliance and Massood would be killed by suicide bomber dressed as a journalist only days before September 11, 2001.

The most radical of the political parties was the fundamentalist party, *Ittehad-e-Islami*. It would take a long time for it to become popular among the muj (mujahidin) because it expounded the extreme Islamic sect *Wahabbism*. This is the brand of Islam practiced in Saudi Arabia, which, at that time, wasn't palatable to most home grown Afghans because of its rigidity. It later found a following among young male Afghans whose families, when escaping the Soviets, had been forced to raise their children in refugee camps on the Pakistan border. Those parents' only choice for education in the camps were the *madrassas* (religious schools) founded and funded by the Saudis and teaching only Wahabbism.

The seventh War Lord, Gulbuddin Hekmatyar, is discussed in full in the next chapter.

Each of the groups fighting the Soviets had headquarters in Peshawar. Each of the groups vied for the international community's military, diplomatic and monetary support.

Like the other political parties, Sibghatullah Mujaddedi's group included a military wing to do the fighting and a political wing to spread the word about its fighting and victories to win converts to its cause. My brothers decided to work with the three moderate political groups that supported the former King, but officially Omar and Sayad joined only the *Jabha-i-Najat Milli Afghanistan* party of Mr. Mujaddedi. Like my brothers, I, too, joined Mujaddedi's group as a volunteer, but later I would become the Director of the Foreign

Relations Office for the *Mahaz-e-Milli* party of Mr. Pir Sayed Ahmad Gailani.

Each of my brothers administered a branch of Mujaddedi's organization: Omar acted as Director of Public Relations and Sayad acted as Mujaddedi's personal military advisor. Sayad also headed all military actions taken in the Province of Paktia for any of the groups fighting the Soviets there. While working with Mujaddedi's organization, my brothers actively sought outside military and political support for those fighting in Afghanistan.

My brother, Sayad, explained to Counselor General Archer that the men covertly supported by the U.S. were referred to as the "seven thieves" among our people. They were artificial leaders created by Pakistan and that none of them were natural Afghan leaders. My brother also pointed out that having many different leaders divided the people into too many ethnic groups. Sayad argued that too many divisions could create problems between the minorities.

At that time, we didn't know that Pakistan had forced a restriction on international aid to the freedom fighters and had chosen the groups that would receive aid. We would later learn that the Pakistan government's leadership plan for Afghanistan did not include a consolidated Afghan front working across its border which could cause problems for it later. A weakened, fragmented Afghanistan was in Pakistan's best interests.

We argued with Archer to reduce the number of groups to one, two or three, but the Counselor General assured us that the decision was out of his hands. He had been ordered to help only certain organizations. If we wanted to join a group, he could help us. Otherwise, we were on our own and we could not contact him directly for financial support. For hours our delegation tried to convince him not to support the fundamentalists, but to no effect.

In the meeting we did win one point, Archer agreed not to send any troops or army officers into our group's war zone.

We explained that we had plenty of soldiers and didn't need any outsiders. He agreed not to get involved directly in our area or in our tribal affairs, but he would supply us with logistic support.

Even though we walked away from the meeting with Counselor General Archer almost empty handed, the discussions went well. We were content when Archer agreed not to interfere with our tribe or in our tribal region. Our family's ancestral home in the Jaji Valley was strategically located for smuggling arms, money and equipment into Afghanistan from Pakistan.

The formidable mountain ranges of the Jaji provided excellent shelter for our forces. We fought hard to keep our valley out of Soviet hands, because if anyone took the Jaji, then they controlled the capital, Kabul. Our history with the British Army had proven that Afghans are good fighters. Unlike other Islamic fighters, Afghans are not suicidal. Afghan fighters prefer to draw an unwary enemy into their territory with a ruse and then attack them. In this way, they hope to kill without dying themselves. This is the first rule of war for any Pashtun tribesman. When the time came, we were able to draw many communists into our Valley.

After invading Afghanistan, the Soviets quickly established seven checkpoints from the Afghan border with Pakistan to the Jaji. These checkpoints were strategically located for stopping the flow of smuggled goods and for shelling the city of Kabul from the mountains.

Soon after the invasion of Kabul by the Soviets, my brother Sayad organized my cousins and others into a fighting force and took out the Soviet's seven checkpoints. This allowed smuggled arms to flow freely into Afghanistan. During the first ten days of war, I lost three of my first cousins. One became famous among Pashtuns when he battled much needed heavy machine guns away from the Soviets before being killed himself.

I went to work for my family and my tribe. My career as a political adviser to the mujahidin began. My brother Omar made it easy for me to work as a muj. Because it was not in our family's best interests for Omar to go to war, he said, "I'll do the work; you do the jihad." As a doctor he was in a position to earn more money than I, so he supported me while I worked for the mujahidin. This allowed me to work with different groups at my own pace.

During this period, I often acted as translator to the U.S. Government in Peshawar and Islamabad. This allowed me to get my family and many other Afghans out of Pakistan and into the United States and Europe. It wasn't until later that we noticed that a brain drain had occurred. It wasn't until *much* later that we became aware of the depth of the vacuum that had been created with so many Afghan civilians running from the fighting. As every student of Philosophy knows, nature abhors a vacuum and where there is a vacuum, it is swiftly filled. As the educated and skilled people of Afghanistan escaped the war, they left behind the uneducated and the religious fundamentalists.

As I mentioned earlier, after leaving Afghanistan my family lived in Peshawar, a town on the northwest frontier of Pakistan. Think of it as a rough, tough nineteenth century Texas town on the border with Mexico. In the town were lots of guns but not much of an organized police presence. A predominate tribe in the area is the Pashtuns, a force unto themselves. Half of my cousins lived on the Afghan side of the border, the other half in Pakistan. Crossing the border for us was no harder than taking a day trip to the country to visit family.

Eventually the Pakistan authorities tried to keep my relatives from moving back and forth across the border. But because the jihad was important to us, we ignored their efforts until one day a Pakistani official came to our house and explained that we were causing too much trouble. He warned us, "We want your fight to be covert and here you are going in and out." Apparently, the Soviets had warned Pakistan that they would commence bombing if crossings were not curtailed.

My brother Sayad told him that if anyone tried to stop us, he and his fighters would consider the Northwest Frontier of Pakistan a Pashtun tribal area. At the time, this was a real threat. It meant that the area could no longer be controlled by Pakistan's officials. He also warned the official that if they kept giving us a hard time, he would join the Soviet's claim to the area.

The Soviets had already claimed part of Pakistan as their own, causing its officials to worry about further Soviet aggression. No doubt it was foremost in the mind of Pakistan's leadership that once the Soviets conquered Afghanistan, they could easily make a dash to the Persian Gulf through one of their sparsely populated provinces, giving the Soviets their much coveted warm water port. Eventually, the Pakistani official backed down, but his visit did make us understand one thing, our future incursions into Afghanistan needed to be more covert.

Before I traveled from the United States to join the jihad in January 1980, I was able to see my mother who I had not seen for six years because I was at university. My mother was a tribal woman. She was four foot nine and weighed about a hundred pounds. My dad was six feet two or three, thin and handsome. He died when I was only four years old. Genetically I take after my father, but I am my mother's son.

Momma always showed pride in her tribe's heritage. She had told me that those of the Jaji Tribe were good fighters, good Muslims and a very hospitable people. She warned me, though, that among the Pashtuns there are two types of people which should be given special heed: the mullahs and the musicians. Although habitually poor, these groups had strong connections to the common people.

"They see, talk, preach and play to many. If you do bad to either mullahs or musicians," Momma warned, "you will have trouble, and trouble with them equaled trouble with everybody." I took her words to heart.

Each mullah has two students called the *talib* (plural *taliban*) who are young students studying in the *madrassas* or mosques. Most of the taliban in Afghanistan are Pashtuns. Because young Afghan women see them as romantic figures, many songs and much poetry had been written about them, until recently, that is.

Because much of the population of Afghanistan is illiterate, the mullahs read and write for almost everyone, and because the country never had a competent postal service, letters are carried by the mullahs. If a villager needs a letter sent to another village, the mullah writes the letter, then the talib, acting as a postman, often takes the letter to the next town. It is passed again and again amongst the mullahs and taliban until it finally reaches its destination. There is no fee for this service. Instead one donates according to one's ability what one can to the mullah and to the mosque. The basic services they deliver make them a very important center of power in the country.

Neither mullahs nor taliban have a steady source of income. Unmarried mullahs usually sleep in the mosques, as do the taliban. Each mosque has one or two guest rooms for mullahs. All other guests and the talib are asked to sleep inside the mosque itself. Its doors are open twenty-four hours a day for that purpose, making it an important center of activity.

Each evening a house, designated on a rotating basis, sends food to the mullah and his students in the mosque. The Pashtuns call this involuntary feeding of the mullah and his students the "mullah's turn."

The mullahs presence ensures that the mosques are the center of village life. Since the mullahs and their families are supported by the people in general, they have an easy time moving about the country. Anyone controlling the hearts and the minds of the mullahs also controls the countryside.

In Afghan culture, as a decision is made by a tribal council, the mullah just sits and listens. He does not have permission to enter into the conversation or to help decide the issue until the *jurga* (council) is over. The council members must first come to an agreement between themselves without interference. After a decision is made in the jurga, then the mullah is asked for his opinion. For example, if there is a land dispute or animosity among members of the council, they first reach an agreement among themselves before asking the mullah what is written in the Quran or whether a religious decree exists on the issue.

Because the mullah knows the members of the tribal council well, most of the time he takes the easiest path and acknowledges the decision already reached by it as being good for the country, God, and the jurga's leadership. Once this declaration is made, everyone must obey the jurga's order or be condemned by the mullah who also decides the penalty for any transgression.

The Paktia jurgas do not have their own homegrown mullahs, rather they are imported from different provinces. The most educated ones usually come from the north of Afghanistan or from the Logar Province. Unlike in the Christian faith, mullahs are not ordained. Instead students are granted that status by established mullahs. They are apprenticed much like evangelists were in the post-Civil War South of the United States.

A mullah, called the White Mullah, visited my family in Kabul each year for a week or two. In exchange for his visit, we would help him out financially. While I was in school in the United States, I lost track of him. After returning to the Jaji Valley in 1980, I asked one of my cousins what happened to him. He said that the White Mullah had died and that they had hired another one, but he was no longer with them.

I found this odd. It is unusual for mullahs to be fired or to leave so quickly. I asked my cousin what had happened. He explained that the mullah had been let go because he disagreed with the jurga too much. My cousin went on to say that when they had needed wood in winter, the White Mullah would tell them that it was okay to chop up the tree of someone else for firewood as long as the owner did not know about it or the act did not hurt anyone's feelings. My cousin said that the White Mullah knew that they were going to act that way, so he gave them permission. Similarly, if the lamb of another crossed onto their land, he allowed them to keep it as a gift from God. The new mullah, however, would look into books and tell them that chopping the tree or keeping the lamb was against the law and the Islamic religion. Every time they tried to take something, the new mullah stopped them. Finally the council got fed up and decided that his books (which they could not read because they were illiterate) were wrong and that he needed the *right* books. His books were burned because they were against the council's and God's will.

"The White Mullah had books, too, but his books were much better," my cousin explained to me. "They allowed the tribe to do the things they wanted to do."

"Why did you do that?" I asked. "What the mullah was saying was the truth."

We know it was the truth," my cousin said without expression. "The council wanted to hear that if you take someone's goods and they don't know it, it's okay since they don't know that you hurt them. This makes the act less sinful."

Apparently the new mullah accused them of sinning and they didn't want to hear it. After burning his books, they blackened the poor man's face, placed him backwards on a donkey, rode him to the border of the Jaji Province, and immediately began searching for another mullah. My cousin pointed toward a man that was their new mullah. I walked over and asked him if his preaching was the same as the White Mullah's.

The man said, "No." Mullahs must respect tribal laws and the people. He explained that the people's wealth is God's will, "So if people are happy, then I'm very happy with it."

Over the years, my mother's advice about paying attention to the mullahs proved useful again and again. Sadly, during my trips to Afghanistan in the last years of the twentieth century, I couldn't pay attention to the musicians as she had also suggested. They had been outlawed by the Taliban government. But I did pay great heed to what the mullahs said; they had come to control the country.

In April 1980, I felt forced to return to America. My marriage was breaking up. My first wife was blond and petite – a real beauty. We met in the university cafeteria and had eloped in September 1978 against our families wishes. After I arrived back in St. Louis, we moved to Texas to be with those members of my family who had immigrated there.

My wife quickly grew to hate Texas. She also had a hard time dealing with my three month absence in 1980, and the fear that someday I may be killed in the mountains of Afghanistan. Much to my regret, we divorced. But this left me free to continue my sometime work as a mujahid.

The State Department invited me to work at the U.S. Embassy in Islamabad. Since I was not a U.S. citizen, it took special permission for me to work for that agency. I was asked to meet with Zalmay Khalilzad, a translator, to check my English.

Immediately before I began working for the State Department, Richard van Devere called and said that he had some bad news. Before anyone could work in a U.S. Embassy abroad, the foreign host must approve of that person being in their territory. Van Devere informed me that the State Department had received a cable back from the government of Pakistan. It felt that my presence in their territory would make the uneasy political situation more unstable because of my family's link to the former royal family. For the second time my diplomatic career ended before it began. I guess it was my destiny to fight as a muj.

While growing up, I had much exposure to tribal people in Kabul. My cousins would often come and stay with us. Having never seen a television or heard a radio before, they entertained themselves – and us – by swapping stories and facts about my parents' tribe. I realized early that the simple life can be seductive when one is removed from its daily grind and hardships. Over the years, I used my cousins' stories to keep in touch with my roots. And, to be frank, I enjoyed their casual style. I eventually became aware of the differences between tribal fighters and those with more education. Tribal fighters were territorial fighters. They just wanted everyone out of their area and their lives. The more educated Afghans wanted to control the country.

Usually the educated had lived in cities for so long that they looked down upon the tribes and called their members *lungi dar* (the turban men). On the other hand, when members of our tribe traveled to the cities, they were amazed at the crime, killings, etc., that they found there. Not respectful of other people's property rights, tribal fighters were very respectful of other members of their tribe. I still find it difficult to explain to outsiders the simple sincerity of this paradox: respect of one's people but not of their material possessions.

During the Soviet war, the tribal chiefs and their followers often clashed with the educated cliques running the war from offices inside Pakistan. When I returned to the fighting in 1981, those in charge of the factions of the mujahidin were in open conflict with the tribal chiefs. A split had occurred and each refused to see the other's point of view.

The tribal chiefs finally asked the muj leaders to leave the tribes alone and let them run their own affairs. The chiefs, knowing the situation on the ground while the leaders back in Pakistan did not, caused problems. I felt it my responsibility to plant myself firmly on the side of the tribal chiefs whenever possible because they were the ones actually doing the fighting inside Afghanistan.

During this period, I traveled freely back and forth across the border between Pakistan and Afghanistan. I often went into Afghanistan with tribesmen to visit their homes. This gained their respect since few of those in Peshawar wanted to venture into the hostile areas. The fighters began to show me respect by calling me *nephew*. I was interested in learning what was happening on the ground in the small skirmish groups. The tribal people always took good care of me. Time and again they shuttled me intact back to either Peshawar or Islamabad after a pitched battle with the Soviets.

By 1982, the leaders of the mujahidin factions suddenly decided that not enough people were fighting. I went to the tribal areas and spoke to the leaders. The chiefs were upset because they were not receiving enough logistical support from the authorities in Peshawar. Many chiefs had become frustrated with the infighting among the political parties, so they simply refused to fight. I tried to explain that the war was a joint effort, but they wouldn't listen. With-out them the war was over, and without them the Jaji Valley would be ceded to the Soviets as would Kabul.

Years earlier my mother said that if I ever needed help getting the Pashtuns motivated to fight the Soviets, she would travel with me to the province and talk to her relatives. Remembering my mother's suggestion, I returned to the U.S. and asked her to come with me to Afghanistan and to encourage our tribal chiefs to fight. At the age of 72, she made the rugged thirty-five hour journey from Texas all the way to Peshawar. I took her to Sada, a border town on the Northwest Frontier where most of the people in her tribe were located.

When we arrived, she got angry with the men. She grabbed a stick and said, "I want you guys to fight tomorrow. I will wait for you until I hear that two hundred of you are dead and that you have killed two thousand of the infidels – then I will forgive you for not fighting." I was proud of her. She really knew how to kick male Afghan butt.

After preparations, the fighters left and I went with them. We managed to get a few Russians without getting knocked off ourselves, but the numbers were wildly short of the two thousand dead communists that Momma had insisted on, but she forgave us later.

The Soviet helicopters were the biggest reason no one wanted to fight. We were good with rifles and machine guns, but we had no defense against the Soviet Hind gunships which we called *jawz* (airships). The Soviets showed fearlessness by flying low between the mountains. They could do that only because we had no defense against them.

In 1982, a group of mujahidin and I were caught by two jawz in the rugged mountains near Jaji. We tried to hide, but they swooped around and strafed us with machine guns. As I clung to the side of the mountain behind a few boulders, I saw the face of the helicopter pilot so distinctly that I swear I could identify him to this day if we ever met on the street.

As a group, we were in big trouble. We mujahidin desperately needed a mobile weapon big enough to take out tons of flying terror.

After delivering Momma back to Texas, I went to Washington to beg for help from every congressman that would grant me an interview. I remember meeting with Tom DeLay from Sugar Land, and another congressman named Brown whose exact name I can no longer remember.

I also visited with the East Texas Congressman Charles Wilson in his office. He was blunt but tolerant. He said that the Pashtuns had been ruling Afghanistan for five thousand years and that it was time for a change. It was time for one of the minorities, a Tajik or a Hazra, to rule. I asked him not to draw distinctions between the different ethnic groups. We were all Afghans facing a common enemy – the Soviets.

Wilson's response, "No, we want to make sure that this time a man from Tajik rules."

I'm sure he was referring to Mr. Burhanuddin Rabbani, the leader of the radical Jamiat-i-Islami group. I had heard the rumor that the U.S. promised him leadership of Afghanistan if we succeeded against the Soviets, but this was the first time I came face-to-face with that prospect. Because Afghans desperately needed Wilson and the weapons he could supply, I wasn't going to argue with him.

U.S. covert operations managed to get us a few Stingers by the end of 1983. By 1986 supplying them became official U.S. policy and everybody had them. With their arrival, we finally had an effective weapon to use against the jawz.

I have personal knowledge of how effective a weapon the Stinger is, even when it misses its target. In a valley near Zarmat, south of Kabul, the Soviets spotted my group of about a hundred anti-communist freedom fighters. The gun ship came upon us so quickly that the man carrying the Stinger didn't have enough time to take a shot at the helicopter. We dropped to the ground looking for cover where none existed. Because of my rank, son of a tribal chief, five fighters jumped on top of me to protect me from the flying bullets. The Hind's fire was so intense, the ground exploded all around us. Stone fragments rained down on our heads; pieces of rock shot up from the earth.

I yelled at the muj with the Stinger, "Get the fucking thing ready."

Prone on his back while another man fiddled with the electronic switch, he growled back, "I can't get the mother fucker ready."

"Just shoot then," I ordered.

He shot. The missile missed the jawz by a few feet and the helicopter sped away. Eight of my men were wounded that day.

Because of the suddenness of the attack, we did not have the time needed to go through all the steps necessary to fire the missile. It always took a few minutes to get a rocket out of its case, aimed and launched. Under fire, it seemed like an eternity.

Nor did the operator want to take a wild shot. Stingers were expensive and each group could only shoot a few missiles before the firing unit had to be schlepped back to Pakistan for re-programming by the Pakistan Army.

We always took special care of the Stingers. We owned our lives to them more than once. And little did the Pakistanis know that we eventually learned how to re-program them ourselves so we could shoot off as many missiles as we could beg, borrow or steal.

I saw Osama bin Laden for the first time while we were on patrol in the Jaji headed toward Khost. While driving through the mountains, we saw a small camp – no more than a few acres. We hid and watched it for a while to see what was going on. The camp contained Arabs that came and went quite often.

At the time, it was believed that all one had to do was join the mujahidin in your thoughts, and help out the *real* mujahidin anyway you could, like donating money or a truck of wheat, and you became a muj. I didn't see anything that would later look like al-Qaida in the camp. Everyone appeared to be mostly rich kids coming and going. They brought food, money and small trucks into the area, made donations to those in charge of the camp, and then left. We watched as lots of photos were taken as evidence that the donor had been in Afghanistan as a muj.

We made fun of them because none of my muj ever saw them in action. We regarded them as tourists offering a bit of material help to the fighters. Because they were foreigners in our valley, we never had much to do with them. I would learn later who Osama bin Laden was when I was asked by the American Counselor General to arrange bin Laden's secure passage through the Jaji. I did as asked, but I never got an opportunity to meet him.

In 1986, I accidentally crossed bin Laden's path in a restaurant when a few of my men and I stopped in a little village to have lunch. Across the street at another restaurant, a group of trucks pulled up and a large group of fighters spilled out of the truck beds. People in the restaurant where we were eating recognized the flags flying from the trucks. Then bin Laden got out of one of the cabs and someone pointed him out to me. I wasn't impressed.

From thirty feet away I could see that the men weren't native Afghans. They had dark complexions. Then one of my men heard one of bin Laden's people call us *mushrekeen* (pro-Westerners who doubt the existence of God). Discretion being the better part of valor, I let the insult slide. But I knew, back in the mountains, my men could take his rabble without dirtying our clothes.

In 1988, President Reagan appointed Ed McWilliams Special Envoy to the mujahidin in Pakistan. A career diplomat, our ideas were very similar and so we became close colleagues. An extremely polite man with a weakness for Afghan food, he knew our culture well. McWilliams revealed that his instructions from Washington were that all aid to the mujahidin was only for the fundamentalists. I learned from him that a man by the name of Charles Dunbar had total control over the State Department's Afghan policy. McWilliams had been trying to get help for the moderates from the State Department and the White House, but Dunbar kept vetoing his requests. McWilliams expressed concern that Dunbar's lack of knowledge about the area and the people would cripple U.S. policy toward Afghanistan.

The factions favored by Dunbar were the fundamentalists. But none of these groups had national experience as administrators or politicians. An historical comparison from the American Revolution would be for the French to take from each American colony a Puritan minister with a local following and hand them control of the national government. It was a strategy for disaster.

About this time, Pir Sayed Ahmad Gailani, leader of the Mahaz-e-Milli party, offered me a position in Washington, D.C. Each of the four fundamentalist groups of mujahidin had offices in the U.S, but the three moderate groups went begging. I gladly agreed to open his office in D.C. I believed that a good place to start my new position with Gailani would be to check in with the State Department. Dropping in unannounced, I found Jim Bruno's office and introduced myself. He gave me an appointment for the next day.

While waiting in Bruno's office for our meeting to begin, a man opened the door and without introducing himself impatiently informed me that there were already four mujahidin offices in Washington. Opening another would only create more problems.

"Excuse me, sir, who are you?"

"Charles Dunbar."

At about six foot two, skinny and pasty faced, I wondered whether he inherited his bad temper or whether frustrations of the job were getting to him. Later I would learn his title, Under Secretary of State for Asian Affairs.

I said, "Sir, the fundamentalist factions in Afghanistan have four offices. "What's wrong with opening one for the moderates? We are the most educated of all our peoples. We will staff the office without any cost to the United States Government. I am only here to consult with you. I really don't need your permission."

Dunbar told me to relay to Gailani that if we opened an office in Washington we would not receive another dime of funding from the U.S. Government. He then huffed out of Bruno's office without further explanation.

Without a doubt, Charles Dunbar was the rudest person that I ever encountered at the State Department. Later Bruno apologized for Dunbar's behavior. Shrugging his shoulders he said, "He's the boss."

By contrast, in McWilliams I always found an honest, open man who understood the people and culture of those he dealt with. He was the first to admit to me that the U.S.

would be washing its hands of Afghanistan as soon as the Soviets left. From him I took it as inevitable. If Dunbar had delivered the same message, it would have come as an insult.

February 1989, the Soviets pulled out of Afghanistan. I turned in two AK47s and a pistol to Pir Gailani and asked for his forgiveness for any mistakes that I may have made during my service. It had been a good fight, but my war was over.

Before leaving Pakistan, I warned a friend staying behind, "Now the mujahidin will kill each other. Someone from each of the muj groups will vie to be Amir. Although they will try, you can't have many kings." I did not want to stick around and wait for the mujahidin to begin fighting each other. Sad to be leaving Afghanistan behind forever, I turned toward my new home in Texas.

By 1992, all attempts to establish an independent Afghan Government failed and the country plunged into civil war. As predicted, the muj groups were at each other's throats for control. Kabul, untouched during the Soviet invasion and occupation, became a prime target for whichever war lord wanted to control the city that week. The once beautiful Kabul was quickly reduced to rubble by a continuous stream of rocket attacks. My life was in Texas. I was no longer involved in the daily battles of the Afghan mujahidin. But I couldn't help wonder whether official support of the fundamentalist factions would come back and bite us on the butt.

Chapter 2: That Cockroach, Osama

Sometime in 1992 after the collapse of the Soviet regime, Mr. Pir Gailani requested that I travel to Afghanistan from Texas. He said it was very important. After I arrived, he asked me to become an ambassador to one of the European countries. I declined the offer. Over the last few years I worked hard establishing myself as a businessman back home and I didn't want to abandon or jeopardize what I had worked to build.

On the flight back to the U.S., I had a heart attack over Germany. My problem began earlier as a pain in the shoulder that lasted for days. By the time the plane landed, I was almost dead. Later I would learn that I had actually died for forty-five seconds, but all I remember of the experience is pain, calm, blue sky and white clouds and looking back at my body and thinking it half rotten. I was finally at peace with myself and the world. But thoughts of my family called me back. I began to fight for the right to live. Recovery was a slow, agonizing process which brought its own horrors, but no horror was half as bad as never seeing my family again.

For years afterward, I was not the same man. One of the few pleasures afforded me was an occasional trip to Europe to see old friends. Volunteering to travel out of political curiosity was no longer an option.

Prague became one of my favorite cities. Its history is knee deep and I loved the people for they, too, had risen up against the red bear of communism. Added to that was the fact that the Afghan Ambassador to the Czechoslovakian Republic, Wazir Faizi, was an old schoolmate. While working as Director of Foreign Relations for Gailani, I had appointed him the muj representative to India.

Faizi and I liked to eat at a small, local restaurant in Prague. It was made famous (or infamous, depending on how you look at these things) by the fact that Hitler was eating there when he first learned that his troops had conquered Czechoslovakia. We ate there not because of Hitler, but because the food was incredibly good and we liked the fact that a small corner restaurant witnessed so much history. Somehow that restaurant always brought things into perspective for me. I identified with that unassuming eatery and its mournful place in history.

In 1996, I received a letter at my home in Sugar Land, Texas, from Dr. Hermat who acted as Mr. Gulbuddin Hekmatyar's representative in Europe. Hekmatyar was one of the four fundamentalist mujahidin leaders vying for leadership in Afghanistan. Hermat contacted me because Hekmatyar wanted an appointment with the U.S. Ambassador assigned to Pakistan. He contacted me by telephone and asked whether I could arrange the meeting. It was ego boosting to receive a telephone call in Texas asking for help in setting up a meeting between two parties residing in countries close to each other but thousands of miles away from me.

For years Gulbuddin Hekmatyar was the most powerful war lord in Afghanistan and one of the fundamentalist leaders nurtured by the Pakistani and the U.S. Governments during the Afghan-Soviet war. It was rumored that he received the most money of any of the mujahidin leaders from the U.S., Saudi Arabia and from the Muslim Brotherhood community. (At the time, the Muslim Brotherhood was known for collecting donations in Europe, America and throughout the Arab world for any type of anti-Western activity.)

While at university, I first learned of Gulbuddin Hekmatyar when other students warned me about him and his anti-Americanism. I eventually came to the conclusion that Hekmatyar was adept at playing both sides against the middle – the middle being those of us in the more moderate muj groups. Once Don Archer asked me to meet with Heckmatyar, but I had to decline. Since my family and tribe were politically moderate, to go to him would show them disrespect.

I asked Counselor General Archer why the U.S. supported Hekmatyar by shipping him money and weapons. Archer explained that technically, Hekmatyar was a good fighter who carried off organized attacks, unlike the independent guerilla actions used by most of the mujahidin. In order to show the U.S. Congress that something was being accomplished against the Soviets, "organized attacks had to occur even if the devil himself led the charge." This enabled action pictures to be taken by satellite so the U.S. Senate, Congress and the American people would see something happening for their money. When the regular mujahidin fought, no one knew where or how they were fighting. Everyone knew they were fighting because Red Army casualties occurred, but there was no way of proving what had happened to people thousands of miles away. Archer said that Hekmatyar was good for everyone: he was proof of a war. At the time I felt that anyone who fought the godless communists, no matter what his past, was fine by me.

In 1996, immediately before the Taliban took over Kabul, Hekmatyar was serving as Prime Minister of Afghanistan while Burhanuddin Rabbanni was acting president. Good sense leads one to believe that as leaders they would work together for the betterment of their country and provide a united face to the world. But unofficially their soldiers often clashed with one another and against those of the Defense Minister who at that time was Ahmad Shah Massood.

At my own expense, I flew to Washington, D.C. to explain to Phyllis Oakley what Hekmatyar wanted. Mrs. Oakley split the deep seas of the State Department and arranged for me to meet with the U.S. Ambassador to Pakistan in Islamabad.

By the way, I greatly admire Mrs. Oakley and her husband, Robert. I first met Mrs. Oakley in 1982 when I worked for

Mr. Sibghatullah Mujaddedi and his *Jabha-i-Najat Milli Afghanistan* party. She was the Afghan Desk Officer and she always helped me anyway she could. By 1996, her title was something like the Deputy Secretary of Immigration. Her husband Robert, a counter terrorism expert in Islamabad during the Reagan administration, was appointed Ambassador to Pakistan in 1988 by the first George Bush (a man I greatly admired at the time) after the previous ambassador, Arnold Raphel, was killed while traveling with Pakistan's President Zia ul-Haq and some of his generals in an airplane.

So I flew to Pakistan to try to arrange a meeting between Heckmatyar and the U.S. Ambassador. I'm still not sure why I agreed to do this.

Before seeing the Ambassador, I met with Tom Williams, the diplomat in charge of Afghan affairs at the American Embassy in Islamabad. Young, energetic and hardworking, Williams expressed anger at having to meet with Hekmatyar. Williams told me that every time they met, Hekmatyar lied to him. He explained that one of Hekmatyar's sons-in-law, Farid Jarrer, had gone on a secret mission to Iran. The U.S. intelligence service quickly discovered the trip. Williams confronted Hekmatyar about it, but the muj said that he never sent his son-in-law to Iran and that Farid had been with him the whole time in Afghanistan. Then Williams confronted him with proof of the visit. Caught in a blatant lie, Hekmatyar threatened to move to Iran. In a show of strength Williams told him, "When you leave the office, make sure the door doesn't hit your rear end." Williams explained to me that Hekmatyar's bout of lying happened in front of the Palestinian Interior Minister, Mr. Baber.

Eventually I was able to meet with Ambassador Simon. Much to my astonishment, he agreed to meet with Hekmatyar on the condition that he stays in power for one more week. At that time I didn't know that the Taliban were poised to take over the Afghan Government by force at any minute.

Soon after my meeting with Ambassador Simon, Mr. Bahir Gharat (another of Hekmatyar's sons-in-law) and I met at my hotel's restaurant. I related Simon's message to him. He appeared as puzzled by the ambassador's statement as I was.

Three days later, I received a call at my hotel from Terry Cook, a Military Attaché at the U.S. Embassy. He invited me to his house in Islamabad for dinner.

In Cook's spacious living room several television sets displayed different news channels at once. He asked me, "Do you know what is happening in Kabul today?"

Confused about which TV he was watching, I said, "No, I have no idea."

"Kabul is being overrun by a group of people called the Taliban."

I had heard a little about the Taliban movement with its mullahs and their harsh Quranic Law, but not much else.

"Who are they exactly?"

"They are from Kandahar, led by Mullah Omar."

"Yeah, I heard that Mullah Omar is ruling Kandahar, but is that his movement?"

"Yeah," he said. "It's a new movement, the Taliban. We are in favor of them coming to power."

"Are you sure? The mullahs can be pretty harsh. Culturally, they are Pashtuns, plus they're Muslims." Last I heard, U.S. policy makers wanted someone from the Tajik minority group to control the country. This was news to me. Now the U.S. wants Pashtuns. What a surprise.

"Afghanistan needs stability," Cook said.

I couldn't agree more. It desperately needed stability. Years of civil war had shattered the people's and the country's infrastructure. So I asked him what should be done if the Taliban arrive at my parents' tribe in the Paktia Province.

Cook said it was up to me, but he suggested that we wave the Taliban through the towns and not start another war. Again I agreed, but I had no influence over the towns. My influence was centered only in the tribal areas. But after all, I reasoned, the Taliban were religious leaders and should be given a chance. They couldn't be as bad as the in-fighting idiots now running the country. If the choice is between mullahs or morons, then I stand by the first. I wasn't about to go in and do it myself; I preferred living in Texas.

Instead I sent a message to Paktia and asked the tribal chiefs to meet me in Peshawar. After they gathered, I told them there was a group of people called the Taliban. They said yes, they knew of them; they were already preaching in the area. I told them not to take up arms against them because they preached goodness.

"They are not here to harm your Muslim ways of life. They are supported by the Pakistan and U.S. Governments." The tribal leaders agreed not to fight them. The Taliban had an easy time entering the south and southeast tribal areas. They were welcomed by most because of the much needed stability they brought to the area.

As the Taliban entered rural areas, in one hand they would hold up the Quran and in the other a Kalashnikov rifle. They told the people they could choose only one. Of course, being devout and simple, they choose the Quran. Using this technique, the Taliban quickly took over many areas of Afghanistan. But in many others, particularly the cities, the people saw them as the enemy and fought hard against them. Eventually Rabbani and Hekmatyar, both occupiers of Kabul, were turned out by the Taliban. As could be predicted, Hekmatyar escaped to Iran. Rabbani ran to Panjsher in the North where he established a base. His group soon gained fame as the Northern Alliance.

The government of the Taliban was quickly recognized by Pakistan, Saudi Arabia and the United Arab Emirates, but other nearby governments like Iran, Russia, Turkey, and the Central Asian states saw the rise of the Taliban as just another problem for the area. The Taliban brought with them a harsh form of stability to those parts of Afghanistan that they subdued. In the rugged, primitive tribal areas, they made few changes to everyone's life. Some changes, however, made everyone wonder, like their very harsh attitude toward prostitution. It suddenly became a death penalty offense. They also banned gambling and the gamblers vehicle of choice – duels between kites with glass or razorblade encrusted strings – making thousands angry with the new regime.

I thought back to a conversation I had in Peshawar in 1984 with Mullah Mutaki. He explained to me that there are 100,000 mullahs in Afghanistan and that each mullah has two talib registered to him, "Which makes us 300,000 strong, with one God, with one Book. We will follow one leader; we will take over Afghanistan and we will give the thugs (the mujahidin leaders) a run for their money."

Of course, Mutaki wasn't a member of the Taliban; it had yet to be organized as a movement. I now realize that he was either prophetic or had been introduced to the earliest stirrings of this political movement.

From 1984 to 1996, the number of religious men in Afghanistan should have grown substantially from the 1984 figure of 300,000. Because there were no public schools in the refugee camps of Pakistan where the Afghans too poor to immigrate lived, *madrassas* supported mostly by the Saudis were the only place Afghan parents could send their male children for an education. Because of the limited opportunities for other types of education, the number of mullahs and taliban had probably increased by a factor of ten or more in the intervening years. A part of me thought a religious state in Afghanistan a frightening prospect. After all, I was the descendent of a man who had worked hard all his life for a civil, secular government.

Sometime after returning from Afghanistan in 1996, I visited Phyllis and Robert Oakley at their home near Washington, D.C. After they welcomed me back to the U.S., Mr. Oakley took me aside and said, "It's all over. Hekmatyar is gone. Rabbani is gone. Mujaddedi is gone. It's all over. It's a done deal." We talked about how the mujahidin leaders had been bad for Afghanistan. We hoped that the Taliban would bring stability to the region.

For a few years I purposely stayed away from any direct or indirect dealings or relationships with officials of the new Afghan Government. I wanted to see what the Taliban would do since the War Lords' record had been so abysmal. Everyone deserves a chance, and I had other things to do.

In May 1998, my old friend Ambassador Faizi called from Prague. He explained that he was coming to the States and wanted to meet with the Taliban's representative to the U.N. Apparently the Taliban leadership wished to ascertain the exact stance of the U.S. on some issues, and since Faizi had been one of the country's more experienced post-Soviet diplomats, they contacted him.

Once face-to-face in Texas, Faizi explained to me that the real reason he came was that the new Afghan Government wished my brother Omar to intervene in a collateral situation that was causing misunderstandings. Contract negotiations between Unocal (Union Oil Company of California which merged into Chevron in 2005) and the Taliban had broken down. Unocal had signed contracts in 1995 with the various War Lords in power. The contracts allowed the company to slink a pipeline across their territories and join Turkmenistan's oil with Pakistan's ports. At that time, each war lord would have gotten a share of the profits. He explained that these contracts had been signed with the help of Hamid Karzai (a Unocal consultant in the 1990's and the current President of Afghanistan) and Zalmay Khalilzad (also a Unocal consultant in the 1990's and a U.S. Envoy to Afghanistan who eventually became the U.S. Ambassador to Afghanistan). Once the Taliban seized control of most of the country in 1996, they wanted Unocal to pay the money into the Afghan treasury and not hand it over to the local War Lords.

Faizi and I drove from Texas to Alabama and spent a few days with my brother Omar. After much niggling on Faizi's part, Omar agreed to travel to Afghanistan to work on the Taliban's problem with Unocal if the prior consent of the U.S. Government could be obtained. In no way did he want to work counter to U.S. international policy. Without our government's permission, Omar warned, the trip was a waste of time.

Thereafter, Omar flew to D.C. and met with Lee O. Coldren, Director of the Office of Pakistan, Afghanistan and Bangladesh Affairs. At the meeting, he did not receive any indication that the U.S. Government was interested in smoothing out aspects of its relationship with the Taliban, so he quickly returned home.

In the Sumer of 1998, I drove Faizi to New York. There we met with the Taliban's Ambassador to the U.N., Hakim Mujahid, at his office in Queens. Mujahid was not a mullah. At first he represented the Afghan Government of Burhanuddin Rabbani, but with the rise of the Taliban, and knowing where his bread was buttered – he switched sides to the new government. Mujahid was a good politician. He understood international diplomacy much better than the insular members of the Taliban, but I got the impression that he was isolated from the Taliban movement and probably had limited access to its top officials.

Faizi and I spent the better part of one day discussing the Unocal contracts with Mujahid. Mujahid and Faizi eventually came to the conclusion that Unocal provided little financial incentive for the Taliban government to sign.

From New York, Faizi and I drove to the State Department in D.C. We met with Lee Coldren, his assistant Don Kemp and the Afghanistan Affairs desk officer, Roberta L. Chew. Coldren explained to us that the U.S. Government was concerned about how the Taliban treated women and its casual attitude toward stopping drugs and eradicating the poppy plants. He also told us that Unocal was pulling out of Afghanistan and that the U.S. was placing Afghanistan on the list of states that supported terrorism.

This broke my heart. The awful mujahidin governments were being replaced by a fundamentalist regime with whom companies and nations could not do business. Where would the Taliban get the money to rebuild Afghanistan, if not from companies like Unocal?

Coldren was the first to bring up the subject of Osama bin Laden.

"Who's bin Laden?" I asked. I had forgotten all about him in the intervening years.

Coldren explained that it was assumed that bin Laden was involved in the Riyadh (1995) and Khobar Towers (1996) bombings in Saudi Arabia. (Later these crimes would be assigned to other groups having nothing to do with bin Laden.) During the 1980's, the CIA had supplied him with money, weapons and training. Also he had been one of its conduits for the distribution of large contributions of money to the mujahidin. I began to wonder whether he was the same rich Saudi that I had been asked to protect as he traveled through the Jaji Valley in the 1980's. Coldren said that he probably was.

"Look what became of him," Coldren added. "Unless the Taliban gets rid of this man, the U.S. will slap sanctions on Afghanistan." Coldren really didn't care what happened to bin Laden as long as he was turned out of Afghanistan. He suggested that I help.

"But where should I start?" I said to everyone in the room.

Kemp suggested that I visit Afghanistan. He said women are oppressed, drugs flow freely out of the country, and bin Laden is protected by the Taliban. Coldren and Kemp explained that the people of Afghanistan should be told that an uprising needed to be started against the Taliban.

I promised to do what I could, but the problems in Afghanistan in the 1980s seemed easier to solve than the current batch. I said, "In the 80's I went to my group of followers and told them, "Rise up in the name of God, against the Soviets, who have no God. Rise up against them! They are telling us to follow the communist manifesto and not the Quran."

"When I go back, they will ask me, "Why should I do this thing?" Am I to tell them, "Rise up because the mullahs are telling you that there is a God and that you must follow the Quran and the Old Testament?" When the people ask, "What is wrong with the things the Taliban and the mullahs are saying?" I won't have a plausible answer. The mullahs are the leaders of the Afghan religion. As in America, people usually follow the advice of their religious leaders."

Confounded by these dilemmas and after not getting a suitable answer from the people in the State Department, doing nothing seemed to be the best policy, so I drove back to Texas.

On August 7, 1998, the American Embassies in Nairobi, Kenya and Dar es Salaam, Tanzania were bombed. On August 20, President Clinton fired almost seven dozen Cruise Missiles at six Al Qaida training camps in Afghanistan and at a pharmaceutical plant in the Sudan.

In a hotel room in Biloxi, Mississippi I flipped on CNN at about ten that morning. Across the TV screen news flashed the bombings of the two U.S. embassies in Africa – Osama bin Laden – American bombs hitting Afghanistan and the Sudan. I wanted to cry. I had first-hand knowledge of how much Afghans appreciated Americans because of the support given to the country in their fight against communism. The bombings would sever the once close bonds between the two countries.

CNN explained how some Americans believed that the bombings were created by President Clinton to divert everyone away from the Monica Lewinsky problem. They were calling it – "Wag the dog." People were openly making fun of the president on the news. I didn't care about that; I aligned politically with conservative Republicans. But I did wonder how Clinton could function rationally under so much pressure from something that – in the world order – seemed so insignificant. I would later learn that Clinton hadn't "wagged the dog" but rather had "wagged the flag" at bin Laden's acts of terrorism. Unfortunately, he had wagged it at the very tribal people that I knew and loved.

When I returned home to Texas from Mississippi, my phone rang non-stop. Afghans from Afghanistan and Europe were calling. Local chiefs even called me. Some of the missiles landed in their villages and had killed innocent people. They wanted to know if it was true that the U.S. had bombed them. They neither believed it nor understood it. Some thought the news was just another Soviet conspiracy and that the missiles had been fired from Russia. Every Afghan I spoke to first blamed the attack on the Soviets because "only they are that low."

I explained to the chiefs that U.S. Tomahawk Cruise Missiles had hit their country. They asked why it had happened. I told them that a man named Osama bin Laden was the cause of their problems. He blew up two U.S. embassies and killed hundreds of innocent Africans, most of whom were Muslim, to get at a handful of Americans.

The tribal chief's responded, "Screw Osama! Who is that piece of shit? We know where he lives, down in the valley? We'll get him! They don't have to bomb us." I asked the chiefs to stay away from bin Laden and not join his movement because he was hell-bent on killing Americans.

I realized that I had to find out more about this man. I contacted Mrs. Oakley at the State Department and asked her about bin Laden. She extended an invitation for me to come so I drove to Washington.

I met with Lee Coldren again. Coldren handed me a little book entitled the *al-Qaida Manifesto*.

"What's this?"

"It's from Al-Queda."

I took the little book back to Texas. Written in 1996, I could see how some of it would make sense to people living in turmoil ridden Arab countries, but I didn't feel it was right for Afghans, who considered themselves from Central Asia and didn't identify with Arabs. But then I got to the part where bin Laden declares war on Americans – *all* Americans – civilian and military. I said wait a minute and reread that part.

"Shit!" Ninety percent of my family was now American. All our babies are Americans. How could he declare war on children? Besides that, his philosophy cut across Islamic teachings. And I knew from personal experience that America wasn't just for Christians, as he said it was. It also welcomes Muslims. I felt that I knew better than bin Laden that America welcomes everyone. God had chosen this place for the oppressed, the destitute, the homeless. My family was living proof of the breadth of America's open arms. For the good of the world, everyone needs to defend this country. I refused to believe that anyone was that ignorant and hated so blindly. I would be proved wrong.

The Nairobi and Dar es Salaam bombings of the U.S. Embassies were very upsetting to me and my family. Because the media freely intermixed the name of that Arab, bin Laden, with that of Afghanistan, I hated him. I hated him for all the pain and confusion that he was bringing down upon my relatives back in the tribes. I hated him for all the death he so nonchalantly called upon others to inflict.

From that day forward I called bin Laden the *Cockroach*. He had crawled into my homes in America and Afghanistan and was fouling them. It was time for someone to hunt him down wherever he was. But it couldn't be me. I had much to do back in Texas. Afghanistan was far away and I was afraid that my contacts had dissolved with time. It was much easier to do nothing. So I returned to Texas.

On August 15, 1998, Mohammed Sadiq Odeh was arrested at the international airport in Karachi, Pakistan with a fake Yemeni passport. A Palestinian born in Saudi Arabia and educated in Jordan, he quickly confessed to being part of the conspiracy to blow up the U.S. Embassy in Nairobi, Kenya, and implicated bin Laden. He would later receive life in prison for participating in the bombings.

On October 28, 1998, Judge Nur Thaqib of Afghanistan's highest court called the Islamic court into session to determine whether bin Laden had committed the African bombings. The judge requested that every nation with evidence against bin Laden submit it to the court so it could be determined whether he should be tried for the crimes.

I heard later that no country even bothered sending proof of bin Laden's guilt to the court, not even the United States, Kenya or Tanzania. Of course sending proof to the high court meant recognition of the Taliban court and state as legitimate government entities which the world community was not prepared to do as long as the Afghan state harbored terrorists.

So everyone was caught up in a conundrum: How to get rid of bin Laden through legal channels without recognizing those legal channels as legitimate. It would prove to be a puzzle that no one could solve. But as history would soon prove, the world would have a hard time getting rid of bin Laden without officially recognizing the newly established government of the Taliban.

In February 1999, Dr. Hermat called again and asked me to get a visa from the State Department so he could visit the U.S. I complied with his request. Again I drove him to Alabama to meet with my brother.

Dr. Hermat had a letter from Hekmatyar to my brother Omar. The letter offered peace between the U.S. Government and Hekmatyar. It was an attempt to repair the damage that Hekmatyar believed had brought the Taliban into power and had kicked him out of the Afghan Government.

After talking with Omar, Hermat and I drove to D.C. There we met with Mike Malinowski. He had replaced Lee Coldren and was now the acting director of the Office of Pakistan, Afghanistan, and Bangladesh Affairs. Also present at the meeting were Don Kemp, Malinowski's assistant, and a man named Jim.

Malinowski asked Dr. Hermat why he came to the State Department. Hermat said that he was on a mission to establish a dialogue between the U.S. Government and Hekmatyar. At these words, Malinowski became angry. He said that the night before, Hekmatyar had been interviewed by Iranian television and had condemned the United States Government. Malinowski explained how Hekmatyar had gone on and on about America's propensity for world domination.

"And now he wants a dialogue?" Malinowski asked. "He's two-faced. This is no way to conduct business." Malinowski then slapped onto the table before us a transcript of the television interview in Iran.

We sat and read it. I was embarrassed for having taken Dr. Hermat to the State Department and felt a little sorry for him. He had no idea that Hekmatyar had been making slanderous statements on Iranian television. Visibly the man's shoulders slumped in dismay. I'm sure he didn't know what to do or say next.

Hoping to save face for Dr. Hermat, I suggested that the best course was for everyone to get together and talk. I realized my mind was no longer in control of my mouth when I heard myself volunteering to act as a bridge between the U.S. and Hekmatyar's group.

That's when Assistant Director Don Kemp caught me off-guard, "Afghanistan needs people like you. If you want to do something, go and speak with the Taliban and the Afghan people about Osama bin Laden. Save Afghanistan from becoming a terrorist country." I had no idea what he was talking about.

Kemp explained that the Taliban was taking every route possible to get itself recognized by the world community, but they would never receive recognition as long as they harbored Al-Queda. If the current Afghan Government could be convinced to turn over bin Laden, then they would be in a better position to get recognition from the U.S. and other nations.

He handed me the opportunity to go to Afghanistan and negotiate with the Taliban. How could I pass this one up? I decided to give it serious consideration.

I took the problem back to my brother, Omar. Later he informed me about the rich oil and gas deposits outside Mazar-e-Sharif and Sara-e-Pul and the fact that U.S. companies were not willing to go into the country because of the violence.

"Life is good," I thought. "I can go into Afghanistan, get signed contracts for the natural resources and convince the Taliban to hand over bin Laden, all in one trip." Of course hind sight only proves how naive I was at the time.

I called Mujahid, the Taliban's Ambassador to the U.N. in Queens, and explained the business purpose behind my need to visit Afghanistan. He suggested that I meet with his brother-in-law, *Mulawi* Ahmad Jan, Afghanistan's current Minister of Mining and Industries. *Mulawai*, like mullah, denotes religious study. However, a *mulawai* had studied religion in a school outside of Afghanistan; a mullah inside the country.

Soon thereafter, I called the State Department and volunteered my services – free of charge. Not working for the government allowed me to travel as a business man and to have the freedom to negotiate with the current Afghan Government if the opportunity presented itself.

I freely admit that I had mixed motives for setting upon this course of action: I wanted the rich oil and gas contracts for myself plus I wanted the Cockroach for the U.S. Government. I firmly believed that both courses of action would help the Afghan people. But in order to obtain the former, the later would have to be accomplished. From my point of view, a difficult but not impossible task lay before me.

ATT:MR MOHABT
FROM:AL HAJ MOULAWI
AHMAD JAN
SUB: INVITATION
DATE:4/5/99 7:39:04 PM

DEAR MR MOHABT

ASALA MU LE KUM

I VERY MUCH APPRECIATE YOUR TELEPHONE CONVERSATION ABOUT THE CRUDE OIL REFFINERY THAT WE INTEND TO CONSTRUCT IN AFGHANISTAN IN THE NEAR FUTURE.

I HEREBY INVITE YOU TO COME TO KABUL WITH YOUR ASSOCIATE AS YOU MAY LIKE TO COMPANY YOU TO DISCUSS MATTER OF MUTUAL INTEREST REGARDING THE CO-OPERATION BETWEEN YOUR FIRM AND OURS IN CONNECTUION WITH THE CONSTRUCTION OF OIL REFFINERY AND OTHER MUTUALLY BENEFICIAL ECONOMIC VENTURES

I HOPE TO SEE YOU IN KABUL AT YOUR EARLIEST CONVENIENCE.

SINCERELY YOURS
AL HAJ MOULAWI AHMAD JAN
MINISTER OF MINES AND INDUSTRIES
OF EMIRATE ISLAMI OF AFGHANISTAN

ATT;MR KHABIR MUHABAT

FROM:ENG,K.N.MANDAR KHAIL

SUB:REQUIRE INFORMATION

DATE;4/5/99 7:15:46 PM

DEAR SIR,

ASSALA MU ALE KUM

AS PER OUR RECENT TELEPHONE CONVERSATION.WE WANT TO BUILD A CRUDE OIL REFFINRY WITH AROUND 20000 BARREL PER DAY REFFININNG CAPACITY .AS YOU MAY WELL KNOW WE HAVE OILRESEVES OF NEARLY 20 MILLION METRIC TONS IN THE NORTHERN PARTS OF AFGHANISTAN AND ARE GOING TO EXPLORE FOR MORE IN THE WESTERN PART OF THE COUNTRY. OUR CRUDE OIL HAS A GRAVITY OF AROUND 0.9.

WE WOULD LIKE THE REFFINERY TO PRODUCE A GASOLINE,DIESEL, KEROSENE, ASPHALT ECT. WE ARE INTERSETED TO KNOW THE APPROXIMATE COST AND SPECIFICATIONS OF THE A SUID REFFINERY IT SHALL BE HIGHLY APPRECIATED,IF YOU COULD SEND US THE REQUESTED AND MORE RELEVANT INFORMATION ABOUT THE REFFINERY AT YOUR EARLIEST CONVENIENCE.

SINCERELY YOURS

ENG.K.N.MANDAR KHAIL

PRESIDENT OF THE AFHGAN

NATIONAL OIL COPMANY

Chapter 3: Where's Your Beard?

In June 1999, with an official invitation to visit Afghanistan as a guest of the government and at the behest of the U.S. State Department, I flew from Texas to Frankfurt, then to Dubai and finally to Kabul. While waiting at the gate in Dubai for the flight to Kabul on Ariana Afghan Airlines, I noticed that everyone in the waiting area wore beards and turbans. The complete change in dress from my last visit made me curious, but styles change everywhere. When a fellow passenger walked up to me and asked, "Excuse me, sir. Do you work for the airlines?" his question made me realize how different I looked from all the other passengers. I was the only person on the flight into Taliban country in a suit and sporting a clean shaven face.

Once on the small plane, the captain introduced himself to me. It really is a small world. He knew my brother, Sayad, from the Afghan Army. We had met a few times, but I didn't recognize him. He now had a long, grey beard. I had never seen a pilot with a bushy beard before. Somehow his appearance didn't give me much confidence in his abilities as a pilot. He invited me into the cockpit and said, "Where do you think you're going?" Since I was on his flight to Kabul, one would have thought the answer obvious, but I mumbled "Kabul."

"Where's your beard? Do you know there is a penalty for not having a beard in Afghanistan?" he warned and then added, "Plus you're wearing Western clothes!" as he eyed my Italian cut suit.

Apparently the penalty for dressing out of fashion in Afghanistan was ten lashes. Not exactly good news to me! I returned to my seat and looked up and down the aisle. I stuck out like a woman dressed in a bright red dress at a wedding in the Southern United States. For the first time, I began to have second thoughts about the trip, but I was stuck. The plane wasn't going to turn around just because I was worried about someone beating me senseless with a whip for being follicly challenged and having little fashion sense.

The pilot's question "Where's your beard?" would greet me at each and every stop of my journey around this once familiar country. By the end of the trip, the number of times I was asked that question reached epic proportions. Going without a beard in Afghanistan would be like chanting a Hindu mantra in the middle of services in the biggest Baptist church in Sugar Land, Texas. If my trip was made into a Hollywood movie, the words "Where's your beard?" would be put to music and become my theme song. If burned to a CD, I'm sure it would top the Afghan charts, that is if the Taliban allowed any music – or movies – or television – or singing for that matter.

From the airplane window I caught my first sight of Kabul since the War Lords grabbed leadership of the country after the Soviets left. It lay in ruins. The years of civil war had destroyed my birthplace. I began to doubt whether my old house even stood.

While in the cockpit, the Ariana pilot told me the one thing he liked about the Taliban was the fact that they did not razz the city after conquering it in 1996. Although still a monument to the devastation of civil war, he said Kabul was in worse shape than when the Taliban took it over. I had to give them some credit, at least they were trying to clean up the mess. I wished them good luck, but from the looks of things they had a long way to go.

After the passport control officer did a chorus of "Where's your beard?" he surprised me by declaring my passport invalid. It had been issued in Prague by my old friend, Ambassador

Faizi. Since Faizi represented the overthrown government of Burhanuddin Rabbani and he was now one of the leaders of the Northern Alliance who disputed the authority of the Taliban in Afghanistan, my passport was useless. To add to my fears, the officer told me it was a fake.

"It is not!" was the best response I could come up with on the spot.

"The dates do not match anything on the calendar of Afghanistan," he pronounced officiously. "In true Afghan passports there are only *Shamsi* dates."

I leaned over and peeked at the date on my passport as he held it in his hand. It looked normal to me, but he was right. The dates corresponded with the Western calendar. The difference between it and the Shamsi calendar was more than six hundred years. The person issuing the passport in Prague obviously did not know the correct date on this side of the world. Still at a loss about what to do or say, I just stood there worrying about not getting into the country – or out of it for that matter – after spending a small fortune to get there. Then a group of turbaned men approached me. By their appearance, I guessed they were trouble and thought, "Here's where the dragging out onto the street for a whipping begins." My adrenalin surged.

Instead, one of them identified himself as Mulawai Elmi, the Taliban's first deputy in the Ministry of Mining and Industries. Mr. Elmi then introduced me to Mr. K. N. Mandar Khail, the President, Department of Oil, Ministry of Mining and Industries, and a few other Taliban officials whose names and titles have slipped my mind.

Elmi snatched up my passport from the clerk's hands, said I was a guest of the state – the Islamic Emirate of Afghanistan – and whisked me away to a waiting car.

In the car, I became more nervous by the second. I said to the Taliban officials that I had heard that they beat people without beards. "I refuse to grow a beard. I would like to go to the Ministry of Vice and Virtue now to get my beating over with. But I will do this only once," I said in defiance.

They laughed at me and then assured me that the Taliban was very respectful of its guests. Since I was a guest of the government, beatings did not apply to me.

For the first time since landing, I relaxed – but only a little. Asking for a beating had broken the ice and I was very glad they declined my request for one. I had heard about the Ministry. It was not a good place for the country's citizens or its tourists.

We sped off to the Spen Zar Hotel in downtown Kabul. A sleek modern building constructed in the 1960's, I was surprised to see it still stood after all that had happened to the city during the rule of the War Lords. I was told that I was getting the exact rooms reserved for the old deposed King of Afghanistan when he came to town. I anticipated a royal suite splattered with gold this and silver that. Looking about the humble room, I guessed that the old king's tastes must be pretty basic. I was disappointed. I wanted the royal treatment, you know, the wretched excess we hear about kings getting on television. Instead I got Anywhere, U.S.A.

We arranged to meet the next morning. After the marathon flight, I needed time to recover. I lay down on the bed and stretched out.

My first encounter with the reclusive Taliban had gone well. They weren't as scary as portrayed on the news. I made it into the country without receiving a whipping for my lack of virtue. Life is good! But as I lay there, my mind running amuck, I wondered what the new day would bring.

Early in the morning the hotel staff woke me an hour before Mulawai Ahmad Jan, the Minister of Mining and Industries, and his entourage were to arrive at the hotel. I dressed again in my suit. Although I owned *shalwar kameez* (traditional clothes), I had left them behind in Texas. I preferred the Taliban to see me as I am, part Afghan and part American. I slipped on my cowboy boots and Winsored my tie.

An hour later Ahmad Jan, his two deputies, Mulawai Elmi and Mullah Salam Zaeef, and a few others arrived. On behalf of his government, Ahmad Jan formally welcomed me to Afghanistan. I was up and running, but beginning to wonder where the race would take me.

After a lengthy exchange of platitudes and pleasantries, we began to talk openly. Of particular interest to the Afghan officials was the U.S.'s "unprovoked" hostility toward the Taliban (another mantra I would often hear repeated). They didn't understand what the problem was between our countries. They assumed since we fought the Soviets together, we were friends.

I believed that the Taliban's senior officials must realize that their relationship with the U.S. was quickly approaching the point of no return. Unless we resolved our differences, there would be no oil deal which we both wanted. Their Ambassador in New York had probably explained to them that I had met with the State Department and was there to resolve issues. He may have also let slip that I had been a muj and a political officer to the mujahidin.

I explained to the officials gathered in my hotel room that they should not doubt that the Americans were angry. Two of their embassies had been bombed and bin Laden had claimed responsibility.

They quickly countered that bin Laden himself never took responsibility for those acts. They argued their point by whipping out news articles showing that bin Laden never claimed that either he or his men participated in the bombings. "He never ordered it and was never a part of it, but he did say it was a good thing to do," one of them volunteered, convinced this would sway me.

Not knowing at that time about Mohammed Saddiq Odeh's arrest at the Karachi Airport for the bombings of the U.S. Embassies in Nairobi, Kenya and Dar es Salaam, Tanzania on August 7, 1998, or that he had implicated bin Laden in the embassy bombings, I was not prepared to argue back. I had no news articles to flash. Rather I quietly insisted that bin Laden *was* the man behind many of the terrorist attacks in the world. I warned them that Afghanistan would soon be considered a terrorist state if bin Laden was not ejected. Then I explained how Mike Malinowski at the U.S. State Department had warned me that international sanctions would soon be placed on Afghanistan, but that I had no personal knowledge of this fact. And there we left the argument for another time.

Minister Ahmad Jan suggested that I visit Mazar-e-Sharif (the headquarters for the Ministry of Oil) and Sara-e-Pull in the Sheberghan Province as their guest. These fields, rich in oil and gas, lay in the northern part of the country. He advised me to go there, take photos and meet the people in charge of the fields. I quickly agreed. But before traveling north, I wanted to catch up with some of my family and friends that hadn't immigrated after the Soviet invasion.

Because I had no beard, I traveled around town mostly at night or, if I had to during the day, I used a Jeep with blackened windows. In addition to family members, I tried to connect with anyone who grew up in the old neighborhood. Probably because our house was located behind the old Soviet Embassy, not much remained of it. It broke my heart to see it in ruins, but my life was now in Texas, so it quickly mended. I stopped and asked shopkeepers about people

I once knew, but not one person remained in the neighborhood. I understood why. The devastation by the War Lords was complete.

A few days later, I flew to Mazar-e-Sharif with one of Ahmad Jan's staff members. Since there were no movies or music on the plane, there was little to do during the 1-1/2 hour flight except talk with those sitting around me. Everyone on the plane thought I was a foreigner until I opened my mouth and Pashto came out.

I was surprised to learn that the pilot of the plane was from Virginia. He had come to Afghanistan to join the Taliban's war against the Northern Alliance. I thought his decision a little odd. Why would he want to leave beautiful, tree covered Virginia for this bombed out wasteland. "He may be CIA," I thought to myself as he warned me that it wasn't a good idea to run about the countryside bare faced. A statement of monumental proportions, but growing a bushy beard in a week was not an option.

When the plane landed at Mazar-e-Sharif, the pilot told everyone to remain in their seats. We watched as sport utility vehicles approached the aircraft. I looked out the window. A knot grew in my stomach as armed men rushed the plane. "I hope this isn't about the beard," I thought but quickly dismissed it.

Suddenly the cockpit radio jumped to life. The pilot listened intently and then turned to me and said, "Mr. Mohabbat, you go first." Adrenalin shot through my body like a bullet from a jawz. This can't be good. I hesitated momentarily before realizing that I had no option but to do as told. I had nowhere to go and no one to help me get there. I smiled back at the bearded pilot from Virginia and asked whether I should have the guys in the SUV's dry shave his beard. He laughed at my empty threat.

The SUV's proved to be my security escort. I felt privileged and afraid at the same time at so much attention being paid to my visit.

Mulawai Abdul Rahman Rhamani, the General Director of Oil and Mining of the Northern Provinces, met the plane. He was about twenty-eight years old. He wouldn't have witnessed much of the fight against the USSR. He couldn't have been more than a small boy when his relatives fought the Soviets.

Rhamani's news was not good. The oil and gas fields at Sara-e-Pull were another two hundred or so miles and the roads were so bad a round trip journey of that distance could take days. Rhamani suggested that we rest, have supper together and take off in the morning.

Before dinner another mulawai, Ghulam Nabi, the Director of Factories of the Northern Province, joined us. Nabi asked whether visiting the chemical fertilizer factories in Mazar-e-Sharif was agreeable to me. They wanted to upgrade them and wished my opinion.

"Why not? The info could prove valuable in the future to me and to U.S. authorities." I wondered whether I should get to know Nabi better. I had heard that he was a high ranking member of the Taliban, but establishing a friendship wasn't meant to be. I had little contact with him after that night.

The governor of Mazar-e-Sharif finally appeared and we all sat down to dinner. I soon learned that eating, conversation and visiting fertilizer factories and oil and gas fields was what passed for entertainment in this part of the world.

After dinner the representatives of the Taliban government asked me why the U.S. felt so much animosity toward them. They didn't believe they had done anything to warrant such hostility.

"Hadn't our fathers fought with the U.S. against the communists?" they argued.

I could see their point of view. Every one of them had lost a father, brother, nephew or cousin in the fight against the Red Army. I soon came to the realization that they knew nothing about the U.S. I tried to explain that America was not against them because of religion. I told them the history of the U.S. and how it was founded. It was not a country like

Afghanistan, Germany, France or England that has special nationalities that claim the land as their own. The U.S. had been put on earth to help those neglected, oppressed and persecuted.

"It is the place that God has chosen for all kinds of people. It is one of the unique places on Earth. When you go there you immediately see the diversity of the country. It's a great country, a country of laws! You are allowed to practice any religion you want whether Hindu, Jew, Christian or Muslim. And no one can grab your property or your money. The police are there to protect you not help the government take property, as in some countries."

They asked me whether the police were white or black. I explained they were from every nationality. This surprised them; they had only seen white American diplomats.

Everyone began to relax as I answered their questions honestly. Then it became my turn to ask questions. "What is the Saudi Arabian, Osama bin Laden, doing in Afghanistan?"

"Osama is our guest," one of the officials explained.

"Oh, crap!" I thought. Guests are given a very high status in the Pashtun culture as long as they have enough good sense not to overstay or abuse their welcome. It would take a jack hammer to crack through the ancient tribal customs for the correct handling of guests to get him out of Afghanistan.

After some hesitation I said, "How long should you keep a guest in your home?"

"As long as it takes."

"No," I said. "You are wrong. Let's say you have a family and I come to visit you. I spend a night with you, then a week, a month, six months, a year. Even though, according to custom, you should be very nice to me – your guest – don't you think that someday your family will tire of me? They won't want to cook for me anymore. They won't want to treat me the way I demand to be treated as your guest. Being a guest does not mean you can stay in a place forever."

One of them said that Osama was a "special kind of guest."

"Then you mean to tell me that he is here for *nanawati* (sanctuary)," I asked in disbelief.

"Yes. He has asked for nanawati."

Suddenly I understood why the Saudi was still skulking around Afghanistan after all this time. They had given him protection which implies permission to stay as long as he wants. "But why would they give him nanawati?" I wondered. I was never able to latch onto enough information to figure out why he was given nanawati. Because arguing against nanwati is almost impossible, I choose to shock them by stating, "This man is nothing but a terrorist!"

Rhamani's face grew red with anger at my statement. He began to look like he was swallowing fighting words that he would like to shoot in my direction, but because I was a guest of his government, he was forced to eat them. I had not known that Rhamani was an admirer of bin Laden's, but I knew it now.

His boss, Minister Ahmad Jan, visibly tried to distance himself from me. Then Ghulam Nabi, the factory director, gestured for me to stop talking. Rhamani brought himself under control enough to say "No matter what the cost, we will keep this man because he has asked for nanawati!"

I did not need to waste any more time or words on Rhamani. He had made up his mind. Nor was he in any position to help me achieve my goals. But, since I had gone far enough to call bin Laden a terrorist, I could not back away quickly or easily. I decided to attack and to hammer my point further. I said, "Okay, you are keeping a man who has declared jihad against all Americans – against me – I am your brother, your countryman. He is a foreigner."

"No, he hasn't," Rhamani said.

"Yes he has. You need to read his writing – his book. I have." By their silence I knew I had won this small point.

I explained that bin Laden was a thug and was not good for the current Afghan Government. He was bringing onto the country United Nation sanctions. I let this sink in, but it didn't sink far enough because most of those gathered around me were so parochial they had no notion what that meant.

Generally what I said was well received by the group until Rhamani argued a second point. He said that bin Laden had sworn on the Quran that he never committed any of the acts for which the West accused him. They had seen him in front of Mullah Omar swearing that he had not committed the bombings against America and that America was doing everything themselves with the aid of the Jewish State. It was all a conspiracy against him. He told the mullahs and the Afghan public every chance he got that he was an innocent man.

I began to wonder whether bin Laden was lying or whether he was making a narrow argument when he said that *he* never committed these acts. In point of fact, it was true that *he* hadn't done them himself. Instead ideologically driven young people were called upon to act. And these bastards before me were too simple-minded to see that when asking bin Laden to swear on the Quran, they could be making him swear broadly rather than narrowly, an oath that was the truth but still a lie. Oaths are constructed around details. If the details aren't just right, an oath can be taken that is meaningless. Watching the movie *A Man for All Seasons* taught me that much.

About ten minutes into my speech about bin Laden, Rhamani lifted his drooping head and said to me, "Mr. Mohabbat. You are our guest and we welcome you. You have traveled a long way. I know you are a mujahid and used to fight the Soviet invaders and we have a lot of respect for those who fought them. Anyone else but you, I would have withdrawn my hospitality for saying what you did about Osama. I am not saying that I would be hostile toward them, but I would have withdrawn my attention."

"Well, if you are upset, remember this is my country, too," I said.

Rahmani added, "I know it's your country, but we have Osama as a guest."

"If you are going to defend Osama in front of me, then we really have nothing in common. Why should I travel to the oil and gas sites? We already have animosity between us."

"No, that's not true," Rhamani said obviously worried about what his boss, the Minister, was thinking.

"This is my country. This is where I was born and this country is a part of me. In everything that happens in this country, I have a share. I am here to explore the oil and natural gas fields and I plan to take my rightful share. If you are going to betray me – if you are mad because of a foreign man who has done nothing but bring harm to Islam and to the Taliban movement and to the Afghan people, then so be it. I will take your hostility and I'll *take you to the mountains* (fight you to the death).

"That's not necessary." Rhamani backed down and sounded sheepish. "No harm! I just told you my opinion." Frustrated by the vast chasm between our points of view, we called it a night.

Rhamani arranged for me to see the sites at Sara-e-Pull, a vast Afghan reserve of gas and oil fields that had been partially explored by the Soviets in the 1960s. Before the breakup of the U.S.S.R. into numerous bits and pieces, it and Afghanistan had been divided by the Amu Darya River. Soviet exploration of the natural gas field showed that on the Afghan side of the river the ground level is higher than on the Soviet side. Since gases seek the highest level, any digging in the area causes the natural gas to pool on the Afghan side of the field. The Soviets delivered King Zahir a warning to not explore anywhere in the area. They feared any type of development because they would lose gas. So the Soviets built a natural gas pipeline that ran from the Afghan side of the field into the U.S.S.R. Basically this gave the Soviets a monopoly over Afghan gas.

The amount of gas siphoned out of Afghanistan by its northern neighbor can never be determined. The meter showing the amount of gas exported was located on the

Soviet side of the river. The Afghan engineers explained to me that the meter broke at least once a year – like clockwork – and it always took the Soviets four to five months to fix it. The Soviets always said that they were shutting down the pipeline when this occurred, but they never did. Unregistered Afghan gas flowed freely into the adjoining country year after year. To say the Soviets took advantage of the government of the Afghan King is an understatement. But little could be done about it until the King, and then the Soviets, were ousted.

When President Daoud expelled the King in 1973, eventually he hired a French company to explore the fields. They were the first to discover the drain of Afghan gas. Then the Soviets warned Daoud not to touch the oil and gas fields, but Daoud was an Afghan through and through. He warned Leonid Brezhnev in 1978 (I believe) that he was withdrawing from their contract. I know this happened because my cousin, Joma Mohammadi, one of Daoud's cabinet ministers, was present at the meeting of the two leaders in Moscow.

I left Mazar-e-Sharif for the oil fields in Sara-e-Pull with a group of Taliban officials. The area near the northern border of Afghanistan is a very rough place where one must always travel with body guards. Thankfully we were able to travel the two hundred miles from Mazar-e-Sharif to Sara-e-Pull without incident.

On the road to Sara-e-Pull, our caravan stopped for afternoon prayers. Before a Muslim can pray he must cleanse his hands, face and privates. The mullahs ordered the SUV's to pull over at a small river for this solemn ablution.

I leaned out of the sport utility vehicle and peeked down at the grimy, black water. Turning to the highest ranking mullah, I said, "Mullah, *Sahib* (Sir), I am not going to wash in this water. Islam calls for clean water. This is filthy! It won't purify me; it'll make me unclean." I made it clear that I drew the line at religious rituals that called for washing in rank sludge just because I peed a few hours earlier.

The Mullah laughed and kindly taped me on the arm, "I'm sorry you feel that way. Of course you are forgiven, if that's how you feel."

The others washed in the muck, but I couldn't watch. I skipped that prayer session. Prayer is something one can always do later.

Rising from the black earth in Sara-e-Pull were twenty or so oil wells in about a ten square mile area. Surrounding each well was dirt soaked black with oil. The field was in a state of neglect and the equipment was antiquated. Looking around me, I had to assume that only a very small portion of the natural resource was being pumped out of the ground.

At Spindeltop the Texans were forced to drill a deep hole to reach oil. The authorities told me that at these Afghan fields all one needed was a bucket and a shovel and you were in the oil business. Dig down fifteen feet and you had black gold and the hole you dug would seep crude for days. You could not walk around for all of the bubbling oil. After just a few minutes of walking the field, I looked down and saw that my shoes were ruined.

Primitive equipment was scattered around each well and people were converting crude into diesel fuel using small homemade refineries. The area was an appalling mess and should have been of environmental concern due to the run-off. I asked the people working the little refineries if they knew that they were killing themselves. Their common response, "You have to make a living." The poorest nation on earth filled with so much untapped wealth. I promised the Afghan officials that I would do whatever I could to bring modern refineries to the area.

A little further up the road, my guides showed me a large hole in the ground. It measured about twenty feet in diameter. The hole was made when natural gas leaking from a fissure exploded. My guides grabbed a scrap of paper, lit it, and threw it in the hole. A fireball fifteen feet high suddenly exploded in front of us. That hole leaked natural gas 24/7.

I was told that children loved to play there despite warnings to stay away. But making exploding fire balls was probably the only fun around this desolate area. Unlike the adults, at least the children put the natural gas to some use.

I promised my hosts that I would tell the U.S. Government about the potential of these fields. Clearly investors with modern technology would be interested in what I had witnessed. I believed that if diggers could make a living, a modern refinery would bring undreamed of wealth. I took photographs and we returned to Mazar-e-Sharif.

During the trip back to Mazar-e-Sharif, I became dehydrated. I requested some water, but we had used up all our bottled water. The only thing left was the melted ice where the bottles had floated. Unfortunately an inch or two of dirt lay on the bottom of the cooler. I thought, "What's worse – dehydration or drinking dirt?" I chose dehydration and drank the water.

By the time we got to the oil ministry's guest house in Mazar-e-Sharif, I was sick. Doubled over in pain, I pled with one of my bodyguards for help. He called for a doctor and one soon came. He examined me and pulled a needle from his little bag.

"What's in the needle?"

"Morphine."

"I don't need any of that shit."

The doctor reassured me that it was appropriate for my condition. I was in pain and there wasn't any other remedy available. He tried to reassure me that this particular dose of medicine had been left behind by a French doctor and wasn't something generated in one of the country's poppy fields. What I was being offered was all there was to relieve my condition. Given the choice between excruciating pain or dope, I chose dope. Relief and then black sleep quickly overtook me.

Through the remainder of the trip, I closely watched my health. I decided that in this country, the cure could be worse than the illness.

Mulawai Rhamani and I flew back to Kabul together. Since he was a close associate of Mullah Omar, there was heightened security for our flight back. Rhamani explained that he used an assumed name for the flight.

At the airport, I was told to hold back and get on the plane last. As our car approached the plane resting on the runway, Rhamani ordered the driver to return to the terminal.

"What's happening?" I asked.

Rhamani said that he wanted to see the plane start its engines and turn at the end of the runway before we got on.

"Is that much security really necessary?"

He explained that he feared problems because people had noticed me in the country. My death could mean that their relationship with the West would also die – something that more conservative members of the Taliban craved.

As the plane turned at the end of the runway, Rhamani ordered, "Let's go," and we drove toward it. As we pulled alongside the aircraft, its door swung open and I climbed on board. Once air borne, I was free to ask Rhamani questions that had been on my mind for days.

"Why do the Taliban cut off so many people's hands? Don't public executions occur almost daily?" I was interested in having him go into details about what I had heard back home.

The Director of Oil explained that the Taliban uses the radio to announce things that *could* happen more than events that actually happened. For example, they announce over the radio that two hands were cut off for stealing today.

"Trust me," he said, "in the last three years we have only cut-off the hands of eight people."

"You mean the radio announcements are propaganda?"

He laughed. "Well, I can say it's a lie. It's good for the people." He explained that before the Taliban came to power, the people acted against each other. "You couldn't even carry around five dollars in your pocket. Worse, if you had a young daughter, you had to call your house all night long out of fear that someone would kidnap or rape her."

I had heard how bad it had gotten between 1992 and 1996 from one of my cousins. She was head of a girl's school. She said that men would break into the school and kidnap young girls and carry them off. Often girls would commit suicide rather than live with their captors. It was true that in some nearby countries kidnaping was considered the best way to get a wife, but it was never a sanctioned practice in Afghanistan.

I began to understand the Taliban's purpose behind some of their actions, even though I didn't necessarily agree with their methods. They were trying to reign in some of the chaos that was unleashed during the time of the War Lords. But their methods – I don't know. I didn't think anyone could convince me their methods were *good*. Perhaps they were just the least egregious of the bad choices available. I'd have to think about it.

By the time we got to Kabul, Rhamani seemed convinced by our conversation that bin Laden was bad for Afghanistan. I said again that the Saudi had claimed responsibility for some terrorist acts, which condemned him in the eyes of the U.S. The only way that bin Laden could save his skin was to publicly prove to the world that he had not done these things. But he wouldn't do that because he wanted to be a big Islamic stud.

"I mean look at the man," I said. "He must get a makeover before going in front of the cameras. Look at those eyebrows. That's not for a man! To me he is a poser who loves to have his name heard all over the world. He loves to hear everyone talking about him on the radio."

I warned Rhamani again about the sanctions that were coming. I explained how much they would hurt the Afghan people. He saw my point of view. Would he do anything to help? I had my doubts.

The daily schedule of the Taliban differed greatly from my own. They woke at dawn for prayers, worked until 1:00 in the afternoon and then broke for lunch. This concluded their work day. The reasoning behind going home early was to give government employees the rest of the day to do their own business. I guessed this was done because they weren't paid much – if anything – and they had to supplement their salaries somehow. I wondered how most of them did it. Poppies? Heroin? Smuggling?

It was hard for me to keep their schedule. I am not a morning person. Meetings at 6:30 in the morning, no matter how congenial the host, are not my cup of tea.

Back in Kabul and after morning prayers, Rhamani knocked on my hotel room door. He asked if we could have breakfast together. With him were several of his close associates, but I can't remember their names. Rhamani said that he had heard of my appointment that day with Mr. Ahmad Jan (Minister of Mining and Industries), Maulawi Azam Elmi (deputy to Ahmad Jan), and Mullah Abdul Salam Zaeef (another deputy). With a grin on his face, he dared me to talk about bin Laden at the upcoming meeting. I told him that I had plans to do just that.

About 9:30 a.m. Land Cruisers from the Minister of Mining and Industries pulled up to the hotel. They found me in my room and swept me away to the ministry. Rhamani was at the meeting, as was Minister Ahmad Jan.

I thanked my hosts for the trip to the north. I told them about the ecological disaster posed by the oil and gas situation in Sara-e-Pull. "This country needs help really badly."

Ahmad Jan laughed and replied, "That's why you are here. You're from Texas. I have been to Texas, to Stafford, where the Unocal office is."

I asked him what had happened with their deal with Unocal. He said that the Taliban had offered the American firm sixty to seventy percent profit for the pipeline, but the contract proposed by the Americans was unrealistic. It offered only about ten percent to the Afghans for their gas and for the pipeline. So the negotiations had broken down.

Rhamani interrupted. He confirmed that I was there to help with their oil and gas problems, but there was something bigger that they needed my help with.

"What is it?"

"Osama."

I took my cousin Esmat Zaqomi, to the meeting with Minister Ahmad Jan. From a small village, he liked to accompany me around Kabul whenever I was in town. At meetings, Esmat would only sit and watch. When we stopped talking about oil and began discussing bin Laden, he became very uncomfortable.

"I must say what's in my heart," I said.

"That's why you're here and you should tell us what you think," Ahmad Jan said.

"I have been warned repeatedly that as long as Osama is in your country, no American corporation will come to Afghanistan. The U.N. sanctions that are coming will work against you even more. They will prevent me and other people from coming here and doing business with you. For example, after November there will be no flights into Afghanistan. You know the country. The roads are awful; the airports are bad. Because of the War Lords, there is no infrastructure left. How are businessmen supposed to get here?"

"We have talked to the Americans about Osama, but the Americans would not give us any kind of documentation that he is guilty. We simply can't hand over a person just because somebody tells us that he's a criminal."

"Let me explain to you what I have learned in my years as a politician," I said putting it in the simplest terms available to me. "There is something called power. The Americans are very powerful people. Nobody can match them anymore and they know that. They will take Osama from you, one way or the other. They can destroy you in the process." I paused to let the words sink in. Out of the corner of my eye, I could see Zaeef fidget.

I broached the subject of the bombing of the two American embassies in Africa by bin Laden. I related a conversation that I had with Steven McCain, deputy for South Asian Affairs in the State Department. His son's playmate in the American embassy in Nairobi, Kenya was a little Muslim boy. "He wasn't even an American, but he was killed in the bombing. Hundreds of Muslims were killed to get at a dozen U.S. embassy employees. These bombing are making enemies, and you are making enemies because you are host to the man accused of the bombings.

"Let's do something different," I said. "Let's announce to the whole world that we Muslims are not fanatics – we are not wild. We have a good book named the Quran, and the Quran says that you should not kill others and that you should not kill yourself." They all agreed with me. So what is holding them back from acting, I began to wonder.

I moved in for the diplomatic kill by insisting that bin Laden be returned to Saudi Arabia. The Taliban officials sat quietly on the floor contemplating my words.

Minister Ahmad Jan broke the silence, "Ok. We will talk among ourselves and see what we can arrange. But it will be impossible for us to hand him over directly to Americans. You find us a country, preferably a Muslim one, and we will talk among us."

"That's fine, because the United Nations resolution that's coming calls for a third country," I said.

"We will think about this and let you know what we decide."

One of the officials said, "We'll we just can't hand over an innocent person. It's very possible that we can be convinced by the Americans that Osama is guilty. I have seen Osama. I have met with him quite a few times. This man cries every time we meet. He cries in front of Mullah Omar. Then he swears on the Quran that he has not committed any of these crimes."

"You guys could be pretty popular here because you brought stability to Afghanistan," I said. "You have brought back something that Afghanistan had lost – honor – and that is the only good thing going for you. In the rest of the world, you are nothing but a bunch of barbarians because you don't respect human rights. My point is this, on your road to power, I am sure hundreds of people died. Do you agree, Mr. Minister?"

Puzzled, Zaeef replied, "Yes."

"There was a war."

"Yes."

"And in war time, people die."

"Yes."

"Let's assume that five thousand people died," I said. "Are you going to tell me that not a single *innocent* person was killed on the way?"

"I'm sure there were."

"That's exactly what I mean. These people are powerful. In order for you to be in power – to stay in power – what is one more life to be sacrificed to save millions?"

I could see on his face that my argument affected Zaeef. I would later learn that he, too, was a close confident of Mullah Omar's.

I ended the conversation by stating that there was nothing that I could do to stop the international sanctions. "I cannot afford for the American government to get mad at me because ninety percent of my family lives there. I don't really know if the man is innocent or not, but I know one thing, if you want to bring stability and peace to Afghanistan, somebody has to sacrifice. Maybe Osama is that sacrificial lamb. If he's innocent, he will go to a better place – heaven." We agreed to meet again.

While hopping onto the Land Cruiser outside the ministry, my cousin Esmat said, "You know what you said inside?"

"Yes."

"I hope the Taliban didn't mark me as your relative. I don't know what kind of power you have behind you, but I am really scared for your life – for my life. Maybe as a guest they won't do anything to you, but I'm afraid that they will kill me."

"No. No, they won't."

I asked him to stay, but Esmat felt safer returning to his village. He was sorry he attended the meeting and had no plans to show up in Kabul again. I explained that what I said was the truth. Afraid to get into the car with me, the Taliban driver asked him where he was going. Esmat replied that he had something else to do downtown. I told the driver to let him go.

Esmat's comments left me wondering whether I had gone too far. The whole world was talking about the Taliban, al-Qaida, Mullah Omar and bin Laden. And here I had just thrown myself into the mix. I wondered if Esmat was right and I should be concerned for my life.

At the hotel, I continued to worry. Uncharacteristically I ate dinner by myself in the room. I tried to go to sleep, but couldn't for thinking about what I had said. Rumors bubbled into my memory. I had heard that the Cockroach was very tight with Mullah Omar, the he had married his daughter. Worry about Omar being friendly with bin Laden became panic and fear that they had a close family bond. It wasn't until later that I learned from a member of the hotel staff that a wedding couldn't be possible. Omar's daughter was only three years old.

About 6:00 a.m. there was a knock on the door. Not anxious to answer it for obvious reasons, I finally gathered the courage to see who was out there. Standing in the hall was Minister Ahmad Jan. I opened the door.

I apologized to the Minister for my disheveled appearance.

He laughed. "Yes. I came to wake you up. I thought that you may not have slept well last night."

"Well, I guess you can tell. I doubt that you slept very well either," I said.

Bravely he answered, "We really don't like our guest Osama, nor do we want to dishonor our guest. Don't worry!

Everything is going to be fine. We could see that you were speaking from your heart."

"I don't fear anyone but God," I bluffed.

"Yes, I could tell. Otherwise it's a very fearful subject when it comes to Osama. You know the Taliban are very simple people and they think that he's an innocent man. God knows, Mr. Mohabbat, whether he's guilty or he's not guilty. Some of us are convinced that we must sacrifice somebody. Osama must be ejected from Afghanistan."

I said, "I honestly don't know whether he is guilty or not, but you need to join the world community. America is one of the most powerful countries in the world, but they always seem to need an enemy. The country is run mostly by businessmen who like competition. If they don't have competition, they will create it. Osama is the competition. He is gaining the wrong kind of fame. Osama must go."

In my zeal to oust bin Laden from Afghanistan, I had forgotten about the issue of drugs which members of the State Department had asked me to mention. I decided to bring it up now.

"By the way, I have another message from the U.S. Government – about stopping the drugs."

Ahmad Jan said, "This we can do something about. That's not a problem because Afghans understand. We know drugs are bad for society. There are lots of addicted Afghans. We do not know about a lot of things, but we know opium is not good for anybody. We used to make a little because of addicted people and for local cultivation as a pain killer. People also used it as a medication for colds. But now it's really getting out of hand. We hear it all the time that there are billions of dollars of business in heroin."

That subject was finally out in the open so I jumped back into the issue of bin Laden. "What are your thoughts about what I said about Osama? And what can you do about it?"

"Mr. Mohabbat, why don't you go back to the United States and come back in a few months. Let me talk to the mulawais who are opposed to having Osama here. He has been a liability." This was a big admission on his part.

I asked him whether he had ever met bin Laden.

"Yes, I have a few times, but he does not mention on the radio anything that we heard from you. On the radio, he shows no animosity toward any kind of foreigners."

I told him that I had read his manifesto and that he called for the deaths of my family.

"Your family! You are joking!"

"No. You must read it yourself. I am sure you can find a copy of it. Or you could ask Osama, if you know him very well. This man has declared war on every American, whether a child, woman, man, old or young, Army officials, civilians. He has declared war on all of us. Your Excellency, it really is my war. I will fight him out of self-defense."

Jokingly Ahmad Jan said, "What if we tell him that you're a good Muslim?"

"It won't work. Maybe you could save me, but he would kill my family."

Ahmad Jan told me they had given me enough information about the oil fields and the natural gas in Afghanistan to propose a package to an American corporation. He said that the Americans are welcome to come and do honest business. Since Americans have the technology, he was willing to give a company about sixty percent of the natural resource and retain forty for the Afghans. He told me to find the right people and talk to them.

"By the time you return," he said, "I would have spoken to our group of moderate mulawais, headed up by Foreign Minister Wakil Mutawakel." Ahmad Jan agreed to have an appointment with him ready for me whenever I came back. He said that Minister Mutawakel was a very open person who did not like Osama at all and he understood international politics.

Ahmad Jan and I visited for several more hours. Then my relatives began showing up at the hotel room to wish me well and we all had lunch together.

After lunch, Zaeef and his entourage appeared at my hotel door. Surprised to see him, I served tea. He asked to speak with me privately, so I asked my family to leave. Because of his rank within the Taliban, his request made me uncomfortable. Ahmad Jan had explained to me that Zaeef was one of the closest confidants of Mullah Omar. They spoke almost daily and once a month he traveled to Kandahar to spend a week with him. Everything that occurs, Zaeef reports to Omar. Even though he was only a Deputy Minister of Mining and Industry, he was a very powerful man in the Taliban.

I should pause a moment and explain that sometimes the most powerful person in a department of the Taliban government is the deputy. Among Afghan Muslims it shows great integrity when offered an office of importance to decline and agree to act as deputy. So contrary to Western culture, the actual person running a department was sometimes the assistant department head. Every time I met a deputy minister, I automatically assumed that he could be the power behind the office. This applies to high offices too, like that of Mullah Omar's, which I will explain in the next chapter.

Zaeef laughed at me and said, "Mr. Mohabbat, you are a very brave man."

"Sir, I am one of you. You're Pashtun; I'm Pashtun. That's something every Pashtun has to have – bravery," I said with pride.

"Well, you have spent much time in foreign countries, but you really have not forgotten the way of a Pashtun." Looking me up and down he said, "You talk like a Pashtun. You walk like a Pashtun. I think I could be fond of you. And I am very proud to see someone coming from another country and retaining their heritage and their language."

I returned the compliment. I extolled Zaeef courageousness in fighting for the peace and stability of Afghanistan over the years. It was rumored that he had several bullet wounds from the wars, but modesty kept me from asking where.

Zaeef explained that after I left the Ministry of Mining and Industries, he had spoken to Mullah Omar by satellite phone. He told Omar that an Afghan named Kabir Mohabbat from Jaji, Paktia is in town. He is the son of Allah Mir Kahn from the South, the one who made Zahir's father a king. He is beardless and dressed in a Western-styled suit. He has come to this country as an Afghan and as a Pashtun. Zaeef told Omar that if there was any punishment for not having a beard, I had volunteered to take it since I had broken the law. He said that Omar had laughed and said, "That's a very courageous thing to do." Zaeef spoke at length with him about our meeting the day before. Mullah Omar agreed to think about all that I said. He asked Zaeef to take personal responsibility for my safety and hospitality. He also suggested that Zaeef encourage me to grow a beard, but, Omar had added, there would never be punishment for not having one.

Chapter 4: In the Belly of the Beast

During the June 1999, trip to Afghanistan, I explained to the eight Taliban officials gathered in the office of Mulawai Ahmad Jan, the Minister of Oil and Industries, that I had met with representatives of the U.S. State Department who told me about a troublesome man by the name of Osama bin Laden living in Afghanistan. He was implicated in many terrorist activities throughout the world. It was suggested in the meeting that bin Laden be expelled from Afghanistan and extradited to the U.S. or to another country. I warned the gathering of men that for them to stay in power, this must occur – they had no choice. They understood the gravity of my remarks and saw the need for bin Laden to leave the country.

Minister Ahmad Jan thanked me for my bluntness. He apologized that they were isolated and did not know much about the outside world. They had requested that I open up direct contact with their American friends who had helped them defeat communism.

"Without America's help," Ahmad Jan said, "we would have lost our country and our God to the Soviets. We heard that in the U.S. they are very much a godly people. It even says *In God We Trust* on their money."

I explained that I, too, had recently devoted my life and my work to God. "It was my faith in God that gave me the strength to enter your country." I told them that I trusted the American government and that I would do my best for our two countries. I gave Ahmad Jan my hand and my word that I would not betray him.

They freely admitted that Osama had been a liability to Afghanistan. He was a leftover from the fight against the Soviets. Ahmad Jan did not know what I had done with the mujahidin, but for Osama, he was little more than a CIA whore. He had taken U.S. dollars during the Afghan fight against communism and now he could be using some of those dollars to fight his benefactor. They asked for a few months to work out the problem of Osama. The moderate mullahs swore that they would do everything within their power to help me get rid of the Cockroach.

As a final note, I told them if growing a beard would help sway their decision in my favor, I would happily grow a beard down to my belly button.

While on my way back to the U.S. from Kabul, the Taliban provided me with a Jeep and my bodyguards and I drove to the city of Jalalabad. We then traveled to the Afghan border with Pakistan. I wanted to determine how bad the roads had become. As a teenager the trip from Kabul to the Afghan border and the Pakistani town of Torahum took three hours. This time it took about nine. The highway was in such bad repair that our vehicle could not go faster than five to six miles an hour. The pot holes posed such a problem that I wished I had brought along a bicycle helmet. My head kept hitting the roof and sides of the Jeep. I was afraid that I would become brain damaged. Once across the border at Torahum, I rented a taxi for the trip to Peshawar and on to Islamabad by car.

Before leaving the U.S., Phyllis Oakley asked me to visit the U.S. Ambassador in Islamabad, so I called at the Embassy. The Ambassador was not available; an emergency had occurred and he was meeting with the President of Pakistan. I was, however, able to meet with his deputy, John Schmidt.

Schmidt seemed straightforward enough, but at first he assumed I was one of the Afghan refugees wanting to immigrate to America. He made me uncomfortable staring at my Pal Zaliri suit and my Moreschi Italian boots.

I assured him that I had attended university in the United States and was not a refugee. I patiently explained that I had been visiting the Taliban at the behest of our government. After we sat down he said, "Well, I'm glad that we have someone coming from Afghanistan who saw with his own eyes how horrible things are."

"I didn't see anything horrible; I saw peace. A few years back I went to Kabul and it was horrible. No one could travel outside the city. Yesterday I drove from Kabul all the way to the border of Pakistan and nobody bothered me. There was that much security."

"We know about the security. What about other things?"

"The country has no infrastructure. It doesn't have a police force. They're trying to do their best to secure the country. Other things will have to wait."

Schmidt explained the current U.S. policy toward the Taliban government. He said this is the last time that the U.S. wants to hear about the Taliban. If anything happens to Americans, like the bombing of the embassies in Africa, we are not going to hold bin Laden accountable. "I promise you Kabir, we are going to hold Mullah Omar responsible. You must give this message to them."

"What is the message?"

"We will bomb the hell out of Kandahar next time anything happens to any Americans."

"Mr. Schmidt, I'll make sure that they get this message." It was good to hear a strong defensive stance taken by a representative of the U.S. Government.

I told Schmidt of the Taliban's agreement to do something about the drug problem. They understood that Afghanistan was creating a bad name as a world neighbor. For the poor relations being created over drugs, the money wasn't worth it. A kilo of heroin could be bought in Afghanistan for $300, but it fetched $300,000 in Europe. The Taliban's tax on the kilo was about $30. Neither the

Afghans nor the Taliban was making big money on drugs. For the big bucks, they had to look elsewhere, like to the dealers or to the War Lords.

Once back in the U.S., I reported the results of my trip to Mrs. Phyllis Oakley and to Mike Malinowski of the State Department. They encouraged me to keep in contact with Zaeef, and Mr. Mutawakel once we met.

I had not realized how anxious my family was about my trip. We had a joyous reunion. I showed my brother Omar and his son Aziz all the information that I had gathered regarding the natural resources in Afghanistan. Most of the work on the Afghan natural resources was decades old and done by the Soviets. Omar realized that with very little effort a lot of gas and oil could be removed from the ground. Once a well or two were set, it would provide enough income to explore the rest of the country.

I had promised members of the Taliban that I would return by October of 1999. I asked Aziz to get together investors for the trip. I realized that no one would put any money into our projects without first seeing for themselves the country and the rich bounty held in the oil and gas fields.

In July 1999, the United States imposed economic sanctions on Afghanistan. These included the freezing of the country's assets and the curtailment of its airline's flights to the U.S.

By October 1999, we had gathered together a group of U.S. and European investors for a return trip. Traveling to Afghanistan was a group of men with easy access to large amounts of money who, for the most part, were interested in Afghanistan's oil and gas possibilities. Traveling with me were my nephew Aziz and his friends, Nick Antoine and Jay Faltz. My party flew from Houston to Frankfurt where we spent the night. The next day we flew to Dubai where German investors Steve Schultz and my long-time friend and business partner, Michael Albrecht, met us at the Dubai Airport in the United Arab Emirates.

On October 10, my 42th birthday, we flew into Kabul. Everyone was frightened about flying into Afghanistan. They had heard awful things about the Taliban from the media. I told them, "I've been to Afghanistan twice in the last eight years. In 1992, I couldn't even travel ten miles across Kabul to see my old house. Now the country is more secure." My reassurances calmed everyone. After all I had just made the trip last summer and I was still alive and kicking.

When we took our seats on the Ariana Afghan Airlines plane, Jay pointed his index finger up toward the ceiling. We all looked up and cried in disbelief. The lining of the plane's ceiling had been pulled back, a few wires hung down, and some type of dark liquid dripped down to the floor. Jay's face blanched white. He shook his head while telling us that the broken bits were the plane's hydraulic system and the leaking fluid was hydraulic fluid.

"We have no choice," I said. Unsure myself and suppressing the need to bolt from the plane, I stayed put. "It's the only plane going to Kabul." I doubted that much maintenance had been done to the planes since India refurbished them earlier in the decade. We tried to strike a devil-may-care attitude. Everyone laughed at our predicament except

Jay. He knew more about planes than we did. Sometimes knowledge can be a burdensome thing.

Flying over the rubble pile formerly known as Kabul was embarrassing. I felt the need to explain that the mujahidin governments that fought for control of the city between 1992 and when the Taliban took over in 1996, caused most of the mess. During that period over 60,000 of the city's residents died because of the factional fighting between the War Lords. In part it was that chaos which brought the Taliban to power.

I admitted that the Taliban, too, had recked havoc on the city in 1996 during their efforts to oust the government of President Burhanuddin Rabbani. Once the Taliban conquered the city, they began to repair the demolished buildings rather than raze them.

When we arrived at the Kabul Airport, representatives of the Ministry of Oil and Mining and Mullah Zaeef were there to meet us. We were taken to the Spen Zar Hotel as guests of the Ministry. We had dinner there with Minister Ahmad Jan and a few others. At first the investors were frightened. The sight of all those beards and turbans was disturbing, but they eventually relaxed in the pleasant atmosphere provided by Ahmad Jan and his entourage.

The next day we traveled to Mazar-e-Sharif. We brought still cameras and a video camera in order to document the condition of the oil fields. At Mazar-e-Sharif we met the governor and the oil directors of the Northern Province. We were given jeeps and an escort to the local fields.

At the fields, when the investors saw people digging their own crude and purifying it in homemade refineries, they were surprised and agreed with me that it was the biggest ecological disaster they had ever witnessed. We asked the local people if they were paying any kind of money to the government for digging their wells. They said, "No." In fact they wished that the government would repair the area.

Several engineers from the Ministry were with us. They explained that of the twenty or so oil wells on the site, only four functioned. They produced about 2,000 barrels of oil a day per well using forty-year old technology. With modern technology the field could produce perhaps as many as 6,000 barrels a day per well.

That night we stayed in Mazar-e-Sharif. The next morning we visited the fields in Sara-e-Pul.

While returning to Mazar-e-Sharif from Sara-e-Pul, one of the investors mentioned that what he had heard about the lack of security in Afghanistan had been untrue. We were out late and, so far, we hadn't been stopped by bandits. We decided to find out whether there was a show of security for our benefit. Issues of security are very important before companies will invest money in an area. At that time, no oil or gas company wanted to inject its personnel into an extremely violent place.

Along the side of the road a few trucks had pulled off the highway. We pulled alongside one of them and asked the drivers whether they needed help or whether they were spending the night on the road because there were no hotels. They explained that they had been sleeping. One of the drivers admitted that the area had been so bad when the War Lords ran the country that they could only drive between the hours of 8:00 a.m. and 4:00 p.m. After 4:00 the bandits and highway robbers took over. He said now they were able to travel day and night and spend the night on the side of the highway. Of course, they were moving in heavily armed groups. I supposed that they were still too afraid to travel alone and unarmed, as was I. Only the foolhardy ventured out alone without arms in Afghanistan even under the Taliban.

The city of Mazar-e-Sharif had an eleven o'clock curfew. We were making our way back from Sara-e-Pul well past the curfew. As we got close to the city, the lead Jeep was stopped by three Taliban soldiers guarding the road. The guards demanded a password before allowing us to pass into the city. Of course, we did not know the password, so the guards began to search my nephew's vehicle.

The driver told the guards, "We have guests of the government here. If you are after guns, they're right here. If you want machine guns, they are in the trunk of the car. If you want to know where the rocket launcher is, it's there." He patted the weapon lying beside his seat. "What are you looking for? Food?"

Their spokesman said, "Yes."

"There is another car coming behind us in a few minutes. That car is full of food." Elated at the prospect of a full stomach, the guards waved them on. My car was stopped next. The Taliban's Deputy of Oil and its Director of the Northern Oil Office rode with me.

"Why are you going to Mazar-e-Sharif? Don't you know it's after curfew?"

The Director told him, "You should know me. I am a top official here in Mazar-e-Sharif. I am sorry, but we have guests." But the soldiers would not back down and let us through their road block. Finally the Director asked, "What are you looking for?"

"Your friends in the first car told us that you have a lot of food in here. We want some food."

"We don't have any food. The people in the first car were joking with you. They were making fun of you."

The soldier wasn't amused. They decided to detain us all for questioning. I got out of the Jeep and approached the soldiers. "Look, I am your guest." I figured if it worked for bin Laden, it should work for me.

The soldier explained it was his duty to stop everyone, no matter how high the official. I apologized to them for the lateness of our arrival. They decided to let us enter this one time because the Jeep "contained a guest." But before allowing us to move forward, the soldier lectured us on the importance of officials obeying their own orders.

This brought home to me the fact that although the Taliban government placed a premium on security, it had a lot more work to do. If soldiers were going without food, one could only wonder what the hard scrabble citizenry had to do to get it. Grow poppies? Manufacture heroin?

Three days later back in Kabul, Minister Ahmad Jan asked if we were interested in visiting the Ainak Mines which were about forty miles southeast of the city. Ainak is a green valley about sixty meters wide in a rough range of mountains in the Logar Province. I had heard about them as a child but had never seen them.

"Why not," I asked my guests and they agreed. Ahmad Jan said they were one of the world's largest copper and iron ore mines. We happily accepted the invitation for the next day.

In no particular hurry, we drove around and stopped to see things of interest. In the Jeep with me was Mr. Mandar Khail, President of the Afghan National Oil Company, a department of oil in the Ministry of Mining and Industry. In his sixties and with a bushy grey beard, he had been in the ministry for the last forty years. I asked him how he lasted through the half dozen changes in government. He replied that he worked for the country and not for the governments. I marveled at his political flexibility.

At that moment, we came upon a heavy wooden gate blocking the road. We could see barracks on both sides of the road about fifty feet in front of our vehicles. Warning shots rang out from armed men on the other side of the roadblock.

Mandar Khail uttered, “Oh, my God! It’s Osama’s people! So this is where the son-of-a-bitch is now!”

Our four jeeps came to a screeching halt and our bodyguards jumped out and took defensive positions on both sides of the vehicles. I could see people wearing ski masks scurrying about on the other side of the gate. One group worked to set up a heavy machine gun. There seemed little we could do. I had a video camera with me. I started to take a shot and then realized they might kill anyone with a camera.

“These are all Arabs,” Mandar Khail said. “I don’t know what language to use. I don’t speak Arabic.”

“Let’s try English. Maybe that’ll work,” I replied.

Suddenly one of the drivers, Pacha Khan, was pulled from the Jeep by the masked men and thrown to the ground. Pacha was frisked and his identification taken. They asked who the car belonged to in Arabic. Pacha responded in Pashto, “Mulawai Ahmad Jan, the Minister of Mining and Industry.” Not understanding, Pacha was told to shut up by a boot in his side.

The masked men moved closer to our vehicles with AK47s held ready to fire. I got out of the car and took two steps toward the mercenaries asking in both Pashto and English whether any of them spoke English. One of the hooded men pointed a gun at me and called me *walad al gahaba* (son-of-a-whore). Even though I spoke only a little Arabic, I knew the meaning of those words.

“Another step and I’ll blow you away,” someone growled in English.

I ordered Pacha to stand up. He tried, but half-way up the butt of a gun got him on the shoulder. From where he fell on the ground, Pacha bid me to get back into the car.

I looked down and saw our AK47 on the front seat. I reached my arm out and asked Mandar Khail for the gun.

"For God's sake! Don't do anything! There are about fifty or sixty of them in this gorge. Don't touch anything. That's what they want – trouble."

I slowly got back into the Jeep and put my hand on the rifle. Mandar Khail told me that this was the most horrible thing that he had ever experienced, but I doubted we would have much trouble once they figured out we weren't soldiers. In the back seat, Nick Anton was slowly turning white.

In the car behind us Abdl Khaliq, the Director of Industry in the Mining Ministry, got out and ran towards us.

"Don't you have a radio telephone or something?" I asked. "You need to call somebody. Call Zaeef!"

"I have a telephone connection to Mullah Obaidullah, the Minister of Defense."

"Then get him on the phone!"

Obaidullah reassured us that he had issued orders to everyone not to do anything to us while we traveled around. He then asked, "Is Osama there?"

"I think so," I said even though I hadn't exactly seen him.

"I'm sorry. He must have moved into the area."

"Do something!" I pleaded. "We cannot move for fear of being shot."

Six or seven minutes later a soldier ran up and ordered the men to leave us alone. He then ordered us to turn around and leave. So much for security! We lost all interest in sightseeing. That area was now forbidden to everyone because of one foreigner playing soldier in a country that wasn't even his own.

Later Pacha said that being thrown on the ground by a foreigner in his own country was insulting, but he was more upset by the fact that they had insulted my mother. Slandering someone's mother is like cursing God in the Pashtun culture – it just wasn't done. How could I not have feelings for this simple Afghan driver who was more upset by my insult than by the harm he suffered at the hands of thugs.

Later I would learn that Pacha was given six months compensation by the Taliban government for what he had endured.

That same afternoon we ran into bin Laden's men again, but this group wasn't protecting their camp. Instead they had been shopping at a local bazar and were headed back to camp. Three trucks stopped our lead jeep which held my nephew Aziz, Steve Schultz and Michael Albrecht of Germany. Again guns were pointed and we were ordered not to move.

They interrogated Aziz, but he handled it fairly well. It helped that one of the soldiers spoke English. He explained to Aziz that they had gotten word that an armed American force was in Kabul and that we were them. They asked Steve to get out of the Jeep and searched him. So I got out of my Jeep, approached them and asked, "What's the problem?"

"You've got a pretty boy with you," the soldier said salaciously as he motioned toward Steve, the young, blond business man.

"Don't even think about it," I spat worried what they might do to him. Then their phone rang and I heard what sounded like human barking on the other end of the line and they turned to leave.

"You better go, you bunch of *harami* (bastards)," I called after them.

Finally we arrived at a barbeque that Zaeef was hosting for us. When we pulled up in the jeeps, he was on the satellite telephone yelling at the provisional governor of Logar. It was surprising to hear curse words roll off the mullah's lips.

After he finished dressing down the provincial governor, I told Zaeef, "This is the first time I have been detained in my own country by a thug who wasn't a Soviet. At least I admired them because they were my enemy. I don't know who the hell this guy is. He must be an enemy, too."

Zaeef shook his head and said, "All I can do is apologize."

"Well, I don't know if I will accept the apology unless you are willing to do something about it," I said trying to push my own agenda that bin Laden wasn't good for Afghanistan when Zaeef's telephone beeped. It was Obaidullah, the Minister of Defense. Zaeef handed the phone to me.

"We are sorry," Obaidullah declared. "We'll investigate this."

"Yes, thank you. Investigate! But what if something had happened to these people?"

The Defense Minister agreed that if something had happened to one of the investors, it would have been impossible to find others. I hated the Cockroach. He was proving to be a detriment to the redevelopment of Afghanistan and to me.

Later, Zaeef accompanied us back to Kabul and apologized again for what had happened. He said, "What do you want me to do?"

"You know what I want you to do. Kill that son-of-a-bitch, Osama. He is no good."

"I cannot have innocent blood on my hands. But, please, we'll do something."

Mandar Khail interrupted, "It says in the Quran that something bad can happen, but it might be good."

"What do you mean?" I said.

"I'm glad this happened to you because I can't talk to the mullahs the way you can. Maybe you can talk to them and explain what Osama did and who Osama really is." Mandar Khail grinned at me.

Back at the hotel in Kabul, I tried to forget what had happened earlier. I surrounded myself with chatting friends, relatives and mullahs. Then suddenly the door to my room swung wide and it was Minister Ahmad Jan. "Mr. Mohabbat, may I talk to you privately." I agreed, so we left the party and borrowed Michael Albrecht's room.

I guessed from Ahmad Jan's twitching left eye that he was smoldering with anger. Ahmad Jan explained that he had decided to resign his position over what had happened to us. He was taking a letter of resignation to Mullah Omar the next day. He explained that Omar never calls anyone unless it is an emergency. This was the first time Omar called him personally and told him to go to the hotel and deliver an apology to me and my guests from the Afghan Government.

Omar and the whole Cabinet had found out about the incident. Apparently bin Laden had called Kandahar and told the Taliban leader that there was a commando force coming after him. It wasn't clear, but I assumed that he was seeking military backup. At that point Omar's deputy cussed bin Laden out and told him that we were not commandos but businessmen who wanted to help explore the country's natural resources.

Ahmad Jan suggested that perhaps something good would come of the incident. Mullah Omar had ordered Ahmad Jan to send Mulawai Wakil Mutawakel, the country's Foreign Minister and the head of the Taliban's moderate faction, to meet with us. Mutawakel spoke with authority for the government. Anything said by him could be taken back to the U.S. Government as gospel.

This was good news. Mullah Omar was now personally involved. The sending of Mutawakel to talk for the Afghan Government let me know I was getting closer to the core of the Taliban's power – the Council – of which Omar was just one member, and the weakest member at that, I was told. But more about that later.

Mutawakel would arrive at the Spen Zar Hotel in the morning. I informed my family and business associates that the Foreign Minister was coming to visit us tomorrow.

The next morning at ten o'clock, Minister Mutawakel came to the Spen Zar. He was surrounded by about fifteen to twenty people. The Minister of Information, the Minister of Interior, Minister of Education, the Chief of Kabul Security, and the Chief of Intelligence accompanied him to this meeting. During this two hour meeting with Mutawakel, my nephew Aziz, Mike Albright, Nick Anton, Steve Schultz and Jay Falz were present.

The hotel's conference room wasn't big enough to fit us all, so we met in the lobby. Many of the hotel's employees stood around and listened to the meeting. Mr. Mutawakel probably allowed this to happen so that the people of Kabul would be informed of our conversation. Since there were very few radios and even fewer televisions in Afghanistan, news at this time was passed mainly via the rumor mill. Thus it's plain to see how the arrival of businessmen became the arrival of commandos by the time bin Laden got the news. And since Kabul is a small city with a large population, word gets around fast.

For the first part of the meeting I wanted to talk about bin Laden. I thought, "Why not get it off my chest quickly so we could go on to other, more pleasant things. Perhaps even end on a high note."

I described to Mutawakel the meeting that I had with Minister Ahmad Jan earlier in the year. I related that after leaving Afghanistan in June, I met with John Schmidt at the American Embassy in Islamabad. I explained Schmidt's warning that if anything else happens against the U.S., the government will hold Kandahar responsible and it will be bombed.

Mutawakel also learned about my trip to Washington, D.C. and my conversations with Mrs. Oakley. I explained that every U.S. official that I spoke to told me that this was the Taliban's last chance. From now on responsibility would transfer from bin Laden to Mullah Omar himself. I added that the Americans knew that if Omar ordered the capture and hanging of bin Laden, "he would be hanging by his toes within a day."

We discussed how the pipeline and the U.S. oil industry works. I explained that the U.S. was very interested in having the pipeline across Afghanistan and that they wanted it no matter what the cost.

Mutawakel informed me that the last U.S. delegation had told him that the pipeline would bring either a "carpet of gold" or a "carpet bombing" to Afghanistan if the pipeline deal did not go through.

I questioned the truth of this statement without appearing to question Mutawakel's veracity. He repeated that he had been told this fact very bluntly.

"Perhaps these statements indicated American policy?" he said.

I confirmed that they may have and asked him to take it very seriously.

He said, "I am taking it very seriously."

"I spoke to many officials in the State Department of the United States in Washington, D.C. They all mentioned drugs and Osama, as problems with the current Afghan Government."

"Well," Mutawakel replied, "the drug issue is also very important to us. We want to show the world that we don't need that stuff; we don't need to ruin people's lives."

Michael Albrech explained the European point of view to Mr. Mutawakel. Michael told him that the Afghans could still do business through Europe even though the U.S. had sanctioned their country, but that very shortly international sanctions would come down on Afghanistan. All flights except for those of the United Nations and those containing humanitarian relief would soon be cut off.

If Mutawakel could do something about drugs and bin Laden then the whole problem would be solved. I suggested that he be handed over to a different country. Since he had been the guest of Afghanistan for some time, "you don't need him anymore. He can go to one of the Arab countries. He could be a hero there. We have plenty of heroes here in Afghanistan." Mutawakel nodded as I spoke, as if in confirmation of my words.

I asked for the forgiveness of the Afghans present if I had been too blunt. I repeated that it would be beneficial to them if they took what I said seriously. I knew my words would be bounced around the country and eventually get back to bin Laden. He had ears and hands everywhere in Afghanistan. I was assured by Mutawakel and Ahmad Jan that whatever we said would be relayed directly to Mullah Omar.

In our meeting, Mutawakel asked me what could be done about the oil and gas fields in northern Afghanistan. He was eager to have Americans return to the country. They could establish the gas fields and the transnational pipeline between Turkmenistan and Pakistan. It was the Afghan position that the American company Unocal wanted them to sign unfair contracts.

I assured him that there was no shortage of help – financing, refineries and pipelines – that could be made available to them. If Unocal was no longer of interest, then perhaps the bigger firm of Halliberton may be.

Mutawakel thanked us for coming to Afghanistan. He explained that what I had related was his understanding, too, and that we had no disagreements. He joked that I seemed less concerned about the forty day prison term or the public lashing that I could receive for not having a beard than I was about what occurred inside of Afghanistan.

I laughed, "It takes just as long to grow a beard by force. You could put me in jail for not having one but as soon as I got out I would shave it again. My beard would not help you. You are a mulawai. You are a holy man and I did not mean to disrespect you, but there are wicked people that grow beards as a sign of righteousness and then work to give Islam a bad name. And here I am with no beard. I am a good Muslim and I am a good Afghan-American and I will do everything in my power to help you."

When what occurred at Ainak was mentioned, Mutawakel shook his head angrily. I said, "As an Afghan, I would have taken it very lightly. But the reason that it makes me angry is because I had foreigners with me and I was stopped by a bunch of masked, foreign Arabs with hoods on their heads in the country of my birth. It was shameful! I was almost searched. They thought we were American commandos. I thank the Defense Minister for getting us out of there."

Mutawakel said that he did not think anyone in his right mind would take us for commandos, we were too well dressed and too old, but he thanked God nothing happened. He assured me that Mullah Omar had ordered an investigation into the matter. "We can promise you this," he said, "it will never happen again, no matter who comes into Afghanistan."

"You mean to tell me that Osama is under investigation?"

"Yes, I assure you – we assure you – that Osama and his people are under investigation and Mullah Omar has asked for a report that should be given to him in less than a week. We don't know why they pulled guns on you. We don't know why they had to hide their faces. They even had rocket launchers pointed at your cars!?!"

Then Mr. Mutawakel said something that I had not heard before, that the Taliban saw themselves as interim ministers. They needed time to bring normalcy to Afghanistan. They had taken music and television away to bring security and decency to a country fraught with violence and aggression. I could tell by his words that he deplored the loss of entertainment, but they needed a little time to calm the country down before bringing it back.

He said that Mullah Omar had not been appointed ruler of Afghanistan. He was only acting as interim Amir. They were going to have a *loya jurga* (a grand assembly of elders, clerics and tribal chiefs) in January of 2000. After the government is established and – if the people approve – they will stay for the next four or five years until people begin to return to Afghanistan from foreign lands.

I wondered about this. I knew that in 1996 Mullah Omar had legitimized his control of the country by wearing the Cloak of the Prophet Mohammed before a large group of followers gathered at the Shrine of the Cloak. If he became Amir by proving (through the use of the cloak) that the office had been granted to him by God, how could he thereafter resign? I wondered whether they really would commit to turning over the government once stability had been regained. Mr. Mutawakel then asked that a distinction be drawn between the Taliban and their predecessors, the War Lords.

Mutawakel freely admitted that they were just a bunch of country mullahs who had been waiting for the bureaucrats and those with education to return. Even though they had begged, the educated citizenry did not want to come back to Afghanistan. The country had become worse than the Wild West in America. Any crackpot Napoleon with a few guns and followers could take the law into his own hands. He thanked everyone at the meeting for being there. He was very blunt about bin Laden and admitted from the government's point of view, he was an unwanted guest that they were stuck with.

At the airport the next day, Minister Ahmad Jan took me aside and for security reasons, asked me to be the last passenger to climb aboard the plane. He then hinted that a surprise awaited me. On boarding the aircraft, the pilot motioned for me to sit in a seat on the first row.

My nephew, Aziz, was sitting across the aisle from me. He leaned over and whispered that Minister Mutawakel was sitting in the seat next to mine. Surprised at not having noticed him, I turned and asked the minister, "Are you going to Dubai with us?" The plane was scheduled for a non-stop flight from Kabul to Dubai.

"No. We have diverted the plane to Kandahar. I am going to accompany you to Kandahar and I will get off there and you can go on." He explained that since everywhere we went we were followed and listened to and this ruse would give us a few hours to talk without being overheard. Then the plane's door closed and it began to taxi down the runway.

I said to Minister Mutawakel that I was there with the approval of the U.S. Government and that Phyllis Oakley, the Deputy Secretary of State for Intelligence Affairs, asked me to speak to you. He replied that it was good news because then everything said would be conveyed to a higher authority.

Mutawakel asked me to tell the Americans that he had attended a madrassa funded by the Americans. Since he was educated by Americans, he did not understand why they thought he was a fundamentalist. He explained that the Taliban was very different from the Shiite Islamic sect. As Sunni Muslims, they were moderates who wanted to join the world community. Because of what had been happening to the people of Afghanistan, the Taliban felt forced to take over in order to stop the chaos and carnage.

"When educated people show up in Afghanistan, we will leave them the government and return to the mosques," Mutawakel assured me. But no one was willing to return to Afghanistan because all the publicity was against the Taliban. "Everyone is scared to join us, especially Afghans who are educated in the West – Europe and America." He expressed hope that they could eventually be convinced to return.

Mutawakel changed the subject to bin Laden. He said, "I have contacted the Saudi government." The Taliban now understood that they would have to deport him somewhere, so they began with the Saudis. "Did you know that the Saudi government has taken away Osama bin Laden's citizenship?" This fact surprised me. I didn't know a country could do that to someone born there.

Mutawakel had called the Saudi Ambassador in Islamabad who acted as liaison to Afghanistan. He talked to the Ambassador and told him that Afghans were sick and tired of being accused of something that they had not participated in. "This man is wanted in your country and wanted in the United States. Because of the Islamic relationship we have with you and because other Muslims are not really educated to know who this man is, you take him to your country and whatever you want to do with him you just do it," Mutawakel told the Saudi.

The Ambassador replied, "Sorry, we do not accept him and we do not want him. You can have him and keep him."

Mutawakel explained that he then threatened to expel bin Laden from Afghanistan and send him directly back to Saudi Arabia by plane.

The Saudi Ambassador said rudely, "We will not allow any plane carrying Osama into our air space. Any plane containing him will be considered a hostel act by the government of Afghanistan. We will shoot it down."

"We cannot take that chance," Mutawakel replied.

"Then what is the solution?" I asked perplexed.

"Talk to the Americans. We don't want him." Mutawakel made it very clear that the Taliban wanted to wash their hands of him.

"What about a third country, another Islamic country? Send him over there," I suggested.

"If you can find another country, good luck! No Muslim country is willing to take him because the man is so popular. In most Islamic countries he's a hero. No government would dare take him and put him on trial. There would be revolt and revolution."

He paused and shook his head, "Mr. Mohabbat, I'm stuck with this dilemma. I tried my best to send this man away. I have taken this initiative on my own. Not too many people know about it. Please tell those people in America who are very responsible and can keep this a secret that we would be willing to do this. If you can help us open the air space to Saudi Arabia we will ship the man over there."

I, too, felt that the system of nations had created a structure that permitted a problem like bin Laden to remain almost unsolvable. The United Nations needs to step up to the bar and create a way to handle world situations like this. No nation should be allowed to evade responsibility for one of its citizens, no matter how popular or wicked. My colleague, Mike Albrecht, would later suggest that perhaps we could use one of the European Union countries or the World Court in the Hague as a depository for bin Laden.

"Please let anyone you talk to know that we are trying to get rid of Osama. And, if this becomes an open secret, we could be in danger."

Mutawakel gave me his private telephone number. After speaking with American officials, I was to call him when we decided on a date to return to complete the delivery of bin Laden. He insisted that it would be preferable from the Afghan point of view for the Americans to come and get bin Laden rather than have him tried in an Afghan court. "Let's make extradition treaties which international law normally requires," he said. "We should not just put somebody on a plane and fly him to another country without benefit of treaty."

When he reached Kandahar, Mutawakel promised to immediately see Omar and discuss the issue of bin Laden's extradition with him. But he stressed this point with me, "Once I get Mullah Omar to issue a warrant for his arrest, this man is not about to surrender himself. He could escape across the Pakistani border. He could travel to northern Afghanistan, to the untamed wilderness of the Hindu-Kush with its thousands of hiding places." Mutawakel was certain that he would not surrender; he would put up a great fight.

As an afterthought, Mutawakel asked, "If Osama dies somewhere in the mountains, would the Americans stop their feelings of hostility toward the Taliban?"

I interpreted this question as an invitation for me to say, "Please take bin Laden into the mountains and we'll forget about the current misunderstandings." I came to the conclusion that if bin Laden's death is what it takes to rescue twenty-five million Afghans from international sanctions, then so be it. But I was not into killing anyone any more. I did not want his blood on my hands. Nor was I in a position to supply Mutawakel with instructions on the point. First I needed to check with the State Department.

Mutawakel left me with his words rattling around in my brain, "Ask America – How do you want Osama?

Chapter 5: Changing the Hearts and Minds of the Mullahs

In October 1999, after our plane landed in Frankfurt, Michael Albrecht invited me to spend a few days with him and his girlfriend in Germany. He suggested that it was in my best interest to meet one of his friends, Rainer Wieland, who was a member of the European Union. Why not? I thought.

On the flight from Dubai to Frankfurt, Michael and I talked at length about the changes that could be made in Afghanistan. I saw drugs as a big problem. While there, I told both Foreign Minister Mutawakel and Mullah Ahmad Jan that growing poppies was harmful to individuals in Afghanistan and in the international community. I explained that if they stopped growing poppies, it would prove to the international community and the U.S. Government that the current Afghan Government was serious about making positive changes.

The issue of the Taliban's treatment of women had not yet become a major negotiation point for the U.S. Government. I had been told in D.C. that it was just a public relations problem for the Taliban government; however, U.S. Government representatives had explained to me how serious a problem the cultivation of poppies, opium and the processing of heroin in Afghanistan had become. Michael suggested that I talk with members of the European Parliament because heroin was one of the big problems in Europe. The eradication of poppies was a very important issue to the European people.

Michael made an appointment for us with Rainer Wieland, the member of the European Union from Stuttgart, and we went to dinner with him. He seemed surprised that Michael had come back *alive* from Afghanistan. He had advised him not to go, but he was impressed that Michael had met with the Taliban's Foreign Minister because everyone in Europe saw the Taliban as frightening and hopelessly out of reach. At dinner he again asked Michael whether he had actually met with the Taliban. I confirmed that Michael had indeed met the Foreign Minister and the Minister of Oil and Industries. To quiet the doubts of the representative from Stuttgart, we showed him pictures taken in Kabul.

At dinner with the E.U. representative, Michael and I discussed how the eradication of the poppy crop in Afghanistan would help Europeans. We also asked the representative to prepare a list of the changes that the E.U. would like the Taliban to make. I volunteered to carry the proposal back to Afghanistan on my next trip.

Michael Albrecht reminded me of an adventurer right out of a boy's novel. The same morning that Mutawakel was coming to meet with our group in Kabul, I discovered that Michael was not in his hotel room. I asked if anyone had seen him, but no one knew where he was. Finally I learned that he had gone – alone – to a street bazaar about a quarter of a mile away. I learned from the hotel manager that Michael had refused his security escort; he wanted to explore downtown Kabul by himself. Upset by his devil-may-care attitude, I sent several of our bodyguards to look for him. They found him being escorted back to the hotel by three members of the Afghan security force. He had been wandering the busy market in a Polo shirt and khaki pants, beardless and blond when they grabbed him and put him in a car to question him. He explained that he was with a group of Westerners at the Spen Zar Hotel.

I was angry at Michael's cavalier behavior. The Taliban guard told me that Michael had been approached in the market by someone offering to sell him hashish and he agreed to buy some when they grabbed him. Michael, who couldn't speak the language, said he did not know what the guy was saying.

I told Michael, "For God's sake do not go out alone again." I then asked the security officer to leave him in my custody. I made sure the guard understood that Michael promised he would not go wandering around again, but they insisted that something be done about the problem of the hashish.

"No," I bullied them. "He does not smoke and that is the final word on it. Leave." I explained to Michael that Mullah Omar had issued a decree that even smoking cigarettes was a condemned act and smoking any kind of narcotic brought a public lashing.

Michael reiterated that he had no idea what the guy was talking about and swore that he would never leave my sight again. Nonetheless, I assigned security guards to shadow him at all times.

Later the hotel manager took me aside and explained that since few foreigners come to Afghanistan, the Taliban government was very careful with them. Some visitors felt they were being harassed, but the Afghans knew that the world had them under a microscope. Their worry was not whether anyone was smoking or drinking as much as what would happen if a visitor died. For that they would answer to the world. If something had happened to Michael, the Taliban's relationship with Europe would be forever damaged.

During the first week of November 1999, I traveled to Washington, D.C. by car. I met with Mrs. Oakley at her office in the State Department. When I entered her office, she acted surprised, "Well, you still don't have a beard!"

"No. I didn't grow one."

"Well it took a lot of courage to do that."

"They were really nice and hospitable to us, Mrs. Oakley," I smiled. "By the way, I can get Osama on a silver platter for you. How do you want him served: rare, medium or well done."

She laughed and congratulated me on a job well done. We briefly discussed what occurred on the trip. Then Mrs. Oakley placed a call. Someone from the National Security Council (or Agency, I forget which) appeared. A young man in his thirties asked me to repeat the details of my meeting with Mr. Mutawakel.

I explained that Mutawakel agreed to *covertly* hand bin Laden over to the U.S. or to a third country if the U.S. did not want to get involved. Egypt, Jordan or one of the European countries seemed like good possibilities to me. But the Taliban could insist on proper legal recourse like extradition, or putting him on trial in Afghanistan first. Bin Laden was very popular and they wanted everything to be above board and legal. If the U.S. has documents proving his guilt, then they have no use for him. If the Americans or anyone else would supply proof of his guilt, then they will order bin Laden's trial. I explained to her about justice in Afghanistan, how trials only last three days and then the perpetrator, if found guilty, is immediately punished.

"If he is guilty," I said, "it would take the Taliban only seventy-two hours to convict him. The man would be hanging off a tree somewhere by the end of a week."

Mrs. Oakley said that we didn't believe in their form of justice nor did she believe that the Afghan Government would put him on public trial. Even if they did, he would probably be acquitted, she said.

I told her that she was wrong, "If we have any kind of evidence, let me have it."

She said that they had already given the Taliban documents publicly, but the television news magazine show *20/20* made a joke out of this gesture. The program thought the documents were ambiguous.

"We have no direct proof of bin Laden doing any of the crimes. If the American Broadcasting Company is making a mockery of our proof, how can we convict or extradite a man to the U.S. with weak evidence."

Since Afghan officials had tentatively agreed to his extradition, I didn't understand what the problem was, "Just give me something that will implicate this man. For Mullah Omar to issue an official warrant for bin Laden, proof of his hand in terrorist activities is needed. Since we do not have an extradition treaty with Afghanistan, they cannot just simply extradite him. So let's sign extradition treaties and get him out of there."

Of course what I didn't realize at the time was the fact that neither the U.S. nor most countries in the U.N. wanted to recognize the current Afghan Government as legitimate. Signing an extradition treaty with them would have immediately given them status as the ruling regime of Afghanistan which no one wanted to do. I didn't quite understand this position since the Taliban looked to me like the choice of those living in Afghanistan at the time. I didn't think they were necessarily the best choice, but it was the country's choice – not mine – and we should recognize it.

Oakley asked about *nanawati* (sanctuary). I explained that nanawati had been the most convincing part of my argument with the Taliban about their need to give up bin Laden. "If you give sanctuary to a person you must provide for them as long as he is a *good* guest. If bin Laden gets on the roof and starts shooting at everyone walking by – which, in essence, is what he was doing – then the host is justified in withdrawing hospitality. If someone's in sanctuary, you advise them to shut up until you investigate what's going on." I explained that is how I convinced the Afghans that this man bin Laden is taking advantage of the Pashtun cultural code and that Minister Mutawakel understood my reasoning.

I confided to Mrs. Oakley the fact that Mutawakel admitted to me that when bin Laden comes to see Mullah Omar, he cries like a baby out of self-preservation. I also told her that Mutawakel had said, "Would you believe me if I told you that this man, many times, has asked us to supply his followers with food? We don't have enough food for ourselves. And we don't know what to do with his entourage. They are not as modest as we are because most of our soldiers just eat bread while bin Laden's people drink their tea with sugar. Sometimes we even have to supply his men with meat. They are foreigners, they are our guests so we have to give our food to them, but we are very sick and tired of these people. When Osama sees Mullah Omar, he cries and swears on a stack of Qurans that he hasn't done any of the things that he is accused of doing. He says it's all propaganda. But once out of Omar's sight, bin Laden disseminates all kinds of anti-American statements that implicate him. We see it, but we can't really talk to Mullah Omar about him because Omar is a very straight forward sort of man who believes what people tell him, especially if they swear on the Quran and before God. That is our biggest problem. But if you give us something to work with – just a piece of paper – an official request from the United States government – I will take it. Mullah's Omar's orders are absolute. If he says show up and bin Laden doesn't then he's a dead man."

I explained to Mrs. Oakley that Mutawakel was concerned that the international resolutions against Afghanistan didn't mention anything about bin Laden's death. Mutawakel said, "What would happen if he died fighting against us? Would the resolutions be lifted?" I posed the question to Mrs. Oakley and others, but unfortunately, Minister Mutawakel would never get an answer to this question from the U.S. Government.

Mrs. Oakley asked me many questions. She was very interested in the internal condition of Afghanistan. I described it basically as a big prison, "but with a few changes from our side, it would open up." I told her that right now the country was in the hands of a few local people who understand only local politics. But there are people outside the circle of leaders who could influence them to change. For example, until I met with Mr. Mutawakel, he had no knowledge of the internet. After discussing it, he saw its potential for the country and suggested that it be installed in the Foreign Ministry. But as far as the rest of the nation having similar access, getting approval would take time.

Mrs. Oakley promised she would forward my information to the top security levels of our country. She promised to send Mike Shaheen, the State Department's Director of Counter Terrorism, to Texas to meet with me. She believed that my coming to the State Department so often might not be a good idea because I had just returned from Afghanistan and the State Department was watched by all sorts of people. It would be much easier if someone dealt with me at my home.

I thanked her and explained how I had admired her since the early 1980's when Don Woodward introduced us. She laughed and thanked me for getting the current Afghan Government to agree to turn over bin Laden. She then invited me to dinner that night. My new contact, Mr. Shaheen, would come to meet with me in a few weeks.

When I arrived at the Oakley home, I reminded Mr. Robert Oakley of what he had told me back in 1996 when I visited their home after flying back to the States from Pakistan.

At that time he said to forget every mujahidin leader that I knew because the Taliban were taking over Afghanistan. I now agreed with him that they were, indeed, in charge of Afghanistan but that I had made some good contacts within their group. I also initiated negotiations for the surrender of bin Laden. I explained that they saw their biggest problem arising once Mullah Omar issues a decree for bin Laden's capture because he would resist.

Knowing the region and the culture well, the Oakley's understood that once Mullah Omar issued a decree, if he didn't surrender, the killing of bin Laden and his entourage would occur quickly. It would be a clean, easy way for the U.S. to get rid of the terrorist. Because the Taliban wanted the sanctions of the United States to be lifted, they would cooperate. Bin Laden appeared to be the only obstacle between the U.S. and the new Afghan Government, but they were afraid that no matter what they gave the U.S., we would want more. We had to put that fear to rest.

I gave Mr. Oakley their point of view toward women as it was explained to me. In a country as backward as Afghanistan, having been blown back into the middle ages by the Soviets and the War Lords, every time there was a revolution or revolt, the women and the children become victims and no one wanted their family to be victims. Normally in that area of the world you could count on three things occurring during someone's rise to power: factional violence, murder, and the kidnaping of a rival's women and children which in primitive societies is a method used to humiliate the enemy. The Taliban hoped to put a stop to the raping and kidnaping of women and girls that began in 1992 with the reigns of the War Lords by confining women and children to their homes until the country settled down. I reminded him that the Taliban still believe they are at war because fighting against the Northern Alliance was on-going.

With respect to drugs, the current Afghan Government was convinced that the drug trade was not in the best interest of their country or their religion. The mullahs in control were aware that the growing drug trade deeply stained the religious impression that they wished to convey. They agreed to do everything in their power to stop it. They asked for help from the U.S. They wanted to join our efforts in the eradication of drugs.

The Oakley's were pleased to hear this. I asked to meet with one of the Drug Enforcement Agency's people and they assured me that could be arranged, but no one from the DEA ever contacted me. Who dropped the ball? I would guess it wasn't the Oakley's.

Nonetheless, I spent a very productive evening with the Oakley's. I left their home grateful for an opportunity to discuss the issues once again. I suggested that perhaps we should go to Kabul together so that Mr. Oakley could talk with the Taliban himself. He agreed.

Back in Houston, I waited for a few weeks before calling Ms. Oakley to find out when Mr. Shaheen would be arriving for a visit. I hadn't heard from her and I promised Mutawakel that I would get back to him quickly. Mrs. Oakley's secretary informed me that Mrs. Oakley had taken early retirement. I waited a few more weeks and then called her at home. I asked why she had retired at such an important time?

She explained that she was tired and needed some time off.

I suggested that she had chosen the wrong time. I negotiated for the head of Al Qaida and now I didn't know who to deal with.

She told me that people in the State Department were very interested in what I had done and that I would find my way. If needed, she agreed to help out. She assured me that she had left detailed instructions with the national security people and with the director of the South Asia Desk at the State Department.

I wondered whether she had a disagreement with people at the national security level and her retirement was forced, but I respected her privacy, so I never asked. It would not have surprised me if that had happened since she and her husband were staunch Republicans, friends of Jim Baker's, and this occurred during the Clinton presidency. Building a trusting relationship with someone in the State Department is always a daunting task taking years and we were running out of time to act on bin Laden.

Not having heard from the State Department for several months after my telephone conversation with Mrs. Oakley, I tried to contact them, but I did not feel comfortable discussing bin Laden with just anyone there. Because I had come so far, my family and friends encouraged me to see it through to the end, but I was beginning to get discouraged. I was about to give up when someone in the department mentioned that my report would have gone to the top man at the National Security Council. At the time this was encouraging news, but in the end it amounted to nothing. Eventually Mike Malinowski of the State Department explained that I should get a response about the bin Laden issue soon, but I never did. The whole problem of bin Laden lay like a dying whale on the deserted beach of international diplomacy.

In November 1999, the United Nations imposed strict economic sanctions on the Islamic Emirate of Afghanistan.

In December of 1999, I received a call from Minister Ahmed Jan. He was going to China in about a week. The Chinese had agreed to help Afghanistan with the pipeline and they had already spoken to officials of Turkmenistan where the pipeline would originate. Everyone agreed that it should run through Afghanistan.

Disappointed I said, "I thought I was going to help you with the pipeline and the oil and gas discovery in Afghanistan?"

"Well, you can have my word that anytime you bring help, you have first rights to it." Ahmad Jan replied.

I did not want the pipeline to be built and run by a communist country. I had fought that ideology all my life. The Chinese are not bad people, but I oppose socialism and communism and would do almost anything to destroy them. I was disappointed to the core.

Because the millennium was quickly approaching, I asked Ahmad Jan whether he thought Al-Queda and bin Laden would pose a threat to the U.S. during the holiday and explained that the U.S. media was full of supposition about attacks. I reminded him, if anything happens, it would be explosive and the Taliban would be blamed "even if you gave assurances that you had nothing to do with the attack." The people of the United States would like to celebrate their Christmas and the Millennium in peace.

Ahmad Jan said that he would speak to Mullah Omar, but he also asked me to call Mr. Mutawakel, the Afghan Foreign Minister. So I called Malinowski of the U.S. State Department and told him about my conversation with Ahmad Jan. He asked me to please make the phone call to Mutawakel.

In our conversation with Minister Mutawakel, he promised to broach the issue of the Millennium directly with Mullah Omar. He added that Ahmad Jan was in Kandahar saying goodbye to Omar. The Minister of Mining and Industries had gotten approval to travel to China. Mutawakel suggested that I call back in a week.

Then I called Don Woodward and told him that I was in touch with Malinowski at the State Department about the problem of the Millennium. He suggested that I talk with someone from the FBI.

I kept Sheldon Rapoport, the director of the Afghanistan desk at the State Department, and Malinowski informed of my conversations about the Millennium celebrations. They explained that one of the biggest problems that the U.S. Government had with Taliban representatives was they would come to the U.S., make promises, request a week or two to run it past Mullah Omar, and then return to Kandahar and either never reply or change their minds. The U.S. officials said that they were sick and tired of meeting with them.

I suggested that a problem may lay in the fact that those coming here were only low level officials who may not get to see that renowned hermit Mullah Omar for months after their return and by that time, problems would be old news. I acknowledged their exasperation with the Afghan Government. Indeed, it was a very ineffective way to run a country that longed for international recognition.

I assured them that from this point forward they could talk directly to the Foreign Minister, Mr. Mutawakel. Unfortunately, according to U.S. protocol, the person who must speak to another foreign minister is the Secretary of State, or his or her representative. Because the Afghan Government was not officially recognized by the U.S., the Secretary of State could not talk to the Afghan foreign minister. Mr. Mutawakel had asked me to open up a line to Madeline Albright so he could discuss important issues with her directly, but protocol would not allow this to be done. So I was forced to go back and forth with the diplomatic form of, he said, she said. The situation was a real headache.

My contact as unofficial go-between was Sheldon Rapoport. I realized in dealing with him that he did not believe anything that the Afghans said. I tried to convince him that some things could be trusted, but it was not easy. He finally began to accept something of what I told him about the Taliban, but he was not inclined to accept much that came directly from them. If he had understood the Pashtun culture and the nature of the Taliban's ruling Council and government better, then perhaps communications between the two groups would have improved. However, he wasn't interested in learning the intricacies of the culture nor was the stubborn Taliban interested in learning the intricacies of American ways. I was an intermediary lashed between two stubborn mules.

Minister Ahmad Jan visited China from December 15 to 20, 1999, with a delegation of two or three other mullahs. He called and said, "We're starving." He complained that the delegation had been eating nothing but bread with tea and onions for days.

I asked why they were restricted to such a poor diet.

He said that the mullahs had heard that the Chinese ate almost anything, including cats, dogs and rats. No one in the delegation would eat a thing presented to them. Their hosts tried to give them food, but the mullahs refused to eat anything they didn't recognize. Instead they went shopping in the Islamic section of Beijing for themselves. Even then they were afraid of buying anything but bread, onions and tea.

I had to laugh. Mullahs are renowned for having very meager diets. "You guys are mullahs," I joked with him. "You should be used to that kind of food."

The subject of the Millennium came up again. Ahmad Jan said he spoke to Mullah Omar directly and was assured that bin Laden would be summoned to Kandahar and asked whether he had plans to bomb or create chaos in the world during the "holy month of the Christians." If he did, then he would be warned that a lot of trouble awaited him. Mullah Omar asked Ahmad Jan to reassure the U.S. Government and Mr. Mohabbat that nothing would happen as long as he was in charge of Afghanistan. Omar also asked Ahmad Jan to tell me that he still had no hard evidence that Osama has been involved in terrorist activities.

"The U.S. needs to provide Omar with evidence. Then, if he is guilty, even of killing an ant, he will be hung off a tree somewhere," Ahmad Jan assured me.

I immediately called the State Department and informed them of what Ahmad Jan had said. They asked me to call Mutawakel to determine whether he could confirm the conversation between Mullah Omar and the Mining and Industry Minister. I told them that I would be happy to call him in a few days when Mutawakel returned to Kabul from Kandahar where no one could reach him by telephone.

A day or so later Minister Ahmad Jan called again from his hotel room in China. I asked him how the pipeline deal with China was going. He said that the Chinese would finance the whole thing, the oil and gas exploration in the north of Afghanistan, plus the pipeline. It was a very lucrative deal.

"If you will remember Unocal offered Afghans almost no profit, while the Chinese are offering sixty percent."

"Please listen to me very carefully," I told Ahmad Jan. "In the 1960's, Afghanistan signed a business deal with the Soviet Union. Look what happened! When people started noticing that they were taking advantage of us, the Soviets came in 1973 and overthrew King Zahir. Then his cousin Daoud took over. By 1978, he began asking the Soviets about the unfair deals and he, too, was overthrown. Finally the Soviets decided it was all too much trouble, so they invaded Afghanistan. This would not have happened if they had been ten thousand miles away."

I plead, "Our next door neighbors, the Soviets, invaded our country over oil. The Chinese are our neighbors, too. We share a border. Think about it. There are over 1.5 billion Chinese. All they have to do is go to the mountains that we have in common and start pissing toward Afghanistan. Afghanistan would be flooded. We should learn from our own experiences. I am getting assurances from the U.S. Government that if I bring Americans and American technology to Afghanistan, America will be happy."

"I hope you find avenues to the big oil companies," Ahmad Jan said.

But I didn't really have those kinds of connections, I explained to him. I only represented a small company, but even a small company could cut a good deal.

"Are you sure that you don't want me to sign anything with the Chinese?" Ahmad Jan asked.

"I'm very sure. Mr. Minister, if you sign any kind of contract with the Chinese, you will make me mad and you will make the Americans mad." I wanted those contracts for myself, my company and my country.

Two days later Ahmad Jan called again from China. He said that the Americans were pushing for sanctions against

Afghanistan. The Chinese had informed him of this because they were part of the U.N. Security Council. They promised that if we signed a contract with them, they would veto the international sanctions against Afghanistan. They had the veto power in the U.N. Security Council and their proposed contract was very lucrative for the Afghans. He then put me on hold. Someone that knew me from the Chinese government wanted to talk to me. I was astounded. I knew no one from that government.

A male got on the phone and began speaking to me in almost perfect English. He said that in 1988, as a Chinese diplomat, he had come to my office in Islamabad. He was visiting each of the mujahidin factions with an offer of help. Suddenly I remembered that China had been pretty accommodating in our fight against the Soviet Union. Then my memory of him returned, but unfortunately I can no longer remember his name. He asked if perhaps we could meet in China or in the U.S. Since I was opposed to the pipeline deal between Afghanistan and China, he wished to change my mind.

I explained to him that if the Afghans wanted to have good relations with China, this precluded doing business with them. I told him of the Afghan saying: If you make a profit from your brother or neighbor, then you really haven't made a profit – you've lost money. Relationships between our people were good. Commerce with China, like that done on the Silk Road for the last two – three thousand years was fine, but an Islamic government and communist China have nothing in common but conflicting ideologies. At least in dealing with the Christian U.S., we have something basic in common – religion.

"The Quran orders us not to have any dealings with you. You don't believe in anything that we can relate to." When I realized my voice had taken a strident tone, I backed off, "Listen, it is only opinion that I offer the Taliban. They can do whatever they want. I am not the government of Afghanistan and I have no part in that government."

The man on the other end of the line said, "You have a lot of influence."

"No. That's not true. The Taliban are very organized. They are very strong. They can make their own decisions."

"Is there any way we could meet."

"Of course, when we have time either here in America or I can come to Afghanistan or Pakistan." I declined his suggestion to meet in China. "I would love to go there someday, but the relationship between the United States and the Taliban is not good and I am trying to repair it first. If I go to China this will create more problems for Taliban officials with the U.S. because they might think that I'm really doing a deal with the Chinese government."

Then Ahmad Jan got back on the phone and we came to the understanding that he would not sign a contract with China even if it cost them sanctions by the U.N. He promised to call once he was back in Kabul.

The next week I wanted to place a call to Foreign Minister Mutawakel about the Millennium celebrations, but first I called the State Department and suggested that they listen in. They said no, just report to them afterward.

After exchanging pleasantries with Mutawakel and Ahmad Jan, I asked the later whether he had signed the contracts with the Chinese. He refused to sign with them even though it was a good deal. They had taken my advice and had not signed with an "ungodly country."

"We had nothing in common. With America at least we share a common God. That is a lot for us. But please, do tell the Americans that the contract was not signed."

"What did you tell the Chinese?"

"I told them to let me take the proposal back to Afghanistan and I will consult with the Ministers Council and Mullah Omar and let them know as soon as possible."

"Do you think you will let them know soon?" I asked.

"Think of it as something written on ice and put in the sun."

Responding like a school boy, I said, "It will melt?"

"That's exactly what is happening to this deal. It's melting." I wondered if this was the tactic that the Taliban used during negotiations with the U.S. State Department. Agreeing to do certain things and then writing them on ice.

I promised Ahmad Jan that I would not let him down. At that point, I hadn't a clue that world events would let me down and I would never be able to fulfill my promise.

"Please give me some time. Let's wait for the Millennium to be over."

Ahmad Jan handed the phone to Mr. Mutawakel. He said that two days ago while he was in Kandahar, he spoke with Mullah Omar. Omar sent someone to Osama and told him to show up at ten the next morning at his office. Mutawakel joked, "You know when our Amir sends for someone, they show up half an hour early."

"I'm glad your Amir is showing his muscle to this idiot," I laughed.

"Let me tell you what happened." Mutawakel surprised me by sounding like an old friend sharing a bit of gossip. "Mullah Omar said to Osama, 'Christmas is a holy month for the Christians, and that is their New Year, just like we have New Year. I don't know much about your activities, but the news I hear through Voice of America and BBC says that you are going to do something really stupid in America.' These are Mullah Omar's words," Mutawakel almost giggled with delight at the strength showed by his country's leader. "People are talking bombs in America and explosives here and there. I am going to tell you this, if I hear that a simple fire cracker goes off anywhere, especially in the United States, I will deal with you personally."

"Osama began to reassure Mullah Omar that he was not going to do anything like that, that he was not even interested, that the whole thing was only propaganda by the United States government. Then Omar warned him again – I don't care about the propaganda. I'm not interested in the news media, I'm only interested in my orders. Are you going to obey what I am telling you right now? Or are you not?"

"Osama responded – Yes. You are the Amir of Afghanistan. I love your rules and your laws. I will obey. I can assure you that I am not doing these things. Nothing will happen. In a severe tone Mullah Omar repeated himself one more time – Just a fire cracker. If it goes off, I will deal with you personally. And thank you for coming." Mr. Mutawakel said that before Osama could say another word, Mullah Omar stood up and dismissed him from his presence like a school boy.

Mutawakel explained that he almost felt sorry for bin Laden because of the way that Omar had treated him. He sat with him for a few minutes and explained to him that our friends in America are calling and telling us what is going to happen. Mutawakel said that security is tight all over the U.S. and it has cost them billions of dollars for no reason – "Because you said something about the Millennium."

Bin Laden told him that he had never issued any kind of orders and that he did not even know what the fuss in the news was about. He said that the whole thing had been made up. The Foreign Minister warned bin Laden that Mullah Omar would not forget. He stood up and said, "I obey the order of the Amir of Afghanistan." Bin Laden then asked Mutawakel what would happen if someone else like the C.I.A. planted a bomb and blamed al-Qaida. Mutawakel said he did not know what would happen, but then ventured that Osama would probably still be blamed.

This made me wonder whether the Cockroach was already scheming. It was clear from the Taliban's point of view that Osama had gotten the message, but why he wasn't thrown out of the country, I'll never know.

Mutawakel suggested that bin Laden issue an assurance to the American public and government that he was not involved in these kind of activities and that he would not issue an order to bomb the American people in their "holy and happy times." Unfortunately, no such assurance was ever forthcoming. Mr. Mutawakel confided to me that bin

Laden did not like him much and reassured me that the feeling was mutual.

I prayed daily that nothing would happen during the celebrations; however, one incident did occur. Someone tried to enter the U.S. through the heavily guarded Canadian-American border. I thought this was a stupid, head butting approach to terrorism. At the time I wondered whether bin Laden had been trying to prove that he was beyond the reach of American authority and that he could penetrate the U.S. border "at will," or whether it was the act of a lone nutcase. Thankfully the perpetrator was caught and the Millennium celebrations ended.

A few days after New Year's Day 2000, I called Mutawakel and Ahmad Jan and thanked them for taking steps to ensure that little happened in America during the celebrations. Unsure whether the idiot's attack was ordered by bin Laden, I did not bring up the incident at the U.S. border. I wanted to keep Mutawakel and Ahmad Jan squarely on my side.

Minister Ahmad Jan suggested that I visit Afghanistan as soon as possible. Mullah Omar was anxious to do something about the Northern oil fields since the Afghan Government was importing oil for domestic use. A Spanish company affiliated with Unocal had approached them, but they preferred working with me. If I would please come to Kabul and open up an office or undertake some other action that would demonstrate a desire to establish a relationship with the government, it would be very helpful to keep their interest peaked.

I agreed to come as soon as I could.

The international sanctions placed on citizens of Afghanistan caused me some concern. Even though I lived in the U.S., I was not yet a U.S. citizen, but I held a green card and, for the most part, lived in the country since 1974.

The sanctions against Afghanistan applied to me and yet they did not. On the one hand, if I signed a deal with the Taliban, I could be prosecuted under U.S. law. On the other hand, as a citizen of Afghanistan, I could make all the deals with the Taliban that I wanted. However, unless I involved U.S. companies, I could not use doing business as a lever to normalize relations between the two countries.

Opening an office in Kabul and having one or two employees under a German company owned by Michael Albrecht seemed the only answer. By law, however, we were not allowed to make any kind of deals until the U.N. sanctions were lifted. Since Ahmad Jan signed no contracts with the Chinese, unless he signed something quickly his efforts would be questioned by his government. I made a Machiavellian choice. I decided the best solution would be to sign the contracts but not do any business.

We organized another trip to Afghanistan for February of 2000. Because no airlines were allowed to fly into the country, we flew to Islamabad and then traveled to Kabul on our own. In Peshawar, Minister Ahmad Jan sent his foreign relations director, Assadullah, to accompany us to the Afghan border.

The next day we traveled by car to Torkham which is on the border between Pakistan and Afghanistan. The immigration officer on the Pakistan side noticed that two of the American businessmen with us did not get entry visas when processed at the airport in Islamabad. We were told to go back and get the passports stamped. We split into two groups – one to remain and work on the passport problem and one to leave for Kabul. The Kabul group left with the understanding that the passport group would join them in a day or two. I remained behind to help with the passports.

To get the passports stamped, I sought the help of Mr. Zaeef, the Deputy Minister of Mining and Industries in Kabul. He suggested that I talk to Ratab Popal who had friends in the office of the Minister of Justice of Pakistan. The Minister of Justice then called the chief of airport security, Sardar Azin Khan, who worked for the Federal Investigation Department which controls the border of Pakistan. He personally stamped the passports.

My group then set off by SUV. The conditions of the roads hadn't improved since my last trip, but they were now the only way into the country.

Everyone became discouraged during the journey. They questioned how heavy equipment could move down the damaged roads? Our heads slammed against the roof of the vehicle even though we drove at about five miles per hour. I think riding a camel would have been more comfortable. The German's had built the road in the 1960's, so I knew it had been built to last, but no one had counted on the destruction caused by the Soviets and the resulting civil war. Even though the roads were a nightmare, the scenery was breathtaking for we traveled the Khyber Pass into Afghanistan.

Driving up to the Spen Zar Hotel in Kabul, I noticed that it looked odd. It appeared to yawn as if it had an open mouth. As we got closer I saw that part of the hotel's front wall was missing. Once at the front desk the clerk told me that a bomb had gone off the night before. Explosives had been hidden in a food-vendor's cart that was left in front of the hotel. Everyone was buzzing that the explosion had been caused by the Northern Alliance.

I was glad to see that Aziz, Michael and Nick had not been blown to bits. They had reached the hotel at about four that afternoon. The bomb exploded while they were in their rooms on the fifth floor talking to Mr. Zaeef. They explained that the hotel had jolted and shook, but no one inside was injured. Outside five were killed and about twenty were wounded.

Mr. Zaeef told me that they were pretty sure the bomb was meant for our group. The bomb was positioned near the hotel's restaurant and timed for the dinner hour. Fortunately for us, it had gone off early. Officials believed that someone was trying to stop the flow of foreigners into the country. Later – in private – Ahmad Jan would share the Taliban's true belief, that it was the work of bin Laden. What the Afghan Government got from that man to tolerate him to such lengths, I'll never know.

Like all governments that espouse term limits, the Taliban government believed in rotating its ministers as a method of preventing a build-up of power. The new Minister of Mining and Industries was Mullah Mohammad Esa. Mullah Omar had ordered him to switch jobs with Ahmad Jan. Esa had been the Minister of Water Power. At that time a large portion of Afghanistan's power was derived from the rivers that ran through the country. Esa was a locally trained mullah who had never been out of the country. A simple man, he lacked any formal education. When he spoke, you could tell immediately that he had zero knowledge about his new position. Nonetheless I congratulated him on the new job.

Esa confided in me that he was not very happy in his new job because he had no experience in mining or industries, but *Amir-oul-Mominin* (Mullah Omar) had ordered the change. Esa held his former position over water power for just two years and had taken great pleasure in making sure that everyone had at least one light bulb in their home. But he wasn't so sure about his new job. Trying to put him at ease, I admitted that I, too, was uncomfortable with the change for I had worked with Mullah Ahmad Jan for over a year.

The next morning Esa and Mr. Mandar Khail, the general director of the oil fields, who was with me earlier when bin Laden's men stopped our cars during our last trip, joined us for breakfast. After breakfast, Esa and I returned to my suite. I offered him a chair. Surprisingly he sat cross-legged on the floor. Embarrassed, I motioned to join him, but he suddenly grabbed my right hand. "Do you promise me – to this hand – that your hand is in my hand – that you will not betray me and you will not do anything against the poor people of Afghanistan."

"You can have that promise," I assured him.

Esa reared-up, shifted his weight to his arms and tucked his legs under his body. I felt pain in my knees just watching him sit there in the prayer position. He was a large man, bulked up with muscle. He was almost the same height on the floor as I was in the chair. I knew that if I assumed his sitting position, I would be crippled for hours.

"Mr. Mullah, please. Don't."

"No, no. You have to sit because I am going to say something that you are going to be very unhappy and happy with."

Curiosity overtook me, "Please go on."

In the last two weeks, Esa had heard a lot of things about me through the Kandahar and Kabul rumor mills. "There are a lot of people saying good things about you, but there are a few saying that you are just an American agent coming here to destroy the Taliban." I smiled. We were close in age, both about forty-four.

"I had a dream last night that I was drowning in water and you were struggling too, but you extended your hand to save me. I woke up in the middle of the dream. I don't know what to make out of it. I do believe in dreams – and you were trying to help me. I woke up at that point and thought about you for a long time."

Esa explained that when he left his house that morning there were about thirty beggars, all women, in front of his house. They had heard that he had become the new Minister of Mining and Industries. It was customary when something good happens, for one to give money or food to the poor, but he only had about twenty dollars.

"I tried to divide my money between all the poor women." His large eyes turned mournful. "These women – one of them could have been my sister – my wife – my mother. All these women belong to somebody. Some of them have lost their fathers, their husbands. It was heart breaking. I am kneeling in front of you – I should not do this, the only one I kneel to is God – but I am kneeling here before you to help these poor people, these poor women. I've learned that Afghanistan has enough oil and enough minerals to help the people of Afghanistan."

I was taken aback by his pleas and said, "Mr. Mullah Sahib, I give you my hand as a man that I'll never betray you, I'll never betray my religion Islam, I'll never betray Afghanistan, and I'll never betray America. Please don't forget people will tell you a lot of things. My family – ninety percent of them are Americans: my brothers, my sisters, my nephews, my nieces, my children – all of them. Please remember you will hear a lot of things about Americans, but we are here on a mission. Perhaps God chose me as an ex-mujahid to come and help you."

Esa admitted that he did not understand politics very well. In the 1980's he had preached to his mujahidin that the Americans were on their side. Now everywhere he turned, the Americans seemed angry with the Afghans, but he still wanted the U.S. to come.

"If the Americans are looking for a response about Osama, please tell them as the Minister of Mining and Industries I said, "Fuck Osama's wives! Fuck Osama's family! Fuck Osama's being! I hope the bastard rots in hell and dies. If I were to see him and catch him I would kill the son-of-a-bitch." Relieved that his tirade ended, he grew serious again, "In the name of the God that we share commonly – help us!"

Esa was a simple mullah; a simple Afghan with simple words. Could he help me deliver bin Laden to the U.S.? I doubted it. He saw me as someone who could help him, not the other way around. I hoped that I could.

After my meeting with Esa, Minister Ahmad Jan appeared at the door. He wanted me to meet Mullah Abdul Jalil Akhund, "the hearts and minds of the mullahs." Originally Mullah Omar had appointed Jalil to be Foreign Minister, but within twenty-four hours, Omar changed his mind. He missed him so much that Omar brought Jalil back to Kandahar as a Deputy Foreign Minister. As a deputy, his apparent authority would be diminished but he could spend more time in Kandahar working with Mullah Omar on important matters. Although only a Deputy to the Foreign Minister, he had great influence over the combined day to day operations of the Afghan Government, including finance, military and intelligence.

One should compare the Taliban leadership to a game of smoke and mirrors, the image of power one saw in the mirror was not necessarily the reflection of the person running the show. It was hard for me to determine whether any one person actually held total power in the country, but I quickly learned that it didn't just rest in Mullah Omar and it wasn't just him running the country. Simple mullahs like Jalil, who were more traditional and who had not traveled outside of the country, possessed enormous power, often more than those "contaminated" by outside influences. And even though they possessed only local knowledge and often stayed within the bounds of their village customs and traditions, these mullahs set national policy.

It was standard operating procedure that whenever Jalil was in Kandahar then Mutawakel must go to Kabul. Prior to my arrival, it had been understood between Mutawakel and Ahmad Jan that Mutawakel would stay in Kandahar so that Jalil could travel to Kabul to meet with me. They had agreed between themselves that I – someone they saw as a foreigner

– was the only one in a position to undertake a change in the hearts and minds of the mullahs about the Afghan Government's guest, Osama bin Laden.

The night I arrived in Kabul, Nick Anton, Michael Albrecht, my nephew Aziz and I sat down to dinner with Ministers Esa and Ahmad Jan at the hotel to discuss their oil. The Taliban leadership believed that those in power should eat the same as ordinary Afghans. Ministers were not allowed to wine and dine in fancy hotels because ordinary citizens couldn't afford it, so we invited them to dinner as our guests.

While we waited for their arrival at dinner, naturally we bought bottled water and some cokes to drink. When Esa saw the drinks, he grew angry. He grabbed my hand and said that as the guest of the Afghan Government, we shouldn't have bought the drinks at the hotel. Because the Taliban had a lot of enemies in Kabul, the drinks could be contaminated. He explained that some in the country wanted to shame the Taliban by killing their guests.

This was bad news for us. We were the enemy of those that hated the Taliban as well as those that supported Osama. If caught in crossfire, we wouldn't win.

Esa told us that in the past, poison had been injected into canned drinks. This made all drinks suspect, even those at the hotel. We were told that when guests of the Afghan Government eat dinner with the Taliban, the different ministries provide the drinks. Because members of the Afghan Government had been poisoned, too, they regularly sent underlings in cars to pick drinks up from randomly selected shops around town.

At dinner we decided to begin the oil business in a small way. One small, portable refinery from Ventech, a Texas company, was all that was needed. It would meet the Afghan Government's need for immediate action thereby relieving their importation of so much fuel. We concluded that a portable refinery was the answer to everyone's problems. They were easy to install and could be set in place and then dismantled and moved when more permanent wells were built. And one functioning refinery would show big investors that the impossible could be achieved in Afghanistan.

I knew little about Mullah Abdul Jalil Akhund before we met. At dinner when Ahmad Jan told Esa that we were meeting with Jalil the next day, he acted surprised but wouldn't say why. Esa described Jalil as a very kind man whose word was good and could be taken at face value. After dinner I asked other Afghan officials about Jalil. I was told that if he wasn't equal to Mullah Omar, he was no less than him. Anxiously I awaited our meeting.

The next day when we entered the Ministry Hall, Jalil greeted us at the door. As we walked up the stairs to his second floor office, we saw that he moved slowly with a decided limp. I got pains just watching him ascend the stairs.

When meeting the highest officials of the Taliban it was understood that one addressed them as *Haji Mullah Sahib*. So I said to Jalil, "Haji mullah sahib, are you okay? Is your foot hurting you?"

He said, "Yes, it does hurt when I walk too fast."

"Well maybe we can have it checked by a doctor. My brother is a doctor in the United States perhaps he should look at it?"

"No, more than that is involved, and a lot of people deserve treatment more than I because others are more wounded and can't walk at all. At least I can walk."

"What happened?"

Jalil explained that he had been hit by a rocket in Kandahar as he fought against the Soviets. It struck nearby wounding him and killing eleven of his fighters. He was cut by shrapnel in three different places on his left leg and the back of his left foot had a piece blown out. He reassured me not to worry because it had occurred during a jihad.

Jalil then surprised me by asking if I remembered him at all. I did not. He remembered me from when I worked with Mujaddedi in the 1980's. Jalil said that he, too, had worked for Mujaddedi (whom we called *Hazarat Sahib*). He explained that it was his job to send people to the Haj (the holy pilgrimage in Saudi Arabia) from Mujaddedi's group. Once we got to Jalil's office, we were served green and black tea with milk, and some cakes, cookies and cheeses.

Mullah Zaeef had been ordered by Mullah Omar to be our host in Kabul and to come to the meeting with Jalil. He had become the Deputy Minister of Mining and Industries in the recent shuffle of offices.

As we sat in Jalil's office, Zaeef played with our satellite telephone. Watching him toy with it, I began to laugh. Jalil asked me what was wrong. I explained that Zaeef reminded me of my nephew, Jamal, back in the U.S. "When he sees something electronic, he must play with it and he either destroys it or fixes it. I'm afraid he will destroy our satellite phone and we need it." Jalil and Zaeef laughed when I snatched the telephone from Zaeef's hands as if he were a destructive teenager.

David Alameel was among the group of foreign men gathered in Jalil's office. He was an American-Lebanese Christian born on the Israeli side of Lebanon, a real immigration officer's nightmare. He explained to Jalil that Afghanistan's infrastructure was so bad that the roads alone would cost about twenty billion dollars to repair. (Alameel always seem to think only in terms of billions of dollars, as if millions were beneath his contempt.) He added that an equal amount would have to be spent on the airport because there was nothing left of the old one. He calculated that it would cost the Taliban about two-hundred billion dollars to get everything up and running. They could use the copper mines and oil and gas fields as collateral for loans from the U.S. and the World Bank for the infrastructure repair. Jalil quietly listened to Alameel's proposal while stroking his salt-and-pepper beard. He grinned at the prospect of getting everything fixed.

Jalil also seemed to appreciate an idea that I had run by the Finance Ministry on an earlier trip. The money of Afghanistan was printed in two different countries: half was printed in Russia and the other half in Iran. This disorganization made smuggling commonplace and often put the Afghan Government in the position of buying back its own currency from foreigners. A sudden glut of smuggled currency could cost them dearly, and often did. Due to the black market, one day an Afghani could be worth a dollar, the next seventy-five cents.

Jalil agreed with me that the Afghani note should be stabilized against the U.S. dollar before they began doing business with the world. I knew of companies that printed Euros for the Germans and Swiss. I agreed to make the initial contact with these companies for the current Afghan Government. Jalil agreed that this needed to be done and asked me to meet with the Minister of Finance. I accepted a dinner invitation for that very purpose.

Jalil was a very quiet man, the type of man it is hard to get to know but the type whose face is the book of his moods. I decided not to discuss bin Laden in the same harsh manner that I had used with the hot-headed mullahs who argued with me on the first trip. Jalil was a local mullah, a traditionalist, someone not necessarily easy for me to deal with. I was afraid that if I said the wrong thing it would betray his trust. I was also afraid of ruining my one God-given chance with the man who helped run things. I didn't wish to risk acting too aggressively. I felt it better to approach him through the Afghan codes of honor.

Before meeting with Jalil, I asked my friends to be tolerant and patient with him because I did not want him to think of us as spies. Rather we would plumb for the soft spot in his heart. It would be easier to locate it and proceed from there than to start off doing battle.

I explained to Jalil that bin Laden was the main obstacle to their entrance onto the world stage. It would be hard to conduct business with the Afghan Government protecting Osama. I did not try to persuade Jalil, but he understood.

Jalil took my hand and guided me into another office. Much to my surprise, sitting in a chair was Mullah

Mohammad Rabbani Akhund (who the Taliban called, Mullah Rabbani), Chairman of the Ruling Council, head of the Council of Ministers, one of the principal founders of the Taliban, Prime Minister of Afghanistan from 1966 until right before his death in April 2001, a member of the country's governing council. On that day I had to give my word that his name would never be revealed until after my death, so I stand by my pledge today even though the man is now deceased. Once I am deceased then my pledge will be fulfilled and his name will be revealed."[1]

Jalil introduced us and said that Mullah Rabbani would be a big help in furthering our negotiations regarding bin Laden. I asked him no questions; I just listened. It is human nature that if one asks too many questions, others can become suspicious. If questions are not asked, most of the time a secret will be forthcoming, especially between friends. I was not this man's friend, but we both had a lot to gain by knowing each other and working together.

This important member of the Afghan council agreed that bin Laden must be removed from the country. He asked for my help and the help of the U.S. Government in achieving our mutually beneficial goal. With Mullah Rabbani's guarantee of assistance at the highest levels of the Afghan Government, there remained no obstacles for the U.S. to get rid of the terrorist, Osama bin Laden.

Later that February night, my friends and I met with Afghan officials at the Continental Hotel in Kabul. The main issue of discussion was the stabilization of the currency. The Minister of Finance said that in the past people had appeared in Afghanistan volunteering to print the Afghan note but since no one in the current government knew

---

1 Now that Kabir, too, has passed away, I can reveal Mullah Rabbani's name. He is the man who gave the Afghan Government's consent to dispose of Osama bin Laden and who attended some of the clandestine meetings that supported the seizure/capture/killing of Osama bin Laden. Unfortunately, since Kabir was still shielding Rabbani's involvement in 2003/2004 when we worked on the book, I was not privy to which meetings Mullah Rabbani attended.

them, they weren't trusted. When a country orders a printing of its currency, twenty percent of the total amount being printed must be paid up front to the printer. In the past, Afghan officials were afraid that the printer would disappear with the down payment. My business partner, Michael Albrecht, knew reputable people in Germany who could do the printing. This caught the Afghans' attention. Michael agreed to introduce them to representatives of a company located in Munich that printed notes for governments.

Six months later in August 2000, an order was placed with the German company. It took about a year and two months for the notes to be printed. In the month of September 2001, the Taliban's Minister of Finance received word from the German printer that the Afghani notes were ready to be picked up. The total cost of printing the money was about forty million dollars.

Since the Taliban were under international sanctions, they could neither travel to get their notes nor transfer funds to pay for them. They asked me to talk to U.S. and U.N. officials about obtaining the legal delivery of their money. The money was still awaiting delivery when Hamid Karzai was brought into Afghanistan by the U.S. backed international coalition. As of this writing, if Afghan currency is closely examined one can see that it is the legal tender of the Islamic Emirate of Afghanistan – the Taliban.

Later, at dinner with Jalil, we agreed to return with a proposal for a refinery in Sara-e-Pul in less than two months. We signed a *Letter of Intent* which gave us the right to research and survey the area for further exploration. I wanted a U.S. refinery in northern Afghanistan and I wanted it to be mine.

Michael Albrecht, David Alameel and David's partner, a man named Abdul, left Afghanistan for Islamabad on a three-passenger plane that flew into Kabul once a month (thus breaking everyone's sanctions against Afghanistan). The rest of us decided to take the road out.

Since my airline ticket was from Islamabad to Texas, I stopped at the Pakistan Embassy in Kabul and applied for a visa which would allow me to travel to the airport in Pakistan. At the embassy, the Ambassador to Pakistan asked to see me. He questioned me about why I was in Afghanistan dressed like a Westerner. I explained that I was an American businessman. He asked, what kind of business, and I explained oil and gas. The Ambassador decided to send my visa application through official channels back to Pakistan and not do it himself. He reassured me that the whole process shouldn't take more than two to four weeks. I knew, if he wanted to process it himself, he could do it in a single day.

I returned to the Spen Zar and called Minister Esa. He came to the hotel and was perplexed at the Pakistani response to my visa application. He sent an official from the ministry to Pakistan's embassy who reported back that they demanded two to four weeks to approve my passing through their country. Esa explained that the Pakistanis knew that Afghanistan was land locked and surrounded by Iran, Russia and Turkmenistan with whom their relationship wasn't that good. I wondered whether it had anything to do with my being a muj in the 1980's, but more than likely they were growing suspicious of all my comings and goings.

Since flying out of Pakistan was no longer an option, I wasn't sure which land route home would be best. I wanted to stay out of Iran because it was the enemy of the U.S. Ideological differences and old war memories precluded me from going to Russia. Esa suggested that we contact the Counselor General of Turkmenistan in the city of Herat near the Turkmen border to see whether I would be allowed to cross their territory. So Turkmenistan it was.

I suggested to Aziz and Nick that they go ahead and leave through Islamabad, but they felt it a better choice to stay with me. That way we could all travel through Turkmenistan together.

Next morning we purchased airline tickets for the afternoon flight to Herat. Jalil, Ahmad Jan, the governor of Kabul, and the Ministers of Commerce and Finance saw us off at the airport. We decided that we would come back within the next few months to look at proposals for a refinery and that because of U.S. sanctions, we would form a corporation in Europe.

Herat, about five hundred miles northwest of Kabul, is a very old Persian city. It once was an important seat of education and is sometimes still referred to as the "Bride of the World" because of its reputation as a center of learning. We flew there and were invited to stay the night at the governor's mansion in Herat.

Because of our suits and clean shaven faces, we were a local curiosity to the sixty or so military and civilian officials who arrived at the governor's for dinner that night. My meal was interrupted by Foreign Minister Mutawakel calling me from Kandahar. He was upset by the news that Pakistan officials would not issue a visa to me. He suggested that he expel their ambassador.

"No. I didn't come here to cause trouble between two countries." Besides the whole problem was really my fault for not applying for the visa before leaving the U.S. And because of the closeness of a port in Turkmenistan, this may be the route that we use to carry equipment to the fields of Sara-e-Pul. It was important to get the lay of the land.

Mutawakel wished me good luck getting our oil investments together. He said to remember, "People who own camels must have tall gates to enter into their yards." I took this as an oblique but polite warning to be prepared for trouble.

"Yes, I have seen tall gates. But in fact, I have no gates in front of my house back in Texas, so a camel can enter at any time." We laughed.

After dinner at the governor's, we sat around drinking tea. Among the fifteen or so government officials remaining after the meal, I noticed someone speaking Pashto with an accent. His features were not quite Afghani. His accent was good, but not good enough – probably ISI (Pakistan intelligence). He flattered me by saying that I was intelligent and that the Taliban could learn a lot from me, but added that I had one fault. If I would just correct that one thing, "I would become a good Muslim and then could join the Taliban movement."

"What is that?" I asked politely.

"You don't have a beard."

The next morning in Herat we met with the Counselor General of Turkmenistan. Very polite and friendly, he noticed the Mont Blanc pen in my nephew's pocket.

"That's a nice pen!"

Without an objection from my nephew Aziz, I pulled it from his pocket and handed it over to the Counselor General. Because we wanted to leave the country as quickly as possible, we could afford this courtesy even though he expected no gift.

The Turkmen Counselor General asked us a lot of questions about what we were doing in Afghanistan. Of course, we had nothing to hide. We freely admitted that we were hoping to make an oil deal and that we were trying to bring Americans in to explore the oil and gas fields in northern Afghanistan. I suggested that since Turkmenistan was no longer tied to the Soviets, they, too, could join us and become capitalists. With a grimace, he issued us visas.

We were driven to the Afghan border with Turkmenistan. Cars aren't allowed to cross a neutral zone that lays on either side of the river separating the two countries, so we were forced to carry (and drag) our large suitcases for a half mile over a gravel road and then a bridge before reaching the official border crossing of Turkmenistan.

The people staffing the immigration office were surprised to see three beardless Western guys shlepping luggage from Taliban country. Aziz and Nick were citizens of the U.S. and were warmly welcomed because the border guards had never seen Americans before. Everyone grinned as they took turns vigorously shaking their hands. On the other hand, I was old news with my Afghan passport and was more or less ignored.

Then customs agents appeared and asked us to come with them. We followed the uniformed men into a large room. At their bidding, we opened our suitcases and watched as they examined each article of clothing and toiletry item in detail. It didn't help that their translator spoke only half-ass English. Then they demanded to search our pockets which irritated me to no end. I said, "There is no longer communism here, why are you doing this?" They just ignored me as they rifled through my pants pockets with me still inside them.

We had forgotten that in Aziz's possession were blue prints of a gas project that he had worked on in Alabama, the Turkey Creek Project. He brought the blue prints to Afghanistan to give the Afghan Government's Ministry of Mining and Industries an example of how the gas fields could look. For some reason, his possession of the blue prints agitated the customs agents. They were especially irritated by the words "Turkey" and "Creek" prominently displayed on the top of the plans. Then their interpreter misread them as saying "Turkey" and "Greek." Because Greece and Turkey had on-again, off-again wars for centuries, these simple-minded men believed that Aziz's plans showed a plan for a war between the two countries. They began questioning my nephew about our motives for being in the country. We tried to explain that the plans were for an oil field in Alabama. But like most people in the world, they had never heard of Alabama, so our explanations didn't diminish their suspicions one bit.

Then they discovered our satellite phone and went ballistic. In their minds, it only confirmed their misreading of the blue prints and decided that they didn't want the phone or us in their country. We could be intelligence agents wanting to disclose their secrets. I explained that we were traveling through Turkmenistan and were planning to stay only as long as it took us to get a flight back to Europe.

After much effort on our part, the Turkmenistan authorities finally came to understand our motives and it quickly became clear to us that they had motives of their own. They wanted a bribe. Finally Nick and Aziz bought our entry into the country with several hundred dollars. Then after inquiring about a taxi, we were informed that we had to drag our suitcases another mile to get into the taxi zone. We tried bribing our way into a ride, but weren't successful. So again, we were out in the middle of nowhere dragging suitcases. When we finally reached the taxi station there were a few very small taxis sitting there. We hired two of them and kept up with each other during the long trip to civilization using our satellite phones.

It was a six hour drive from the border of Turkmenistan to its capital city, Eshqabad. We arrived there about eleven that night. Luckily there was a luxurious Sheraton Hotel in town. We ordered the only dish available at that hour, eggs, and then went straight to sleep.

The next morning we scouted around for flights to Europe. There was one flight to Frankfort that day, but the airlines wouldn't allow us on it. Lufthansa had a rule that ticket purchases must occur five or six hours in advance of their flights. We lucked out, however. The very next day there was a flight to Europe on Turkmenistani Airlines, so we bought tickets to London.

Since we had a day to kill, we decided to see the sights. Prominently displayed at every intersection was a huge picture of Saparmurat Niyazov, the President of Turkmenistan who his people call *Serdar Turkmenbashi* (great leader of all Turkmen). We saw hundreds of these gigantic photos. The images that I had seen years earlier in Iraq of Sadam Hussein were nothing compared to this guy's. There was even a golden image of him that turned to meet the sun as it progressed across the sky.

For me the proof that Turkmenbashi was a heavy handed dictator was the fact that he had ordered that his pictures be placed in hotel bathrooms. Not used to seeing a leader's face at every turn, I quickly tired of his presence, especially when it came time to take a leak. To get some peace from his prying eyes, I finally took his pictures down from the hotel room walls. I was tempted to piss on the one sitting on the floor in the bathroom, but decided to let the temptation pass.

The day we were to fly to London, we were told to get to the airport three hours in advance of departure. Eager to leave the country, we arrived three and a half hours early. The airport was enormous and brand new. We looked at each other in disbelief. The three of us were the only passengers in the entire facility and only one plane rested on the tarmac.

We checked in at the ticket counter and everyone began screaming at us that we were late in spite of the fact that we were hours early. Then the ticket counter reps quickly showed us to security. We were turned upside down and inside out by Turkmenistan's security officers. They were looking for goods bought in their country so they could tax them. I explained that we had already declared everything at the border and showed them a list that the customs agents had made, but it didn't stop them from searching. Thank God we hadn't bought a single thing in Turkmenistan. Aziz bribed them with a fifty dollar bill, so they finally let us go.

We were shown back to the ticket counter where everything was meticulously weighed, even our hand luggage, and pushed through a metal detector. It became impossible to ignore the fact that they were going to drag our security inspection out and that we wouldn't be allowed to board the plane until another bribe was handed over. I had enough so I jumped on the scales and loudly dared them to weigh me, too. My tantrum allowed us to move on without forking over a bribe to the ticket counter reps. By the time we passed a third security check, we still had a little more than an hour to go before our scheduled flight.

Everyone kept delaying our departure in order to get bribes out of us. Aziz began handing out money to everyone. The officials reminded him of the Soviets who invaded Afghanistan in the 1970's. The Turkmen uniforms were almost the same as those of the Soviets. A child of about ten when they invaded, the sight of the uniforms scared him. Fearfully Aziz admitted, "I just want to leave this country." I noted his concern and added a few dozen bills of my own.

A military officer came into view. He had the stereotypical Soviet Army uniform covered with metals. I approached him and asked if he could get us out of here – no matter the price. We flashed two hundred dollars. He motioned everyone to back off, which they did, and he escorted us to the gate.

When we arrived at the gate, the stewardesses and pilots seemed to be standing around waiting. When they saw us, they began shouting for us to get on the aircraft because, "It's getting late!"

I looked at my watch. We still had almost an hour to go before the scheduled takeoff. What we failed to understand was that there was no real scheduled takeoff time. They simply got the plane in the air whenever all those booked were finally on the craft. As we were the only passengers, they were more than ready to depart the moment they saw us coming toward the gate.

We got on the plane and the door quickly slammed shut behind us. I tried to explain to the stewardess that we had an hour to go, but she wasn't interested. The plane had come from New Deli packed with people and was leaving the country almost empty. It was a big relief for us when the plane finally left Turkmen soil.

It is customary for airlines to give first class passengers a small gift for traveling with them. Half way through the flight to London we were presented with calendars. They were normal wall calendars about the size of an A4 sheet of paper. After opening it, I noticed that the month of January had been renamed "Turkmenbashi." On the first few pages were photographs of the Turkman.

I groaned and flipped through the rest of the calendar. Each page presented a different pose of their leader. Some were bust shots, others full length photos. Some showed a ring on his index finger, others on his ring finger. I glanced up and noticed, pinned to the inside fuselage of the airplane, was another photo of the Turkman. In disgust, I handed the calendar back to the stewardess. She seemed almost scared to take it from my outstretched hand.

When we arrived in London, I was confronted with the fact that I didn't have the right paperwork to enter England. At that time I was not yet a citizen of the U.S. and only held a green card. Every time I traveled it was a headache because I also held the passport of the Islamic Emirate of Afghanistan – the Taliban. To make matters worse, during my last trip I had to get a new passport since my original passport had been issued by an Afghan Government that was no longer in power.

Believe me when I tell you that holding a passport from the Taliban government makes traveling a wee bit difficult. I eventually began bundling all of my passports and green card together. Whenever I approached an immigration officer, I plopped the mess down on the desk and let them slowly make their way through it answering any questions that they may have.

My Taliban passport had been marked with a *schengen* visa which should have allowed me to travel everywhere within the European Union. Unfortunately, at this point in time, I didn't know that England had yet to recognize all of the E.U. amenities like recognition of a schengen visa.

I explained to the British Immigration Office that I thought my visa applied to England and they assured me that it did not. So I apologized for the misunderstanding and they were very kind and allowed me to stay for twenty-four hours at a nearby hotel until my flight to the U.S. the next day. Since I "voluntarily" deported myself (which means that I bought a ticket and left the country) I would be allowed to travel to England again if I had the correct paperwork.

From that time forward, every time I used the passport issued by the current Afghan Government, I was questioned by immigration authorities about the cause of my deportation from England. After many delays, I finally destroyed that particular Afghan passport and applied for a new one. I got tired of having to explain my stupid mistake everywhere I went.

After returning to the U.S., I reported my progress to the State Department. Because I didn't want to have trouble with my government over the fact that I was doing business with a sanctioned country, I explained everything that had occurred to State Department officials. No one seemed to care. They understood that I wouldn't do business without delivering bin Laden first. They also understood that I had no intention of breaking U.S. law.

Chapter 6: The E.U. Slumbers

One of the most asked questions during my February 2000, trip to Afghanistan was, "How could President Clinton remain in power after confessing to adultery?" The mullahs in power were shocked that he still held office. I told them that the President of the United States never really admitted to adultery, but they insisted that they heard he had on the radio. They also read in newspapers that he had confessed. I wondered how they had heard of this so quickly but had never heard anything about some of the terrible things that bin Laden was accused of initiating.

"According to Clinton, he did not commit adultery. He committed a sin," I explained. "A woman had oral sex with him." They had no idea what that meant. I explained how oral sex is performed to the group of Afghan holy men. After my explanation, half of them said they wanted to puke, the other half laughed. It was a shocking practice for this group of religious war veterans who felt that only animals licked each other. I said that it was pretty common in Western society.

Their next question, "How come it isn't a sin?"

"It probably is a sin, but Clinton didn't think it was adultery," I said.

"Then what is it?"

"In a way he was right. In no holy books – Old Testament, New Testament, Quran – is there any punishment for that kind of sex." This made the mullahs laugh. They wanted to know how Clinton came up with the distinction.

I asked them how they would convict a person who had committed that type of sin. They had no answer and admitted that Clinton was clever and unique.

I agreed that he was good with his words and that he knew what to say and when to say it. I explained his background and that the man really was a genius when it came to public relations and speaking – except for the one small problem he had with his intern.

"Plus, he's really good for America because he makes the economy strong. He comes from a very poor background. He lost his father at an early age and had to make it on his own." The rich people don't want him running things because he tries to watch out for the poor people.

I used him as an example of what America really represents: opportunity to whoever can rise above their original status. They questioned Clinton's judgment but came to admire him nonetheless. In retrospect, this was one of my funnier moments with the Taliban.

Sometime during the February trip, it was decided that I should return around May with a *Memorandum of Understanding*. Similar to an option agreement, it is a mutual promise between the parties to agree to work together. In this case, the parties were the Afghan Government and our small group of investors, but because of U.S. sanctions, I couldn't do business from the U.S.

Together with my European friends, we decided to form either a European or Swiss based corporation and call it the Global Oil and Gas Corporation. During the February trip, we took samples of Afghan crude with us to be examined for quality. A lab in Dubai found it to be heavy crude, one not easy to refine.

While in Sara-e-Pul and Mazar-e-Sharif, we had videotaped the fields. Engineers examined the tapes and confirmed that the machinery at those locations represented old Russian technology. We even laughed when they pointed out that the

Soviets had hoodwinked the Afghan Government by passing off a beer brewery constructed in the 1950's as an oil refinery. Apparently in the 1960's the Soviet's had painted it silver and sold it to the Afghans without it ever having produced a single barrel of oil as proof that it worked.

Once back in Texas, I contacted Ventech, a corporation that constructs modular, portable refineries that produce between 5,000 and 10,000 barrels a day and are suitable for the oil fields of northern Afghanistan. No one in our group thought that we could handle more than 10,000 barrels a day for the first six months.

We were disappointed to learn that because Afghanistan had been put under U.S. sanctions, Ventech couldn't export equipment to it. I explained that my partners and I weren't really interested in making money now, but we would be in the future.

"We want to construct one portable refinery in order to claim the oil and gas fields of Afghanistan. Once I have a contract and register a claim, things will be resolved." But the people of Ventech could not sell us a refinery until all international sanctions had been lifted. The Cockroach had to be eliminated before I could do business in the U.S.

Better organized by May of 2000, we returned to Afghanistan. I left the United States around May 10th. I got to Kabul on May 13th. My partners and I planned to stay about a week.

Upon my arrival, Mr. Mandar Khail called on us. I began to understand the depth of his ambition. In a matter of months since our last visit, Mandar Khail had been promoted to the General President of Oil and Gas Fields of Afghanistan, a top position in the Ministry of Mining and Industry. And Esa, although still heading the ministry, had appointed Mandar Khail to negotiate the final contract with us. For all practical purposes, Mandar Khail was now in charge of the entire ministry.

Mandar Khail would prove to be a hard nut to crack. For some reason, he didn't want to negotiate with us. He erected obstacles out of thin air. Michael Albrecht confided in me that he suspected that Mandar Khail could be involved with a branch of Unocal located in Greece.

Mandar Khail wanted to relegate us to the west of Afghanistan which had yet to be explored for natural resources. To operate in the West one needed a lot of money for surveys and geological studies. In the North, the groundwork had been laid by the Soviets and the French. I tried to turn Esa from Mandar Khail by hinting that he had worked under – and survived – too many governments, but there was little we could do. They had become close.

In the contract negotiations, we got stuck on the word "commission." Mandar Khail did not understand the word. In his defense, although the contract was written in English, it was bound by Swiss law and the Swiss government, making it difficult for everyone. Nor was it particularly easy for the Taliban officials to accept the law of Switzerland when they believed themselves bound only by *Sharia* law. But my partners and I thought it a good thing for everyone concerned to register a company doing business with the Taliban under the laws of the neutral Swiss.

Again and again the negotiations broke down. Eventually we had no choice but to sign a *Memorandum of Understanding* in the form dictated exclusively by Mandar Khail.

Still exasperated over the negotiations with Mandar Khail, I jumped off the plane at Newark, New Jersey hoping to make a quick connection to Houston. Before stamping my passport, a U.S. Immigration officer staring at his computer, asked me to step out of line. He pointed a finger toward the Port Authority Visa Immigration Office, put my passport in an envelope and sent me to that office. I asked him what was wrong, but he didn't know – or wouldn't say. He would only repeat, "Report to Port Authority." I assumed it was the same old problems: 1) I frequently traveled to Afghanistan and 2) my passport was issued by the Taliban's Minister of the Interior.

There were about fifty people ahead of me in line at the Port Authority office. I asked an Immigration officer what the problem was. He told me to sit down and take my turn. I explained that I had been a resident of the United States for over twenty years and had never had any problems entering before. He could care less.

After a while I refused to sit and wait any longer. The two of us entered into a quiet shouting match. Deprived of cigarettes for nine hours, I was a mess. My collapsed negotiations with Mandar Khail probably had more to do with my temper than I'd like to admit. I pleaded with the officer to allow me to leave and have a cigarette. I promised that I would then come back and deal with this problem. Finally feeling pity for me, he got another official over to inspect my passport. He was surprised to learn that it had been issued by the Taliban.

"Mainly you have been traveling to Afghanistan?"

"Yes. In fact, I just came back from there."

"Do you mind if I talk to you?" the official asked.

"Tell me what the problem is and we will talk. I have no problem talking to you," I grumbled. The man in charge of the Immigration Office then came over and asked if they could look inside my briefcase. I didn't mind.

Then someone from Customs showed up. Before I knew it, quite a few people had gathered around me. They asked what the papers were for. I explained that it was a *Memorandum of Understanding* that I had signed with the Taliban for the oil fields in northern Afghanistan. They asked if I was going to be a rich oil man and I jokingly said, "Didn't you know I'm from Texas."

"You people really do smell oil."

"Yes, we smell it and wherever it is, we go after it."

"Well if you ever go public or if you want partners, we wouldn't mind buying some shares." The guy questioning me was named Bill. He was responsible for the airport's Port Authority offices. He asked, "Why is your passport issued by the Taliban?"

I explained that previously I had a passport issued by the Afghan Government of the War Lord Burhanuddin Rabbani. Now to travel inside Afghanistan, I was required to get a new one issued by the Taliban. Since Rabanni was no longer in power, the Taliban did not accept a passport showing his government. "Now I carry two passports stapled together, just in case everything changes tomorrow. I have one from the Rabbani government and one from the Taliban." Bill understood my predicament.

After a few moments, we began talking about bin Laden. I explained how in the past I had worked with the State Department "but now it appears no one cares about him anymore. I guess he's no longer a threat." Bill assured me that he still posed a threat. I repeated the story of how I was offered the opportunity to take bin Laden to a third country by Minister Mutawakel, and that I had told the State Department about it in October 1999, and how they said that they'd get back to me. Now it's May and no one's even bothered getting in touch with me.

"I can't act on the oil and my contacts with the Taliban until bin Laden is out of the country." I explained that there was every incentive for me and the Afghan officials to move him out quickly because we couldn't do business until that had been accomplished.

Bill asked if I would be willing to talk to the FBI.

"I could do that. That's not a problem." I agreed to talk to the FBI if they called upon me in Sugar Land, Texas.

We talked for about an hour and Bill graciously allowed me to smoke during our conversation. After it was over I asked him with a grin, "How many people have you had coming through New Jersey from Afghanistan clean shaven?" He laughed. Unfortunately, I missed my flight. Bill called Continental Airlines and informed them that I was questioned at Port Authority and it was not my fault that I missed my flight. They put me on the next flight to Texas.

A few weeks later a gentleman by the name of Mario Gutierrez called me at home. A soft spoken Hispanic, he informed me that he represented the FBI. Toward the end of May of 2000, we met for a late breakfast at a Denny's restaurant located off the Southwest Freeway and Buffalo Speedway in Houston. After exchanging pleasantries, we talked about my trips back and forth to Afghanistan. He acted surprised that somebody from Texas was so involved with the Taliban.

I asked him about his position with the FBI. He surprised me by saying that he didn't work for the FBI. He had been sent out from the anti-terrorism branch of the City of Houston Police Department.

"Do you have access to the FBI – like one of its agents?"

"Yes, but I'm not as powerful as an agent.

"No offense to you, but why couldn't the FBI send an agent?"

"They didn't send one because they get a lot of calls like this from a lot of people. They try to send us first."

"But we are talking about attacks on the United States. This should be a federal thing," I said in disbelief.

"Don't worry. It's okay for me to deal with it. Perhaps later on, when you prove to them who you really are, they might talk to you." Mario promised to report our discussion to his Police Chief and then to the FBI. When he returned to his office, his superiors had trouble believing him, so he called me and asked for another meeting.

Personally, I was surprised that I had been flying under the local radar. I would have thought that at some point someone in Washington would call someone in Houston to have somebody check up on me and determine what I was up to. I was wrong. Of course that was in the year 2000 and we would learn in another year that there were some very sinister folks that were also flying under the U.S. radar.

Again we met at Denny's. I explained to Mario that I would be returning to Afghanistan soon. I produced the signed *Memorandum of Understanding* and gave him a copy. Mario said it was difficult to understand why an Afghan living in a small town in Texas would have such access to the Taliban. He asked if I would meet with the director of the FBI in Houston. I was more than willing to meet with them, but it had to be quickly for I was leaving for Afghanistan soon. We made a quick appointment.

I went to the FBI office and met Steve Gentry, the director of the Houston FBI. A true professional, he was one of the top FBI agents in the country. Whenever there was a crisis in the U.S., he was one of the team members assigned to handle it. At the time of 9/11, he spent a lot of time in D.C. The rumor was that Steve was very accessible. He quickly put me at ease when we spoke.

Gentry asked me questions about my past. I explained myself. I had some bad habits and had made my share of mistakes. Mainly I liked to drive fast. Lots of traffic offenses lurk around in my past. I also had a temporary problem with drinking, gambling and womanizing in the early 1990's. I told Gentry everything, but he wasn't interested in my indiscretions. He was concerned with criminal acts against the United States, such as acts of terrorism, but there were none in my history.

I explained how America was on the side of the Afghans in their war against the Soviets in the 1980's. I told him about Sid George, an American from Texas who had been wounded in the Vietnam War. Sid traveled to Afghanistan with me and met my leader, Mujadidi. Sid told Mujadidi that he needed one hundred mujahidin plus any old arms lying around. He wanted to hijack and destroy Soviet cargo tankers and ships on the high seas and to attack a border city in Yemen which was full of Soviet munitions. Sid freely admitted that he had a personal vendetta against communists.

Mujadidi rejected Sid's ideas. He said they were not interested in executing them. "We're not Palestinians. We have a war right here on our soil. We will not go beyond our borders. We will only fight on our turf." Sid was mad and called us cowards. I didn't agree with his idea of taking the war of a landlocked country to the high seas.

I explained to the FBI's Steve Gentry that I had been offered a job in the mid-80's by the FBI, but eventually decided that I wouldn't be a good agent – I have too big a mouth. I like speaking my mind. I don't know how to keep secrets because I don't care about keeping secrets. To me there is nothing really secret. Secrets bring troubles and lies. I don't want those types of problems and I don't want to live like that. I am a free man and would like to keep it that way.

Steve asked me when I was going to Islamabad. He had a close friend, Mike Morris, a legal attaché who represented the FBI at the U.S. Embassy there. He suggested that I meet with him.

Michael Albrecht arranged the purchase of used oil refineries from an Italian firm that had bought them in America. Like the Ventech models, they were built to be easily erected and dismantled, but the price was high, about fifty million dollars each. The maximum daily capacity of one of the Italian refineries was thirty thousand barrels, the minimum was fifteen thousand which was more than we could produce.

We decided to upgrade the oil field drilling rigs so we could meet the refinery's minimum daily requirement. Various businessmen in Europe and America estimated it would cost between two and three million dollars to take new technology to the Afghan oilfields to make the wells produce more. We were optimistic that everything would fall in place and we would soon be in the refining business.

On July 21, 2000, I left for Islamabad. To pay for this trip, I took out a second mortgage on my house in Sugar Land. At the time, I felt that I had two obligations: to continue working on a better relationship between Afghanistan and America and to finalize the natural resource contracts with the Afghan Government. If I was able to accomplish both, I would be one of the richest men in the world. But it would take both for me to win – and I could still lose. If I couldn't get bin Laden out of Afghanistan, I would never be able to establish a good working relationship between the U.S. and the current Afghan Government.

A lot was riding on this trip. Having a *Memorandum of Understanding* was great, but it wasn't a final contract. If we worked out a formal contract half of my two goals would be complete. But at that point in time, it seemed a bigger obstacle to work out our contract problems than to remove the Cockroach that had crawled between me and what I hoped would be a brilliant future for myself and Afghanistan.

After arriving in Pakistan, I called upon Paula Thiede, Political Officer of the U.S. Embassy, the contact supplied by the Houston FBI. Paula and her husband both worked for the embassy in Islamabad. She was very professional, but she hated the Taliban.

I agreed with her that Afghanistan was a harsh place for women, but for different reasons than she believed. I explained that yes, women in Kabul were being forced to wear burkas which covered their entire bodies, but in areas outside of the capital, everyone wore shawls not burkas. Especially in the Pashtun areas, women habitually wore shawls. I begged her to be patient because the culture was very different from that of the U.S. and the people were very traditional.

I gave her the example of my mother. My mother and my father's brother were almost the same age, but she would never uncover her face in front of my uncle, even in private. She wouldn't show him her face when he visited her in the U.S. even though she was in her 80s. It was what she had become accustomed to.

"Mom is a tiny woman, but she still ordered us around and no one could force her to show her face. Some Afghans are very traditional and we shouldn't force them to change too quickly." I asked Paula to give them time. "Once the country settles down and the civil war with the Northern Alliance is over, there would be plenty of schools and freedom for women." But the country was torn up by decades of war; survival was the main concern. The finer aspects of life had to wait.

Paula Thiede called me the next day. Mike Morris of the FBI would like to see me. I went back to the U.S. Embassy with my nephew Aziz. He stayed in the cafeteria with Paula while I visited with Mike. Soon after Mike and I began talking, two men walked into his office without knocking. One introduced himself as Ron, the CIA Station Chief in Islamabad. With him was an arm-twister named Harry (probably a fake name).

The Station Chief said, "If you are really a patriotic Afghan-American as you claim, then you *must* deal with us."

"No," I said. "I won't have anything to do with you. It's hard for me to deal with you because I have heard negative things about the CIA." I paused, looked at the scowling faces around me and then blurted out, "I hope you're not here to hurt me!"

"Nobody's here to hurt you."

Thankfully at this point Mike jumped in and said, "Let me explain how the system works. You know that the FBI, the Federal Bureau of Investigation, is responsible for inside the boundaries of the United States.

I shook my head, yes.

"Well anything outside those boundaries is the CIA's jurisdiction," he pointed to Ron. "The FBI has no authority in anything that occurs in the rest of the world. We just take over when it comes time for an arrest."

I hadn't realized that was how U.S. security operated. "Okay," I said, "but I barely said hello to Mike and now you guys look like you are about to grab me and take me away."

"That's exactly what we would like to do. Grab you and take you to our office."

"Are you muscling me?" We all laughed. Ron explained that under current U.S. law he could not talk to me in the presence of the FBI representative.

"Please come to our office. All we want to do is talk to you. And if we convince you, then you stay with us. If we don't, you have no obligation to work for us."

"I don't work *for* anybody, so I will not go to your office. I am willing to work *with* the United States government, but not *for* it." The distinction between *with* and *for* were very important to me. I didn't want them to consider me an employee.

"I want you to work *with* us," Ron said.

Eventually I agreed to go to his office to hear him out. He asked me to wait for about five minutes and then someone would gather me up and take me there. Normally there were lots of employees milling about the embassy. On my way to Ron's office, I didn't see a single one. The halls had been cleared.

When I got to Ron's office, I saw pictures of his family. He looked young for someone in his early 50's. He laughed and said it was because he made such a good living.

I explained again that I had problems with the people in the CIA. For one thing, it was really not easy for me to work with people who – for all their lives – for one reason or another – gave false names. "Like Harry over there. He doesn't even look like a Harry. I don't know who I am talking to – who I am seeing – or what kind of situation I'm in. It's hard for me to have a working relationship with people who won't even give their right names to people. People know me. They know that I was educated in America. If I told them I had nothing to do with the United States government, they wouldn't believe me. I am much better off admitting that I have lots of friends in the United States, at all levels of government. That way people respect me and see that I am telling the truth. It is a known fact that today I walked into this United States Embassy like it is my mother's house. I have visited it quite often in the past. I couldn't hide that and suddenly pretend that I am for the Taliban and against the U.S. Government."

Ron agreed. "Before you leave, can I ask you a question?"

"Sure."

"Would you be willing to establish some kind of contact between the Taliban and us?"

"With the Agency?"

"Yes."

"I can't do that, unless you are willing to admit that you work for the United States government."

"Of course, you're not gonna tell them we're with the CIA."

"Don't even tell me who you are with. If I am asked, I will tell them who you are. I don't want to know who you are going to send to meet the Taliban."

Thereafter we discussed the issue of Foreign Minister Mutawakel. They acted excited by the fact that I could talk to him at any time and asked me to call him. "Yes, let me have your phone. I'll call him right now." They handed me the telephone but before I finished dialing the number, Ron said it wasn't really necessary for me to call. I decided that they were just testing me.

They asked whether I could introduce one of my bodyguards or one of my relatives to be a contact for the U.S. Government.

"No problem." I knew some good people. "How many are needed?"

"One."

"You mean to tell me, you have no contacts whatsoever inside Afghanistan?"

"No."

And there it was, out in the open for everyone present to see. They had no intelligence assets on the ground inside Afghanistan, a country where the Central Intelligence Agency used to have hundreds, if not thousands. How could they possibly have accurate information about what happened there? I was shocked when I realized that they must depend upon rumors for news.

"Where do you get your knowledge of the Taliban? The newspapers?" I said.

The response bordered on malfeasance by those running an intelligence agency, "From people traveling back and forth between Pakistan and Afghanistan." They freely admitted that they got their news from those who may not really know either the Afghan mind set or what was going on inside the Afghan Government. I suggested that I introduce them to a few of its high officials. They agreed and thanked me for meeting with them.

"Before I go, please answer one question. What do you tell people that you do for a living when you are on a plane sitting next to another passenger on a long flight and he or she strikes up a conversation?" I asked.

Ron said, "We usually don't speak to whoever is sitting next to us, but if someone acts friendly and wants to chat about work, we always tell them we're morticians."

I let out a belly laugh and said, "I bet that turns people off."

"Yes, it does. Are you willing to introduce Harry to some people?"

"No problem. I could have someone for him in less than five hours."

Harry called that evening and asked if we could meet and whether I had thought of anyone to introduce him to. I did, but Harry didn't want to meet at the embassy. He wanted another place – somewhere safer.

"I have a relative that lives in the G/9-1 section of Islamabad."

Harry asked if we could meet at about seven o'clock at the Jenah Supermarket. He would be in front of the Chinese restaurant in a diplomatic car. We were to get into the car and drive away.

At 7:00, I arrived there with one of my male relatives and one of my bodyguards, Ahmed. As we got into Harry's car, I glanced at the license plate. It was a diplomatic plate but not from the U.S. I mentioned this to Harry and he laughed. It was the plate of one of the E.U.'s less important countries – Ireland.

We went to the house of one of my female relatives. She had been a translator for the American Embassy in Kabul in the 1960's. I explained that there was a friend coming from the Embassy to talk to me and asked if we could use one of her bedrooms? We followed her upstairs. Once there, Harry informed me that they were very interested in dealing with Mr. Mutawakel.

Earlier I had explained to Harry and Ron that the mullahs' Minister's Council appeared to be the one in power. If they would give me some time, I could get in tight with them. They asked me to give some money to Mutawakel.

"These are men of the cloth. They are very honest with me. I am not going to exploit them. They have never asked me for money."

This surprised him, "Kabir, most of the time, before we even talk to people, they say they have a price."

"I'm a volunteer. Don't offer it to me or to anybody who deals with me. That would degrade me; it would put me in an awkward situation." I explained to Harry that because some members of the Taliban wanted to establish a good working relationship with the U.S. they didn't need to be bribed.

"There is no cost. They are willing to help out on their own accord."

Harry wanted information from Mr. Mutawakel. He asked if my bodyguard Ahmed could go to Paktia and then from there to Kabul to meet with Mutawakel. From my point of view, this was a good thing. It would prove that the Americans were ready and prepared to talk to the current Afghan Government.

"That's not a problem," I replied.

But in order to make it official, Harry said he would have to pay Ahmed's way back and forth to Afghanistan, "Otherwise it will not be an official trip."

"Fine! If you're going to send someone on a trip or a mission, I expect you to pay."

I thought Harry was going to pull a thousand dollars out of his pocket. He pulled out $200 to send Ahmed to Paktia, then Kabul and back to Islamabad. A long trip over bad and dangerous roads, it would easily have cost Ahmed over $300 in expenses. Harry tossed Ahmed the money.

Ahmed took it in his hand but he did not understand what the money was for. I translated that Harry wanted him to go to Paktia, Kabul and Islamabad. Ahmed politely put the money back in front of Harry, laughed and said, "Is this all you're going to pay? What a poor country that you're living in, Mr. Mohabbat."

"Why don't you give him extra money. When we get out of here, I will pay you back."

Harry said, "Here is $200 more."

The whole thing was getting frustrating. "Give him at least $500," I said which he did.

Before we left the house I made Harry promise never to offer money in my name. It would cause problems for me in the future and it would undermine my authority. It would make people greedy. Anyone contacting me after that would be after U.S. money and wouldn't be interested in establishing goodwill between the U.S. and the Afghans.

One of my relatives knocked on the bedroom door. They had made us dinner and asked Harry to stay. He agreed and we all sat down to a lovely meal. Then Harry took us back to the supermarket. There was too much cloak and dagger in all of this for me. I was happy to get away from Harry.

When we arrived back at the hotel, Ahmed said, "Mr. Mohabbat, these people are cheap. I was expecting at least $1000."

I gave him an extra $200. Ahmed offered to give the $200 back, but I told him to keep it. "$700 is enough for you. I'm going back to Europe. You keep in contact with them and go back and tell them whatever Mr. Mutawakel tells you."

Ahmed was happy. He asked me to call Mr. Mutawakel and tell him that he was on his way to see him in Kabul. I picked up the phone and told the Afghan Foreign Minister that I was sending Ahmed to him, a man he had already met in Kabul who traveled with me.

Ahmed made it to Kabul and spoke to Mutawakel. Afterwards he got very excited and called me in Europe from Islamabad and said that Mutawakel had agreed to meet with the American officials. Apparently Harry had asked the Taliban's Foreign Minister to meet with the U.S. ambassador, William Milam. They had agreed to meet sometime in late August or early September. The meeting in the Fall of 2000 would put me one step closer to my two goals.

After my clandestine meeting with Harry in Islamabad, Michael, Nick, Aziz and I went to Peshawar and met with Esa, the Taliban's Minister of Mining and Industries. Again Mandar Khail was with him. We explained that we needed to clear at least $7 per barrel as a refinery fee, but they were only willing to pay $3 per barrel – the international price tied to quieter, more settled countries and far less risky ventures. But we were taking on too much risk for $3. We tried to make him understand that we wanted to reinvest any money we earned back into the Afghan fields by bringing in permanent equipment; plus we would have to do more surveys. We needed at least $7 a barrel.

Because no one was willing to insure our refinery, we were taking a big financial risk putting a fifty million dollar refinery into war torn Afghanistan. If it was bombed or hit by a rocket, that would be the end of us. If our take was held down to only $3 a barrel then the Taliban needed to provide the money for the refinery and allow us to run it. As a negotiation tool, we asked Esa whether they could come up with fifty million dollars, but we knew the ministry didn't have that kind of money.

We argued for days but never reached an agreement. Disappointed, we looked around for a tie breaker. Luckily, Mr. Ahmad Jan, the previous oil minister, was in Pakistan. We left Peshawar and went to Islamabad and asked Ahmad Jan to intervene.

He said no – he wanted to wait until the next cabinet meeting with Mullah Omar and allow Mr. Mutawakel to raise the issue. Frustrated beyond words, we left Islamabad for Frankfurt the 25th of July 2000.

While still in Frankfurt I got a telephone message from Minister Esa. He and five other ministers were in the Slovac Republic. He left me a number to call back. I asked Michael Albrecht whether we should call Esa since we didn't know why he was in Slovac. When we called him we learned that representatives of the Afghan Government were there to sign a contract with a cement factory. From there they planned to travel to Germany to talk to companies in Stuttgart, but the German government refused to allow them inside the country.

Since the Saudi Arabian government was one of the countries that recognized the Islamic Emirate of Afghanistan, they applied for visas to enter Germany through the Saudis. The German government required all members of the Taliban to demonstrate that they were coming in for a business purpose and not for purposes of political propaganda. Even though the Saudi government guaranteed that they were traveling for reasons of business, the German government refused them entry. The Taliban officials were stuck in Slovac for three or four days while the Germans went through the process of refusing their visas. Esa wondered whether I could do anything to help them out of their predicament. I asked him to give us some time to see what my partner and I could come up with.

Michael placed a call to the office of a German representative to the European Union who said he would check with the Ministry of Foreign Affairs in Germany. The Ministry told him that they had received the request, but because the Taliban was associated with terrorists, it was afraid of what they might do while in Germany. We were asked to guarantee that the mullahs' purpose in coming to their country was business.

About three in the afternoon the E.U. rep called back and said that the German government had agreed to issue the members of the Taliban visas for three days, but their activities would be monitored. I called Esa and gave him the news. All they had to do was send somebody to the German Embassy in the Republic of Slovac to pick up the visas.

Michael and I jumped up and down like school boys congratulating each other on our sudden turn of fortune. I suggested that we show the mullahs something different: a hotel in the center of Frankfurt.

Michael said, "The Savoy Hotel."

Upon arriving at the Savoy, we were surprised to find Afghans working the front desk. They acted apprehensive when they learned that we were bringing the Taliban into the Savoy. They had heard that the Taliban were wild and hoped they wouldn't destroy the premises. I couldn't help but laugh at the thought of the mullahs acting like rock-and-rollers. We reserved seven rooms, six for them and one for me.

Then I received a call from the Taliban representative in Germany, Mr. Gullali. He received a call from the Taliban officials who were making their way to Frankfurt on a train. We arranged to meet at the Frankfurt Train Station between five and six o'clock on August 7, 2000, and welcome the Taliban into Germany. Gullali informed me that they would be staying at the offices of the Afghan Government while there. We countered with our gift of hotel rooms.

Dressed in the traditional baggy clothes and turbans of Afghanistan, it's an understatement to write that the Taliban officials were easy to spot as they stepped off the train. Arriving were Mullah Abdul Razaq (Minister of Commerce), Mullah Abdul Jalil (Deputy Foreign Minister), Mullah Abdul Qadir (Taliban Military Attaché to Pakistan), Mullah Mohammad Esa (Minister of Mining and Industry) and the Governor of the Afghanistan Central Bank, whose name I have forgotten.

After welcoming them to Germany, we asked if we could help them carry their luggage. Each held up a briefcase for me to see. They explained that it was an understanding among the members of the Taliban that wherever they go, they take only one briefcase per person which contained a couple of sets of Afghani clothes. Since their country was very poor, it showed others that they are not visiting for personal gain.

"We come with one briefcase and we leave with one briefcase."

Michael joked, "You must do a lot of washing."

"Yes, we wash our own clothes," the official replied, not understanding that Michael was making a joke at his expense. I understood their display of solidarity and frugality, but thought it misplaced. Usually delegations wish to demonstrate to the world their strength and wealth. They looked as if their only asset was poverty.

We climbed into Michael's car and two taxis, and headed toward the Frankfurt office of the Islamic Emirate of Afghanistan. The office had one large room and two very small rooms. Each could be converted from offices into bedrooms if the desks were removed.

"Sir, this is not where you plan to stay?" I asked.

"We don't really have much money and this is fine. We usually sleep on the floor of the mosque. These are much better rooms than those in the mosque. And we have beds!"

As they shuttled into their headquarters I said, "I know you are trying to impress people and your government that you are simple people, but this is no way to do it. If a foreign journalist or dignitary sees beds in the offices and three or four of you sleeping in each room, it will not look good."

A mullah calmly replied, "I agree but we don't have much of a budget. We would like to stay in a reasonable hotel, but cannot."

"Well one has been arranged for you. You are our guests while you are in Frankfurt." Their mood changed to one of sheer gratitude.

Within an hour of the mullahs' arrival, Afghans began dropping by their office. Of note was the number of officials present that represented the Afghan Government prior to the Soviet invasion. In all, about one hundred people came by. Everyone found a place on the floor and checked out the representatives of the new Afghan Government.

At about ten o'clock, I asked the mullah's if they would like to go to the hotel. People at the Taliban headquarters began volunteering to drive them to the Savoy. Along the route to the hotel were German advertisements depicting pictures of naked men and women. The signs embarrassed the mullahs who choose to stare at the floorboards of the cars until we arrived at the Savoy. I told Michael, "This is Europe. Let them get used to it. They will be coming here more often and they will have to see it sometime."

While waiting for the elevator in the hotel, I grabbed a word with Jalil, "The Western media makes fun of mullahs. Everyone makes fun of you. In order to do business in the West, you must change your image. Your office is in the worst part of Frankfurt and it looks awful. No one will look up to you because your office is so poor. People may not want to do business with you. You must convince those in the Cabinet back in Kandahar that you know how to do things in a worldly way. Perhaps you are making a point about your humility, but the world isn't interested in humility."

Michael and I took the mullahs to their rooms. They were surprised that it wasn't necessary for them to share rooms. The costs of putting up the mullahs would strap us financially, but we hoped we would make it up with the goodwill we were spreading.

The next morning the manager of the Savoy Hotel told me there were about forty or fifty Afghans gathered in the hotel lobby. He asked us to come and meet with them. I assumed that the Afghan hotel clerks had informed their friends and relatives that mullahs were in town. I sent Michael Albrecht downstairs to tell everyone that they had to meet with the Taliban at their office in an hour or so and not at the hotel. Michael reported back that most of those gathered seemed to have unresolved grievances back home. Michael and I dodged them and crossed the street to the train station in Frankfurt. We rented a van for the mullahs' use while they were in town.

People began showing up at their office before we arrived. The one question that was a constant all afternoon was the beard law. Many disputed the requirement of a beard by the Quran. It was interesting to hear the Taliban argue that because Mohammad had a beard, as did the other prophets before him, a beard was considered a sign of respect. They explained that they were still debating the point, but some scholars of Islam argue that a man should always have facial hair. It reminded me of the discussions of Jewish rabbis who split hairs over ancient points that modern people care little about.

They spent the day at the office. Afterwards an old friend of mine, Abdullah Mangal, drove the Taliban around town. Unfortunately, I forgot to ask Mangal later whether they looked at the scenery while in the van or continued to stare at their feet.

When they arrived back at the hotel, I asked them if they wanted to eat and they said they wouldn't unless the food was Kosher. We went outside and looked for a kosher restaurant.

Luckily, there was a Turkish restaurant nearby that served kosher meat. We bought them dinner and then returned to the hotel. During the meal, I was able to make an appointment the next day to discuss the oil deal which had gone sour. We agreed to meet at eight in the morning for breakfast in the lobby of the hotel.

After eating breakfast, I explained to the mullahs that Mullah Mohammad Esa was a very good man, very simple to deal with, but the employees under him in the department of oil and gas were creating problems. I explained that we were planning to bring a refinery that cost us about 50 million U.S. dollars to Afghanistan but that no insurance company in the world was ready to insure it.

"Yes," I admitted, "the price we are asking is high, but who else is going to come in and invest that kind of money. We can compromise a little, but not much."

They asked our price and I told them $7 per barrel for refining the crude oil. "Yes, I am asking for a lot of money, there's no doubt, but the investors are really worried about their investment. Once they earn their money back, I can give you a big discount, but for now they are really worried." Jalil and Razaq saw my point of view, but they asked for a $1 per barrel discount.

"There's no problem with $6 a barrel, but I can go no lower than that because nobody will invest with us because of the risks."

Esa wished to check with Mullah Omar first, but Jalil interrupted and said, "We don't have to worry about Mullah Omar. I will answer to him." After he said that, Esa agreed to the deal. I looked at Michael and said "Bingo" in English.

Not understanding what was being said or what I said, my German partner looked puzzled and asked, "What does that mean?" I grinned ear to ear and said, "I'll tell you later." Even without a translation of the spoken words, he was able to interpret the meaning of my ear-to-ear grin.

We drew up and signed a new preliminary contract. Michael and I were almost set to refine Afghan oil for the Taliban. Life is good!

The German authorities had issued the six members of the Taliban a three day visa, but they decided to stay a few days longer. Michael and I took their passports and their visa applications to the immigration office in Frankfurt. We were able to obtain a three day extension, but it cost us close to 300 Deutsche Marks for the extension. That evening, when the mullahs arrived back at the hotel, they were very happy for the extra time in Germany.

I told the mullahs that we now had to talk seriously about a few things that we had talked about before but which we had done nothing about. I explained that bin Laden and the drugs were problems.

"A couple of months ago, I discussed the issue of drugs with Mr. Mutawakel. The people of the United States are very much against drugs and they want it to end." I asked the mullahs to take a walk with me.

Jalil said, "With our turbans and our beards – the way we are dressed – we don't want to scare people off."

"That won't happen," I reassured him.

Jalil, Qadir and I went for a walk. Initially they were disturbed by all the nude pictures about the city. I suggested that they ignore them if they wanted to deal with Western society. That is the way it is. It's a fact of life. There was nothing they could do about it but get used to it.

"They have these advertisements all over the magazines and everywhere you look." I jokingly said, "Sex sells in Western countries."

They asked, "What do you want to show us."

"I am taking you to the train station. It is late and no one will be around." There in the tunnel between our hotel and the station were people lying on the hard concrete floor do drugs. One man was using a small mirror to examine his face. I guessed he was searching for a vein. Finally he injected himself somewhere around his eye. It was a horrifying sight, especially for the religious men with me. Jalil asked what was he doing.

I said, "Sir, this is what you produce for these people. This is heroin."

"I thought people smoked heroin."

"Yes, they do in Afghanistan. But it is so expensive here that they liquefy it and inject it into their bodies. According to studies, it is so dangerous that it will make you an addict the first time you use it." We went further into the tunnel and saw more people: some drunk, some high, and some injecting heroin. After a few minutes Jalil said, "Please, Mr. Mohabbat, let's go back." In the quiet cold of the German night, we walked back to the hotel, each wrapped in our own thoughts.

At seven we met for breakfast. I got the impression that Jalil and the others had spoken amongst themselves. I asked, "Mullah Jalil are you okay? You look sleepy."

"Yes, Mr. Mohabbat, I want to tell everybody that I could not sleep all night because of what I saw in the underground of Frankfurt. They were all human. And it doesn't really matter if they are Muslim or Christian or German. For the first time I saw – something – so horrible. He described to everyone present what we had witnessed in the tunnel. He then said to me, "Are the Americans prepared to help us eradicate this stuff?"

"Yes," I said. "Not only the Americans, but the Europeans. You could get even more help from Europe right here."

"When you come to Afghanistan to finish negotiating a formal contract and get it signed by the Council of Ministers, we will talk about this. Because it must be cleared by them, it could take some time."

I said, "That's not a problem. We have time." Little did I know what the future would hold.

Mr. Jalil suggested that I visit Kandahar. I wanted to visit the Taliban's center of power and I was sure that everyone in the U.S. Government would want me to go, too. Jalil explained that it was an honor to be invited to Kandahar.

"Would I be your guest," I asked. Razaq immediately said, "You'll be my guest."

Jalil said, "Thank God! Now I don't have to worry about anyone taking care of Mr. Mohabbat." Then Esa volunteered that I should be his guest, too. I wanted to see Kandahar. The last time I had seen it, I was a small child. It would be interesting. I wondered what changes their regime had made to the ancient city.

Jalil broke my reverie over the invitation by jumping back into the issue of drugs. He would talk to the Council to convince them to eradicate the poppies and then get a decree from Mullah Omar.

Michael agreed to call European Union people that he knew and broach the drug issue. He immediately called Rainer Wieland, the Stuttgart member of the E.U., and asked if he would be interested in talking to the Taliban. He agreed to meet with them and then he reminded us that he had already given us a short list of things he wanted changed by the current Afghan Government. They were: Osama bin Laden, drugs, and women's issues. The order didn't matter. Any of them would open the doors of the European Union.

Mullah Jalil asked me, "How do you think we can stop the drugs?"

"The best way is to go to the root of the problem. The problem is not the buyers or the sellers as much as the people growing the poppies – the farmers. The farmers always claim that this stuff pays a hundred times more than a regular crop. They get much more than they do from farming wheat, for example. If they make $100 in cultivating poppies, they might get $5 for growing wheat. Couldn't you help them by giving them another $5 for growing a legitimate crop." After all, farm subsidies work well in the U.S.

"We can try," the mullahs said. But they really were not sure how to approach the problem. From my experience in Afghanistan, more farmers growing food crops rather than poppies is a good thing.

While flying through Dallas I had picked up a newspaper with an article on drugs in Afghanistan. It showed that drugs brought about 300 million dollars to the Afghans, but when they hit the world market, the 300 million becomes an "80 billion dollar cash industry." I showed the article to those present and said, "If Mullah Omar will issue a decree, then every mullah in every village will rise up against the drug thugs and farmers." They looked at each other and agreed. "When I get to Kandahar, we will talk about it more," Jalil said.

"Would you be interested in meeting with a representative of the European Union?" I asked. The mullahs agreed to a meeting. Michael called the rep from Stuttgart back. We decided to meet the next afternoon for tea at the Arabella Sheraton Grand Hotel in Frankfurt.

Rainer Wieland, the European Union member from Stuttgart, had never met the Taliban. At first he was hesitant – but excited. He had brought a long list of ten or twelve issues that he wished to discuss with the representatives of the Afghan Government. Of course, his number one issue was the Cockroach.

The members of the Taliban looked at the list and said that since I had convinced them that the first item on the list was important, "Let's talk about Osama, first." The rep looked surprised by their response. "Is it true that the Taliban is willing to hand over Osama to a third country?"

The Taliban said yes, but they requested that it be one of the Islamic countries. Wieland said that it would be difficult to find one, but he would try. He mentioned the International Justice Court at The Hague.

"We can't turn him over to them unless you give us your word that he will receive a fair trial? Then you can either come get him or we can send him out of the country." The member of the E.U. wasn't expecting that generous of an offer.

"We would like to join the international community in prosecuting Osama if it is really in an international court of justice," the Afghan official said. "We will join you because we will want some of our fugitives to be returned someday. There are a lot of communists living in Europe and the United States that have committed genocide and are wanted by the people of Afghanistan. Just tell us when and where we can bring bin Laden to you. Or you can pick him up in Afghanistan."

The E.U. representative began to get nervous. Since this was such a big opportunity, he suggested that we meet with Elmar Brok, the Director of Foreign Relations for the European Union. "We will discuss this with Brok and then perhaps talk to the Justice Department of the E.U."

Wieland then asked the reps of the Afghan Government, "Is there any possibility that you could write a letter to the President of the European Union to explain the current situation in Afghanistan and explain that you want to join the world community." He promised to give the letter to the President of the European Parliament. The Taliban asked me if I could write a letter in English and they would sign it and stamp it with the official stamp of the Afghan Foreign Ministry. I wrote their letter and we sent it to the President of the European Union through the Stuttgart rep.

In the letter, the members of the Afghan Government asked for a meeting. They explained how devastated their country was from over twenty years of war, but that they, themselves, had not ordered any atrocities to be carried out. From their point of view, they had brought security and justice back to Afghanistan. The Taliban's two day shooting spree of the citizens of Mazar-e-Sharif could be counted in the atrocity column, as far as I was concerned, but I wasn't there to act as the Devil's Advocate.

The second issue discussed by the Taliban and the E.U. rep in their meeting was drugs. The Taliban said that they had no problem meeting with others on this issue, but first they needed to discuss it in the Council of Ministers. "But you can have our word that this will stop," they said. Members of the Afghan Government were scheduled to have a meeting with Thomas Pickering, the U.S. Deputy Secretary of State for Political Affairs, soon. They promised to discuss this with him, too.

The meeting between the member of the European Parliament and the Taliban lasted almost two hours. Both sides agreed to do everything possible to establish a "formal" meeting between the Taliban and the top leadership of the European Union. Because Western world governments stubbornly refused to recognize them as the official government of Afghanistan, I had my doubts that any such meeting would occur, but I was hopeful.

About a month later, we contacted the President of the European Union. She denied having received any letter from the Taliban, so we sent her another one. This one, too, was sent through the Stuttgart rep of the E.U. No one from the E.U. ever replied to either letter.

Eventually doubts about a more expansive role for Afghanistan in the modern world crept into the minds of the Taliban. Sometime later one of them said to me over the telephone, "We offered them this man and there is no response."

"That's okay. It's not a problem. I'll think of something," I reassured him. But I, too, was beginning to doubt whether the nation states were ready to help the unworldly Taliban tackle the seemingly insurmountable international problems they faced.

I believed my trip of June 2000, to meet the Taliban in Frankfurt, Germany a roaring success. When I arrived back in Texas, my partners and I rhapsodized about our plans for a refinery in oil rich Afghanistan. At a partnership meeting in Texas, we decided that I should go to Kandahar for the signing of the official ten page contract and then to the ceremony in Kabul which would be the official acknowledgment of the contract by the Afghan Government. While in Kabul, I would get our Swiss company registered. But a visit to Kandahar was also important because it was now the Afghan power base rather than Kabul.

I arrived back in Islamabad on the 6th of September 2000. A couple of days later I made my way to Kandahar. There I was to meet with the members of the Council of Ministers which must approve *every* act taken in the country. Once approved by the Council, then Mullah Omar would sign our contract. I expected a *greased* process. What actually reared its ugly head was a totally different creature.

In Kandahar, I met with Jalil, Akhtar Mohammad Osmani (Mullah Omar's deputy and the commander of the Kandahar Corps) and Mullah Mohammad Hassa Akhund (the Governor of Kandahar and a member of the Council). I had heard of Akhund before. He had lost one of his legs during the 1980's to a Soviet land mind and had a peg leg.) I also met many others, but I have forgotten their names and ranks.

I spent a few laid back days networking, then I left for the capital, Kabul, to have our company officially registered and to sign the oil and gas contract which was waiting for me there and which I thought was a done deal. In Kabul, my partners, Michael, Aziz and Nick were waiting for me. I didn't know that we still didn't have an agreed upon contract. My done deal was in the process of dissolving while I lazed about in Kandahar.

At the time I didn't know that it was a customary part of the Afghan process that approval for government contracts must first go through a commission. The commission then made recommendations to the Council of Ministers who determined what would be sent to Mullah Omar for signing. His signature was the final act in a long list of acts that made a contract binding on the Afghan Government.

They appointed a man, whose name I have forgotten, to head the commission that reviewed our contract. If I remember correctly, he was a member of the Northern Alliance who had been in the Afghan Government for a long time. He started off being very difficult. Every sentence of the preliminary contract, which had already been signed by the Taliban in Frankfurt, was questioned.

Eventually we left Afghanistan without a final contract. The experience convinced me that we had opposition in the Council of Ministers. Someone could have been opposed to dealing with Westerners, so I complained to Jalil by radio telephone. Back in Kandahar, Jalil obtained a special decree signed by Mullah Omar that overrode the commission and the Council of Ministers. By August 10, 2000, Esa and I signed an Agreement. Life is good!

Even though I was happy that everything turned out okay, I wondered how Omar could override the Council, if it was true, as I was led to believe, that he was the weakest member of that body. But I left working that fine point out for another day. Now the only obstacle remaining between me and doing business in Afghanistan was the Cockroach.

Before leaving the region, I visited the American Embassy in Islamabad. There I met with Paula Thiede, the contact between me and Ron, the CIA's Station Chief. I told her of the meetings with the mullahs in Kandahar. Laughing she said, "I knew you would work your way in." She requested that I meet with "my friends with the Agency."

I thought, "Yeah, right, friends." But I agreed to go. She took me upstairs to an office the size of a large broom closet. Ron appeared out of thin air. I told him about who I met in Afghanistan and he said, "Is there any way possible to meet with the Taliban leadership?"

"Definitely, it is possible." I complained that it had been almost a year since the resignation of Mrs. Oakley, when I first reported the invitation for us to act against bin Laden. He seemed happy to see positive moves being made by the

Taliban while I was happy to finally see positive moves being made by the U.S. Government.

On September 20, 2000, I left for Frankfurt. Michael Albrecht and I met with the E.U. rep from Stuttgart again. He asked me to meet with Elmar Brok, the Chairman of Foreign Relations for the European Union. The meeting would be held in secret. I agreed.

We met at B1 Street in Deutshmond, Germany. Mr. Brok and the E.U. rep wanted reconfirmation after my visit to Kandahar that the Afghan Government was willing to address their concerns. He asked if I would be willing to talk to the drug enforcement agency of Germany.

I said that it would be better for me to discuss this with the U.S. Drug Enforcement Agency. I didn't want to appear to be doing anything without the knowledge of the U.S. Government. Brok agreed and said he would contact the U.S. Ambassador to Germany, a Mr. Bloomberg. He requested that I stay for an extra day to see if he could get a response from him.

On September 25, I received a call from Mr. Brok. He had spoken to the American Ambassador. He was willing to inform the people in the State Department about the Afghan Government's willingness to turn over bin Laden. I hoped the American Ambassador would light a fire under the sluggish asses back home. After all, the hills of Afghanistan were alive with oil and I wanted to start refining it yesterday.

[The documents in this and subsequent chapters given to me by Kabir are proof of his interactions with the Afghan Government. Not all of the documents are complete, but they are as I received them. At the time Kabir gave them to me, we had no way of knowing that he would pass away and they would become the proof of his interactions with Afghanistan's Taliban. L.M.]

VON : PETROLAB SPEYER AN : 29813056 1900.02-18 21:01 #089 P.01/0

Laboratorium für
Mineralöl- und Umweltanalytik

PETRO LAB
GMBH

PETRO LAB GMBH · Brunckstraße 12 · 67346 Speyer

Von DASMIN-Deutsche Akkreditierungsstelle Mineralöl GmbH nach DIN EN 45001 akkreditiertes Prüflaboratorium. Die Akkreditierung gilt für die in der Urkunde aufgeführten Prüfverfahren.

MIN-P-07/93 (Kraftstoffe)
MIN-P-01/97 (Schmierstoffe)

Telefax to
Mr. Michael Albrecht
c/o company AMP GmbH
Talstr. 41

70188 Stuttgart

Telefax 0711/9979456

Speyer, 18th Februar 2000/ne
page 1 of 3

c/c Mister Nick ANTON
c/o Arabella Sheraton Hotel
room 660

Telefax 069/29813056
or 069/2981810 (for room 660) **EILT!!!! bitte gleich weiterleiten!!!!!!!**

certificate of analysis

Attention:	Mr. Michael Albrecht, AMP GmbH
Your Order	from 5th February 2000
Sample of:	Crude Oil
Sample Description:	„von AMP GmbH, Talstr. 41, 70188 Stuttgart ex Afghanistan"
Subject:	Minor Crude Assay, only for pre-interpretation of an atmospheric column
Sample Quantity:	ca. 250 ml in Glasbottle
PL.-Number:	38.635
sample receipt:	7th February 2000

The sample we received was analysed and we found the following results.

Bankverbindungen: Dresdner Bank Speyer, BLZ 670 800 50, Kto. 193 600 100 · Postscheckkonto Ludwigshafen: BLZ 545 100 67, Kto. 2 158 18-679

Geschäftsführer: Dieter Mehlis, Sitz der Gesellschaft: Speyer, eingetragen beim Amtsgericht Ludwigshafen unter HRB Nr. 1913 SP

67346 Speyer
Brunckstraße 12
Tel. 06232/330 11 0
Fax 06232/330 15

Niederlassung:
40231 Düsseldorf-Lierenfeld
Lierenfelder Straße 29
Tel. 0211/73 36 67

Niederlassung:
81477 München, vorm. PHL Dr. Mausch
Vorholzerstraße 3
Tel. 089/75 89 77

Niederlassung:
01571 Riesa (Sachsen)
Postfach 32
Tel. 035 25/76 10 56

PETROLAB Netherlands B.V.
NL-3161 VB-Rhoon
Binnenbaan 33
Tel. 0031/10-501-6464
Fax 0031/10 50 -2243

Analytical Results

Appearance black, medium viscosity

Odor odor for hydrogendisulfide

Remark
Because we only have a low quantity of sample it was impossible to analyse a normal crude assay. The keypoints can only give a wide view of the crude oil product quality.

Quality criteria	Method	Dimension	Results
Density 15/4 °C	*EN ISO 12185*	kg/m³	915
Sulfur Content	*EN ISO 14596*	m/m%	2,6 (2,58)
Water content	*ASTM D 1744*	m/m%	4,1
Vanadium as V	*ash, AAS/ICP*	mg/kg	5
Nickel as Ni	*ash, AAS/ICP*	mg/kg	lower than 5

Distillation *ex SIM DIST DIN 51 435*

		FBP °C AET	Fraction m/m%	cummulated m/m%
naphtha	to n-C9	150	8,8	
naphtha	n-C9 to n-C10	175	3,5	12,3
kerosene	n-C10 to n-C13	235	11,5	23.8
kerosene	n-C13 to n-C15	270	9,1	32,9
light gasoil	n-C15 to n-C19	330	16,9	49,8
heavy gasoil	n-C19 to n-C22	370	11,5	61,3
light VGO	n-C22 to n-C30	450	23,3	84,6
heavy VGO	n-C30 to n-C41	530	14,8	99,4

Attention! The results are related only to the evaporated part of the sample.

Distillation *modified to ASTM D 86*

	°C AET
IBP	45
5 v/v%	182
10 v/v%	245
20 v/v%	290
30 v/v%	326
40 v/v%	345
44 v/v%	350*) product starts to crack

Residue 350 °C 56 v/v%

Ne

VON : PETROLAB SPEYER FN : 00692981305б 1900-02-18 21:02 #089 P.03/0

page 3 of 3 to certificate of analysis, AMP GmbH, PL.-Nr. 38.635 from 18th february 2000

Yields (approximatly)

	FBP °C AET	Fraction m/m%	cummulated m/m%
naphtha	to 150	7,0	7,0
naphtha	to 175	2,8	9,8
kerosene	to 235	9,1	18,9
kerosene	to 270	7,2	26,1
light gasoil	to 330	13,4	39,5
heavy gasoil	to 370	9,1	48,6
atmospheric residue	370	51,4	
light VGO	to 450	18,4	67,0
heavy VGO	to 530	11,8	78,8
vacuum residue	530+	21,2	21,2

Conclusions

- high density, high sulfur crude oil (we estimated sulfur content near 5 % in the vacuum residue)
- very low metal content
- We think that distillation in an atmospheric column is possible.
- Problems with the high sulfur content are possible.
- For a crude oil analysis for basic construction informations we need 5 liter product for minimum.

Do not hesitate to contact us in case of any questions.

Best regards

PETROLAB GmbH
Laboratorium für Mineralöl- und Umweltanalytik

D. Mehlis i.V. Dipl.-Chem. [signature]

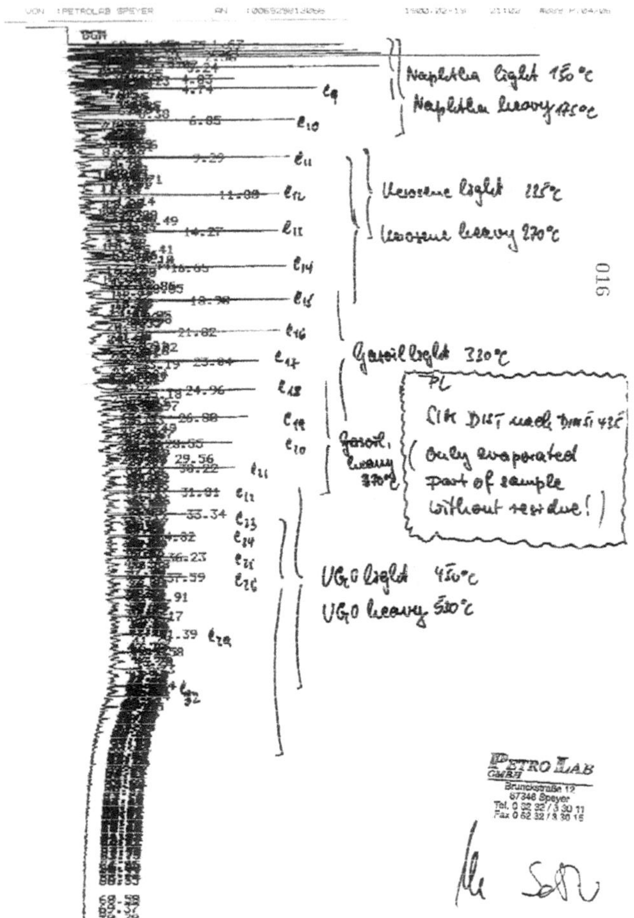
Naphtha light 150 °C
Naphtha heavy 175 °C
Kerosene light 225 °C
Kerosene heavy 270 °C
Gasoil light 320 °C
Gasoil, heavy 370 °C
(Only evaporated part of sample without residue!)
VGO light 450 °C
VGO heavy 530 °C
PETRO LAB GmbH
Brunckstraße 12
67346 Speyer
Tel. 0 62 32 / 3 30 11
Fax 0 62 32 / 3 30 15

Computerunterstützte Auswertung von simulierten Destillationen
Programm der Firma Petrolab Speyer

Simulierte Destillation nach DIN 51 435

AMP, Rohöl PL Nr.: k. A.

Siedeübergang bis	36 Grad C	(entspr. n-C 5)	0.33 Gew. %
Siedeübergang bis	69 Grad C	(entspr. n-C 6)	1.38 Gew. %
Siedeübergang bis	98 Grad C	(entspr. n-C 7)	3.90 Gew. %
Siedeübergang bis	126 Grad C	(entspr. n-C 8)	5.89 Gew. %
Siedeübergang bis	151 Grad C	(entspr. n-C 9)	8.76 Gew. %
Siedeübergang bis	174 Grad C	(entspr. n-C 10)	12.29 Gew. %
Siedeübergang bis	196 Grad C	(entspr. n-C 11)	15.86 Gew. %
Siedeübergang bis	216 Grad C	(entspr. n-C 12)	19.49 Gew. %
Siedeübergang bis	235 Grad C	(entspr. n-C 13)	23.76 Gew. %
Siedeübergang bis	254 Grad C	(entspr. n-C 14)	28.32 Gew. %
Siedeübergang bis	271 Grad C	(entspr. n-C 15)	32.92 Gew. %
Siedeübergang bis	287 Grad C	(entspr. n-C 16)	37.27 Gew. %
Siedeübergang bis	302 Grad C	(entspr. n-C 17)	41.27 Gew. %
Siedeübergang bis	317 Grad C	(entspr. n-C 18)	45.40 Gew. %
Siedeübergang bis	331 Grad C	(entspr. n-C 19)	49.81 Gew. %
Siedeübergang bis	344 Grad C	(entspr. n-C 20)	54.48 Gew. %
Siedeübergang bis	356 Grad C	(entspr. n-C 21)	57.74 Gew. %
Siedeübergang bis	369 Grad C	(entspr. n-C 22)	61.32 Gew. %
Siedeübergang bis	380 Grad C	(entspr. n-C 23)	64.71 Gew. %
Siedeübergang bis	391 Grad C	(entspr. n-C 24)	67.96 Gew. %
Siedeübergang bis	402 Grad C	(entspr. n-C 25)	70.96 Gew. %
Siedeübergang bis	412 Grad C	(entspr. n-C 26)	74.12 Gew. %
Siedeübergang bis	422 Grad C	(entspr. n-C 27)	76.86 Gew. %
Siedeübergang bis	432 Grad C	(entspr. n-C 28)	79.34 Gew. %
Siedeübergang bis	441 Grad C	(entspr. n-C 29)	82.33 Gew. %
Siedeübergang bis	450 Grad C	(entspr. n-C 30)	84.63 Gew. %
Siedeübergang bis	459 Grad C	(entspr. n-C 31)	87.03 Gew. %
Siedeübergang bis	468 Grad C	(entspr. n-C 32)	88.61 Gew. %
Siedeübergang bis	483 Grad C	(entspr. n-C 34)	92.97 Gew. %
Siedeübergang bis	499 Grad C	(entspr. n-C 36)	95.58 Gew. %
Siedeübergang bis	513 Grad C	(entspr. n-C 38)	97.56 Gew. %
Siedeübergang bis	527 Grad C	(entspr. n-C 40)	99.06 Gew. %
Siedeübergang bis	533 Grad C	(entspr. n-C 41)	99.44 Gew. %
Siedeübergang bis	540 Grad C	(entspr. n-C 42)	99.67 Gew. %
Siedeübergang bis	546 Grad C	(entspr. n-C 43)	99.83 Gew. %

Interpolierter Siedeverlauf

Siedebeginn	41 Grad C
5%	113 Grad C
10%	159 Grad C
20%	212 Grad C
30%	260 Grad C
40%	297 Grad C
50%	332 Grad C
60%	364 Grad C
70%	398 Grad C
80%	434 Grad C
90%	473 Grad C
95%	495 Grad C
Siedeende	535 Grad C

111 P03 APR 04 '00 15:18

APPROXIMATE ESTIMATED COST

Purchase Price	$1,000,000	to	$2,000,000
Dismantle, Crate, Prepare For Shipping	$1,500,000	to	$2,500,000
Shipping	$1,000,000	to	$2,000,000
Reconstruct, Prepare For Start-Up	$6,500,000	to	$8,500,000
Total Estimated Cost	$10,000,000	to	$15,000,000

ALTERNATIVE

If it could be established that condensate from natural gas was available in the area, then the crude oil could be blended with condensate (assuming 0.5% sulfur or less) bringing the sulfur content of the blended feedstock below 1.5%. Therefore, more options would probably be available on the selection of a facility, possibly with some cost savings

FURTHER RECOMMENDATIONS

Should it be determined to go forward with this project, we would bring in an engineering construction company (which we know and have a very close association) to help identify the best plant for the project, dismantle, ship and reconstruct the plant in Afghanistan.

111 P04 APR 04 '00 15:18

APPROXIMATE ANTICIPATED PRODUCTS BASED ON ASSAY SAMPLE RECEIVED: (20,000 BBLS Per Day)

PRODUCT	PERCENTAGE	BBLS PER DAY
Unleaded Gasoline	10	2000
Diesel Fuel	23	4600
Kerosene	22	4400
VGO (Cat Feed)	24	4800
Residual Fuel (Bunker Fuel)	21	4200

These product percentages could vary considerably depending upon the processing equipment available with the plant. Also, they may be adjusted to fit a particular product slate with a carefully planned blending program. (A new assay on the crude oil is needed on at least a five gallon sample.)

PROFORMA CASH FLOWS BASED ON $7.00 Per BBL PROCESSING FEE, 20,000 BBL Per Day, and $1.50 Per BBL OPERATING COST

Monthly Revenues	**Refinery Operating Cost**	**Net Monthly Revenue**
$4,200,000	$900,000	$3,300,000

Based on these assumptions, the project would pay out in approximately five months.

111 P05 APR 04 '00 15:19

AVAILABILITY

We have located four plants in four different countries that would possibly meet the criteria pointed out in the above discussions, however, they would all have to be examined thoroughly.

PHONE NO. : 00 92 91 287 655 Apr. 09 2000 11:29AM P01

د افغانستان إسلامي امارت
د کانو او صنا یعو وزارت

Islamic Emirate of Afghanistan
Ministry of Mines & Industries

نمبر______ تاریخ______

From: Alhaj Mula Mohammad Esa Akhund
Minister of Mines & Industries of the
Islamic Emirate of Afghanistan

Mr. M. Kabir Mohabbat
Fax No: 001-281-564-2254

I thank you very much for faxing me a signed copy of the memorandum of understanding that was faxed to you earlier which sure is an encouraging indication of your kind desire to Co-operate with us in the construction of an oil refinery in Afghanistan. I shall very much appreciate your efforts to expedite relevant activities to conclude a mutually acceptable and beneficial agreement.

Form our side, I assure you of our sincere Co-operations,

Sincerely yours,

Alhaj Mula M.Esa
Minister of Mines and Industries.

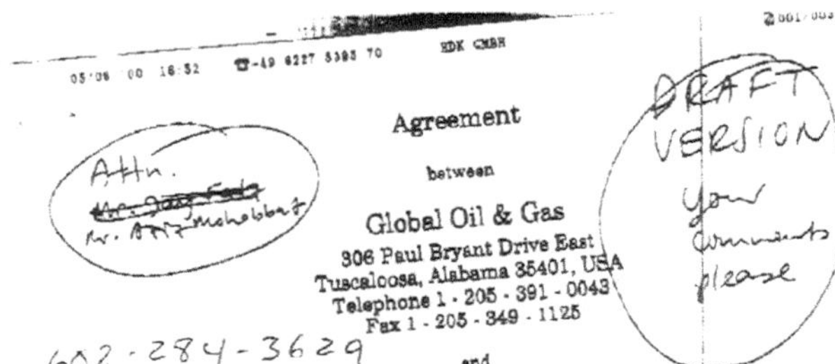

Agreement

between

Global Oil & Gas

306 Paul Bryant Drive East
Tuscaloosa, Alabama 35401, USA
Telephone 1 - 205 - 391 - 0043
Fax 1 - 205 - 349 - 1125

and

HD/K GmbH

HD Kapital Vermittlungs GmbH
Josef-Reiert-Straße 4
D-69190 Walldorf/Baden, Germany
Telephone 49 - 6227 - 83 95 0
Fax 49 - 6227 - 83 95 70

on

Joint Venture

for Exploration, Production, Processing and Marketing
of Crude Oil and Natural Gas projects
in Alabama and other areas

§ 1

Structure of the Company and Division of the Shares of the Company

Global Oil & Gas and HD/K GmbH agree on a joint venture for exploration, production, processing and marketing of crude oil and natural gas projects in Alabama and other areas, with the structure of the company and the division of the shares of the company being defined as follows :

1. The crude oil and natural gas projects are all executed in the framework of the company Global Oil & Gas which acts as the operator of the projects.

2. Because the operator of the projects needs to hold the majority of the company, Global Oil & Gas keeps 51 % of the shares of the company. HD/K GmbH receives 49 % of the shares of the company Global Oil & Gas, and participates with scientific, technical, marketing and economical consulting in the company Global Oil & Gas. In the framework of the joint venture, Global Oil & Gas and HD/K GmbH will cooperate in mutual trust and for mutual benefit with the understanding of a long-term profitable business strategy.

3. The board of the company Global Oil & Gas includes representatives of both Global Oil & Gas and HD/K GmbH, in a relationship that Global Oil & Gas keeps the majority of the seats. The board representatives from the side of Global Oil & Gas are Dr. M. Omar Mohabbat, Mr. Aziz O. Mohabbat and Mr. Jay Klaus Falz, and the board representatives from the side of HD/K GmbH are Mr. Hartmut Thome and Dr. Detlef Mader.

1

05/06 00 18:53 ☎-49 6227 8398 70 HDK GMBH

4. All principal decisions on the operation of the projects of the joint venture will be taken based on mutual agreement between Global Oil & Gas and HD/K GmbH. Mutual agreements of the general business goals and the principal project organization will be concluded during regular or ad-hoc board meetings where generally 100 % consensus should be achieved. The daily executive duties of the projects will be handled by Global Oil & Gas in the sense of the baselines as approved in the board meetings. For task force decisions, agreements and confirmations could also be made between individual board members from the sides of both Global Oil & Gas and HD/K GmbH, in case the other board members support these agreements and confirmations. In all contracts between the joint venture and third parties, which have to be set up exclusively in English language, Global Oil & Gas represents the joint venture, subject that the wording of the text of the contracts has been approved by the board in 100 % consensus.

5. Global Oil & Gas holds 51 % of the shares of the company and HD/K GmbH holds 49 % of the shares of the company, as agreed in § 1 Art. 2, at least until the moment of going public of the company. Any sale of parts of these existing old shares by either party and/or any issue of additional new shares in connection with going public or in case of step-in of an investor into the board requires 100 % consensus of the board members in a special board meeting. Any sale of parts of the existing old shares by either party and/or any issue of additional new shares in case of step-in of an investor into the board requires signature of an additional agreement between Global Oil & Gas, HD/K GmbH and the investor.

6. In case of promising business possibilities, the strategy of Global Oil & Gas does not have to be limited to crude oil and natural gas projects, but could also be extended to other types of projects, for example metal projects. Any decision in this direction has to be approved by the board in 100 % consensus.

§ 2

Acquisition of Investors for Financing the Projects and Division of Net Revenues of the Projects

Global Oil & Gas and HD/K GmbH will acquire potential investors for financing the crude oil and natural gas projects and will divide the net revenues of the projects as follows:

1. Irrespective of the model of financing the projects which a potential investor will choose, it is maintained that Global Oil & Gas holds 51 % of the shares of the company and HD/K GmbH holds 49 % of the shares of the company throughout the lifetime of the projects, as agreed in § 1 Art. 2, unless an additional agreement following § 1 Art. 5 is coming in force after signature.

2. The division of the net revenues of the crude oil and natural gas projects will be determined by the model of financing the projects which a potential investor will choose. Depending on the model of financing the projects, the division of the net revenues of the projects could differ from the division of the shares of the company. The net revenues are the remaining part of the gross return of the projects after deduction of taxes, royalties, operating cost, and compensation of claims of third parties.

3. In the case of a bridge loan model, the investor will receive 50 % of all net revenues of the crude oil and natural gas projects from the moment of investment until the achievement of payout of the investment plus a reasonable profit, which has to be negotiated with the investor. From the moment of investment until the achievement of payout of the investment plus the profit as agreed with the investor, Global Oil & Gas and HD/K GmbH will receive 25 % each of the remaining 50 % of the net revenues. Once the investor has received his payout plus the negotiated profit and has left the projects, Global Oil & Gas will receive 51 % and HD/K GmbH will receive 49 % of all net revenues of the crude oil and natural gas projects until the end of the lifetime of the projects.

4. In the case of a shared revenue model, the investor will receive 30 % of all net revenues of the projects which he will finance with his investment from the moment of investment until the end of the lifetime of the projects. Global Oil & Gas will receive 35 % and HD/K GmbH will receive 35 % of all net

2

revenues of the projects from the moment of investment until the end of the lifetime of the project.

5. The division of the shares of the company Global Oil & Gas as agreed in § 1 Art. 2 and the division of the net revenues of the projects as agreed in § 2 Art. 3 and 4 will be maintained irrespective whether Global Oil & Gas or HD/K GmbH mediates, contributes or acquires the investor of the projects, and will be in force for all projects which will be executed by the joint venture after 100 % consensus decision in the board meetings

Date of Signature of Agreement :

Place of Signature of Agreement :

For Global Oil & Gas

(Mr. Aziz Q. Mohabbat)

(Mr. Jay Klaus Falz)

For HD/K GmbH

(Mr. Hartmut Thome)

(Dr. Detlef Mader)

JUN-01-00 THU 07:23 AM

15.08.00 17:22 49 6227 6095 70 KDE GMNH

Dr. Detlef Mader

International Consultant for Petroleum Geology and Engineering

Hebelstraße 12, D-69190 Walldorf/Baden, Germany, Telephone 49 - 6227 - 1252

Project : Afghanistan Oil Refinery

Evaluation of the project submitted in the meeting
in Tuscaloosa/Alabama, USA, on May 12th, 2000

Introduction

The project of the Afghanistan Oil Refinery has been submitted in the personal meeting on May 12th, 2000 with

- Dr. M. Omar Mohabbat (C.E.O. and founder Global Oil & Gas)
- Mr. Aziz O. Mohabbat (President Global Oil & Gas)
- Mr. Jay Klaus Falz (C.F.O./Marketing Manager Global Oil & Gas)

In this meeting, base information on the above project has been provided by showing a video and various photographs which had been taken in October 1999 when Mr. Aziz O. Mohabbat and Mr. Jay Klaus Falz had visited Afghanistan. In addition, a brochure of various documents (including a feasibility study of the refinery and an analysis of a sample of the crude oil) has been handed out, and oral reports and explanations have also been given. An invitation has also been issued to visit Afghanistan personally with the accompany of Mr. Aziz O. Mohabbat and the assistance of Mr. M. Kabir Mohabbat (brother of Dr. M. Omar Mohabbat) in Kabul.

Summary of base information

Proposal has been made to install an oil refinery in Afghanistan to process sulfur-containing crude oil (gravity abt. 0.9) on-site instead of importing refined oil from abroad. The installation would cost abt. 15 million US $ in the first step with a refining capacity of abt. 20,000 bbl/day of crude oil. The estimated oil reserves in the northern part of Afghanistan are abt. 20 million metric tons. It is planned to make further exploration in the western part of Afghanistan. The refinery should produce unleaded gasoline, diesel fuel, kerosene, asphalt and residual fuel. At the moment, there is no refinery for crude oil in Afghanistan.

The crude oil of Afghanistan has been analyzed by PetroLab GmbH in Speyer, Germany, based on a sample of abt. 250 ml. It is a high-density, high-sulfur crude oil (sulfur content abt. 2.6 %, water content abt. 4.1 %) with very low metal content. From the analysis, conclusion has been made that distillation in an atmospheric column is possible. A sample of at least 5 litres of crude oil should be submitted for a thorough analysis for basic construction information.

A feasibility study of the Afghanistan refinery project has been carried out by Cana Resources Inc. in Houston/Texas, USA. Proposal has been made that an existing refinery (not presently in use) could be purchased, dismantled, shipped to Afghanistan and reconstructed more economically than trying to design, engineer, and construct a new facility. Based on a capacity of 20,000 bbl/day, the refinery could produce daily also 2,000 bbl of [illegible] abt. 4,000 bbl of diesel fuel abt. 4,200 bbl of kerosene etc. Based on a processing fee of 7.0 US $/bbl and an operating cost of 1.0 US $/bbl, the projected cash flow of a refinery with a capacity of 20,000 bbl/day would include: monthly revenues 4.2 million US $; monthly refinery operating cost 0.9 million US $; net monthly revenue 3.3 million US $. Based on these assumptions, the project would pay out in abt. five months.

JUN-01-00 THU 07:24 AM P.02

18.05 '00 17:20 ☎ 49 6227 4345 70 HDW GMBH ☎004

Conclusions

According to the assessment of the presented information, prior to a personal visit of Afghanistan, I recommend to accept the proposal and to invest 15 million US $ for the installation of an oil refinery in Afghanistan for the following reasons:

1. The proposed project is sound from geological, reservoir engineering and economical points of view. Afghanistan has extensive oil reserves which are largely unproduced so far. The extensive oil reserves have certainly been one of the major targets of the Russian invasion into Afghanistan, as being confirmed by the drilling of various wells with Russian rigs. The video shows abandoned Russian rigs after the retreat of the Russian army, and various shut-in wells as the sulfureous oil cannot be used without being refined. Because of very limited production so far, the oil reservoirs are considered as being largely undepleted and can await long production history. As many wells are already installed and are only shut-in temporarily, production would be very cheap, with in many cases only opening of the wells, cleaning of the strings and installation of pipelines to the refinery being necessary.

2. At the moment, Afghanistan wastes an awful lot of hard-currency money for the import of refined oil, which makes no sense in view of the large reserves in the ground which cannot be processed, and the need for enormous amounts of money to rebuilt the infrastructure in the country after the damage during both the Russian war and the civil war. The current expences of Afghanistan for the purchase of refined oil abroad are 50,000 US $ per day or 1.5 million US $ per month. Considering only these expenses, the investment of 15 million US $ for the installation of an oil refinery in Afghanistan would already make sense after an operation of only 10 months.

3. Afghanistan is a destroyed country at the moment after the end of more than 20 years of war. In contrast to the desastrous economical conditions at the moment, the country is extremely rich in oil and mineral deposits. Oil exploration has so far only covered the northern part of Afghanistan, and in the future, considerable potential is waiting for exploration and consequently production in the western part of Afghanistan. Therefore it would be the best chance for external investors to come in now in the stage of start-up of the economical reconstruction of the country.

4. A fast and confident investment in Afghanistan at the moment would secure enormous business possibilities in the future. One of the most challenging other options would be the participation in the development and operation of a copper mine. According to the outcrops at the surface as being seen in the video and the photographs, the potential should be enormous. Confirmation will soon be made during a personal inspection in the field.

5. The Ministry of Mines & Industries of Afghanistan has expressed in writing to Mr. M. Kabir Mohabbat the sincere cooperation of the authorities in Afghanistan in the project. Dr. M. Omar Mohabbat has formerly been Minister of Education in Afghanistan before having been thrown into prison during the Russian occupation. He has now received an offer to act as Prime Minister in the new government of Afghanistan. The Mohabbat family belongs to the largest tribe in Afghanistan and has excellent connections to all the key decision-makers. Mr. M. Kabir Mohabbat is very often in Kabul and would be a perfect contact person on-site. This scenario allows close cooperation with permanent assistance both inside and outside Afghanistan with a very good control of the risk of investment.

Recommendation

I therefore strongly recommend to invest the applied 15 million US $ for the installation of an oil refinery in Afghanistan as soon as possible.

Walldorf/Baden, Germany, May 16th, 2000

(Dr. Detlef Mader)

JUN-01-00 THU 07:54 AM P. 02
25 05 00 17:42 ☎+49 6227 8395 70 HDK GMBH 002

Dr. Detlef Mader / Dr. Martin Oczlon
c/o HD/K GmbH, Josef-Reiert-Straße 4, D-69190 Walldorf/Baden, Germany
Telephone 49 - 6227 - 83 950, Fax 49 - 6227 - 83 95 70

Preliminary Evaluation of Copper and Chromite Deposits near Kabul in Afghanistan

In October 1999, Aziz Mohabbat, Kabir Mohabbat, Jay Falz, Steven Schultz, Michael Albrecht and Nick Anton visited Afghanistan for one week and had the possibility to look on some ore deposits. Based on a video, various photographs and four small rock samples which were taken on this trip, as well as on personal reports of Aziz Mohabbat and Jay Falz, the following preliminary evaluation was established.

Location of Ore Deposits

The copper and chromite deposits are located at two different sides of the same valley in abt. 20 - 50 km distance from Kabul. There is no paved road leading to the outcrops of the copper and chromite ores. The sand and gravel road can be passed by field cars and probably also by a truck with drilling equipment. A one-way trip from Kabul to the outcrops of the copper and chromite ores takes abt. 2 hours. For any regular truck service to the copper and chromite deposits, a paved road would have to be built. No mining has been done at any scale on the copper and chromite deposits up to now. Under the Russian occupation, it is possible that geological fieldwork and even drilling has been carried out on the copper and chromite deposits, but there are no documents on this research left in Kabul.

Type of Ore Deposits

The rock samples as well as the recorded outcrops on the video and the photographs suggest mafic and/or ultramafic host rocks of the copper and chromite ore deposits. The geological map shows also ultramafic rock bodies in the vicinity of Kabul.

The weathered sample of the surficial leaching zone of the copper ore deposits is composed of argillized ultramafic (?) rock with hematite and limonite on fractures which could be weathering products of sulfidic copper ores. Much of the host rock has been transformed into clay minerals near the surface. It could be expected that the top of the sulfidic copper ore body below the surficial leaching zone is located in a depth of at least 20 m. Abundant vesicles and cavities in the surficial rocks reflect intense weathering and dissolution. The absence of sedimentary structures in the surficial rocks supports the interpretation of an ultramafic host rock, because in the case of black shales, at least some bedding planes should still be visible. Green and blue oxidic copper minerals are present in various spots on the rocks. In addition to or instead of weathering and dissolution, also hydrothermal processes could have contributed to the transformation and overprinting of the original rocks in the surficial zone.

The relatively fresh sample of the chromite deposits contains in addition to chromite crystals also either magnetite grains or at least significant diadochous replacement of chromium ions by iron ions in the crystal lattice of the chromite as being reflected by its reaction to a magnet. Some light components in the sample are probably feldspar and olivine. The most probable genesis of such chromite deposits is primary segregation as pockets and lenses in an ultramafic host rock

UN-01-00 THU 07:54 AM
28-05 '00 17:15 ☎+49 6227 5383 70 MDK GMBH

Procedure for Further Evaluation

The video and the photographs show a rather limited extension of the outcrops of the copper and chromite ore bodies. The outcropping rocks are located on the opposite sides of a valley near the boundary to the valley floor. Based on the recorded distribution of the outcrops, the following further evaluation is proposed :

1. Preliminary geological mapping by local field geologists. The mapping should be performed in the area of abt. 1 km2 around the outcrops of the ore deposits and should include :
- mapping of all occurrences of blue, green, red, orange and yellow colours in the outcropping rocks
- mapping of the distribution of outcropping rocks vs. the sand and gravel cover (where no bedrocks are visible)
- sampling of blue and green colours in the outcropping rocks (abt. 20 - 50 samples in the size of abt. 1 - 2 cm taken at various places)
- aerial colour photographs of the extension of the outcrops of the ore deposits from helicopter or small airplane

2. Geological evaluation (including reconnaissance and special mapping) of the extension of the surface outcrops of the ore bodies by one professional western field geologist who would be accompanied by one or two assistants for measuring, sampling etc. Geological special mapping should be performed in the scale of 1 : 2,000 or 1 : 5,000 in the area of abt. 1 km2 for each ore body. The necessary time would be abt. 3 weeks, and the cost would be abt. 10,000 - 15,000 US $ plus expenses.

3. Geophysical survey of the extension and depth of the ore bodies in the area of abt. 1 km2 per ore body by abt. 5 persons with equipment. Again abt. 2 weeks time and abt. 20,000 - 30,000 US $ plus expenses would be required. Surveys of electromagnetics or induced potential are recommended.

4. Depending on extension and depth of the ore bodies, decision has to be made whether to start drilling. In order to evaluate the depth potential of the ore deposits, some selected boreholes should be drilled to at least 100 m depth. For economical exploitation, the thickness of the ore body should exceed abt. 20 m depending on strike and dip extension of the ore body as well as on average grade of the ore body.

Statement on Economical Feasibility

Without drilling of at least some selected boreholes to at least 100 m depth, decision on the economical feasibility of the ore deposits and on the start of their exploitation by establishment of the necessary industrial facilities would not be possible. Earlier estimations or calculations of reserves during the Russian occupation of the country would have to be verified by an actual evaluation according to modern western standard.

Walldorf, May 24th, 2000

(Dr. Detlef Mader) (Dr. Martin Oczlon)

شماره : 01

مؤرخ: 06.04.00

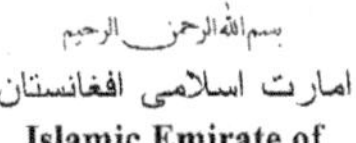

Islamic Emirate of Afghanistan

From: Islamic Emirate of Afghanistan
Ministry of Foreign Affairs, Kabul
Deputy Minister Mullah Abdul Jalil Akhund

To: European parliament
Rue Wierbe 10E216
B-1047 Brussels
Belgium or

Palais De L, Europe
F-67000 Strasbourg
France

Dear Representative of the European Union:

As you may well know, Afghanistan was the battleground of two super powers for many years. Until, with the help of the people of Afghanistan, our movement succeeded to rescue Afghanistan form anarchism, trespassing on women chastity, looting and a destructive civil war. After the succession of our movement to bring stability and peace to the nation, we believed on our western friends that they helped us to fight the invasion of former Soviet Union, for rebuilding our homeland. On the contrary we now understand that peace and stability has no meaning to the United States of America and Russia. They only want to implement their self-interest, which are based on baseless and misinformation. Our nation has been accused of supporting terrorism and has no regards to women's education.

We would like to present the truth to the people of Europe and you, the ladies and gentleman of the European parliament members, listen to our reasons and help you understand our culture, religion and the way of thinking of the people of Afghanistan. The only way to achieve this goal is through talking, understanding and mutual respect in building the bridge of friendship and trust among us and the rest of the world. We are ready and open to any discussion and subjects anywhere any time.
Kindly accept our regards we would like to meet you and discuss upon the issues of unjust imposing sanctions and inhuman treatment against the people of Afghanistan. We also would like to discuss the allegations inflected on us regarding terrorism and Human Right issues.

We hope to discuss these issues in detail based upon reality and friendship for this purpose that the needy people of Afghanistan will not suffer unnecessary difficulties and problems anymore

Sincerely yours,

CORRECTED Version

بسم الله الرحمن الرحيم

شماره :

امارت اسلامی افغانستان

Islamic Emirate of Afghanistan

مورخ :

From: Islamic Emirate of Afghanistan
Ministry of Foreign Affairs, Kabul
Deputy Minister Mullah Abdul Jalil Akhund

To. ~~European parliament~~
~~Rue Wiertz 10L216~~
~~B-1047 Brussels~~
~~Belgium~~

~~Palais De L. Europe~~
~~F-67000 Strasbourg~~
~~France~~

THE PRESIDENT OF THE EUROPEAN PARLIAMENT
Mrs. NICOLE FONTAINE
60, RUE WIERTZ
PHS 11 B011
B-1047 BRUSSELS
BELGIUM

Right honorable President of the European Parliament,
~~Dear Representative of the European Union:~~

As you may well know, Afghanistan was the battleground of two super powers for many years. Until, with the help of the people of Afghanistan, our movement succeeded to rescue Afghanistan form anarchism, trespassing on women chastity, looting and a destructive civil war. After the succession of our movement to bring stability and peace to the nation, we believed of our western friends ~~that they helped~~ us to fight the invasion of former Soviet Union, for rebuilding our homeland. ~~On the contrary we now understand that peace and stability has no meaning to the United States of America and Russia. They only want to implement their self-interest, which are based on baseless and misinformation.~~ Our nation ~~has been~~ accused of supporting terrorism and has no regards to women's education. .... And Drugs.

We would like to present the truth to the people of Europe and you, the ladies and gentleman of the European parliament members, listen to our reasons and help you understand our culture, religion and the way of thinking of the people of Afghanistan. The only way to achieve this goal is through talking, understanding and mutual respect in building the bridge of friendship and trust among us and the rest of the world. We are ready and open to any discussion and subjects anywhere any time. Kindly accept our regards we would like to meet you and discuss upon the issues of unjust ~~imposing~~ sanctions and inhuman treatment against the people of Afghanistan. We also would like to discuss the allegations ~~inflected on us regarding~~ terrorism ~~and~~ Human Right issues.

We hope to discuss these issues in detail based upon reality and friendship for this purpose that the needy people of Afghanistan will not suffer unnecessary difficulties and problems anymore

Sincerely yours

FROM : PHONE NO. : JUN. 12 2000 09:25AM P1

بسم الله الرحمن الرحیم

دافغانستان اسلامی امارت

د بهرنیو چارو وزارت

Islamic Emirate of Afghanistan
Ministry of Foreign Affairs

From: Islamic Emirate of Afghanistan...

To: The President of the Europe Parliament
Mrs. Nicole Fontaine
Go, Rue Wierte
PHS M BOM
B- 1047 Brussels
Belgium

Right honorable President of the European Parliament,

You may well know. Afghanistan was the battleground of two super powers as for many years. Until, with the help of the people of Afghanistan, our movement succeeded to rescue Afghanistan from anarchism, trespassing on women chastity, looting and a destructive civil war. After the succession of our movement to bring stability and peace to the nation, we believed on our western friends that they helped us to fight the invasion of former Soviet Union, for rebuilding our homeland. On the contrary we now understand that peace and stability has no meaning to the United States of America and Russia. They only want to implement their self-interest, which are based on baseless and misinformation. Our nation is now accused of supporting terrorism and has no regards to women's education.

We would like to present the truth to the people of Europe and you, the ladies and gentleman of the European parliament members, listen to our reasons and help you understand our culture, religion and the way of thinking of the people of Afghanistan. The only way to achieve this goal is through talking, understanding and mutual respect in building the bridge of friendship and trust among us and the rest of the world. We are ready and open to any discussion and subjects anywhere any time.

Kindly accept our regards we would like to meet you and discuss upon the issues of unjust imposing sanctions and inhuman treatment against the people of Afghanistan. We also would like to discuss the allegations followed on us regarding terrorism and Human Right issues.

We hope to discuss these issues in detail based upon reality and friendship for this purpose that the needy people of Afghanistan will not suffer unnecessary difficulties and problems anymore

Sincerely yours,

Maulavi Wakil Ahmad Mutawakel
Minister of Foreign Affairs

28.JUN.2000 16:57 WIELAND R 32 2 2849545 NR.742 S.1/1

EUROPÄISCHES PARLAMENT

Rainer Wieland

MITGLIED DES EUROPÄISCHEN PARLAMENTS

Mr Mohammad Kabir Mohabbat

Brussels, June 28 2000

Dear Mr Mohabbat,

I kindly refer to our meeting in Frankfurt on the 22nd of June 2000 and thank You cordially for the copies You handed over. Due to a mistake of the fax transmission I was unfortunately not able to read the whole of the draft letter, particularly in (the) two very (most) crucial lines. I would be pleased if you could send a proper copy in advance to my Brussels fax number.

Considering the readable parts I suggest You, to send a copy of the final version via fax to the President of the European Parliament, Mme Nicole Fontaine (Fax-Nr: 0032-228.49562) followed by the physically signed original by post (Parlement Européen, 60, Rue Wiertz, B-1047 Bruxelles).

I will forward the copy of the final version, you send me, without any delay, to one of my colleagues involved in the case of your country.

I urge You in addition to that, not to hesitate contacting me in the case of new developments on your side or in the case of any response from the European Parliament.

Yours sincerely

Rainer Wieland

Rainer Wieland

Europäisches Parlament, Rue Wiertz, 10 E 242, B-1047 **Brüssel**, Tel: 0032-228.47545, Fax: 0032-228.49545
CDU-Europabüro Region **Stuttgart**, Pf 100164, 70826 Gerlingen, Tel: 0049-711.806074880, Fax: 0049-711.806074894
Palais de l'Europe, F-67000 **Straßburg**, Tel: 0033-3-881.75545, Fax: 0033-3-881.79545
Bundestag IHZ, Platz der Republik 1, D-11011 **Berlin**, Tel: 0049-30.22771739, Tel: 0049-172.9352762

DER SPIEGEL
DAS DEUTSCHE NACHRICHTEN-MAGAZIN

Lieber Erick!

Ich sende Dir zwei (Blatt) für einen Freunde!

Ich habe ihnen geschrieben, dass die "nur" Themen des Gespräches sind! und wir nur autorisierten Gespräch drucken! Vielen Dank für Deine Bemühungen!

Viele Wünsche zum Erfolg bei Dir.

Herzlichst
Dein Adel

ADEL S. ELIAS
ROSENSTRASSE 5, D-88045 FRIEDRICHSHAFEN

SPIEGEL-VERLAG RUDOLF AUGSTEIN GMBH & CO. KG
GESCHÄFTSFÜHRER RUDOLF AUGSTEIN KARL DIETRICH SEIKEL

ERIK MARGRAF +49 7551 51895

28 JUN '00 17:33 DER SPIEGEL ADEL S.ELIAS S.2/3

DER SPIEGEL
DAS DEUTSCHE NACHRICHTEN-MAGAZIN

DER SPIEGEL REDAKTIONSVERTRETUNG ROSENSTRASSE 3 D-88045 FRIEDRICHSHAFEN

حضرات السادة المحترمين ،

تحية وبعد

نرفق لكم "مواضيع" الحديث الصحفي مع السيد الملا عمر

والعميد "مواضيع الحديث الصحفي لصالح مجلة دير شبيغل الالمانية.

ونحن نتعهد بعدم نشر المقال قبل اخذ موافقة

الجهات الرسمية حول نص المقابلة.

مجلة دير شبيغل أكبر مجلات اوروبا عدد القراء اسبوعيا

حوالي خمسة ملايين في المانيا والنمسا وسويسرا وبلجيكا.

فلذلك نتمنى الموافقة على المقابلة الصحفية لنحضر الى

افغانستان في الوقت الذي يناسب الملا عمر.

ولكم التقدير والاحترام

عادل الياس

المانيا / ٢٨/٦/٢٠٠٠

28 JUN '00 17:33 DER SPIEGEL ADEL S.ELIAS S.3/3

"مواضيع الحديث مع الملا عمر"

١- أفغانستان تعاني من عزلة دولية. كيف تريد التغلب على هذه العزلة.

٢- ما سبب العزلة الدولية

٣- لم تتمكن حتى الآن من بسط سيطرتكم على كل أفغانستان لماذا؟ وكيف الحل.

٤- طالبان لا تستطيع وحدها حكم أفغانستان فما هو الحل.

٥- السبب من أحد أسباب العزلة، اتهام أفغانستان بحماية الإرهاب الدولي؟

٦- أمريكا توجه التهمة لكم أنكم آويتم شخصية يعتبر إرهابي كبير؟ هل ذلك صحيح؟

٧- أين هذا الشخص

٨- قلتم أنكم لن تسلموا هذا الشخص لأن الدين الإسلامي يمنع خيانة الضيف. كيف تحل المشكلة؟

Spiegel - Seite 116 - 42/2001

(1)

ملاقات محرمانه در خیابان B1

دفتر رئیس پارلمان حزب CDU دولت آلمان و هیئت نماینده افغانستان می‌خواستند
بن لادن را به امریکا تسلیم نمایند.

فرستنده تیلویزیون امریکا CBS از شهر کویته پاکستان این معلومات [illegible]
خبر داد. با وجود یکه مقامات دولت امریکا این مشوره و ملاقات را رد
کرده اند.

خبر CBS برعکس آنرا انتشار داد.

در ملاقات پنج نماینده رسمی USA در تاریخ 16 سپتمبر پنج روز بعد از واقعه نیویارک
و واشنگتن 5 تحت [illegible] رفیت پولیس [illegible] در کویته در حکومت پاکستان
بین دو نماینده طالبان ملاقات کردند که یکی از آنها مقام بلند پایه ارتش بود.
مطابق شاهد فرستنده CBS بتاریخ 25 Sep. تا حال [illegible]
آنها گفتند [illegible] که حتی [illegible] [illegible] بود [illegible] امریکایان [illegible]
[illegible] کردن و در عین حال بسیار قاطع به [illegible] [illegible] بودند.

~~[illegible] شاهد فرستنده CBS بتاریخ~~

هدف تسلیم کردن بن لادن و همراهان خارجی او [illegible]
با کمک [illegible] او بود.

آنها گفتند که در شهر Houston امریکا [illegible] [illegible] به [illegible] ملاقات
[illegible] دارد. ایشان شناخته شده [illegible] امریکا در آلمان است که قبلاً
همراه شان کار کرده بود.

آنها گفتند از طرف طالبان [illegible] [illegible] که [illegible] تسلیمی بن لادن را
اعلان کند. پلان این بود که طالبان بن لادن را تسلیم امریکا نکنند بلکه
تسلیم [illegible] کشور بی طرف مانند محکمه جهانی در شهر Den Haag.

(2)

در مقابل این تجارت می خواستن خانم‌ها که تجاوزه اشتغالی بالا جنایتشان
برداشته شود و هم چنان دولت پاکستان در سیر جنایی پرابلیک شاهد
شود. [crossed out] دولت کابل توجه بیشتر به حقوق بشر خواهند کرد
در نشر نزد پارلمان آلمان CDU آقای ... توسط ... ایران
شاهد بودند و به این صورت ملاقات با ... کابل یعنی ... به
خصوص H. Hkindshof دیگر Dortmund در سرک B1
صورت گرفت.

بعد از رد و بدل کردن معلومات در خصوص آقای Brok ... گیر
امریکا 4 به برلین John Kornblum اطلاع داد. از بودن حملات به
دولت آن خبر داد. گفت بعداً به واشنگتن احضار شد و
۳ روز تحقیق گردید. [crossed out] دولت فعلی Clinton مجبور است که
خواسته‌های طالبان 4 قبول کند. بن لادن باید به امریکا سپرده شود
علاوه دولت امریکا و هم دولت آلمان میداند که بن لادن 4 ... لادن
در سال 1997 قبل از یک ترور بن لادن در افریقا و یمن امریکا
توسط دستگاه‌های تحقیقاتی ... بوده که بن لادن 4 معلوم کرده بودن
... حمله هوایی در همان زمان ... امکان بپذیرد
ولی رئیس جمهور امریکا در همان موقع Bill Clinton از ...
پاکستان 4 ندارد و به این [crossed out] صورت بن لادن ...
به سلامتی ... [illegible]

حاجي ملا صاحب!

السلام علیکم!

د لوی خدای (ج) دی له تاسو ملګرو سره جوړ او کامیاب غواړم.

دا خلک به په مجلس کښې اشتراک وکړي.

1 ویلیم مائیلم، سفیر په پاکستان کښې.

2 آلن ایستم، معین د وزارت خارجه.

3 جف لنډنشتید، رئیس د جنوب د آسیا.

4 فرانک، د تروریسټ په ضد رئیس.

5 (۳) درې تنه نامعلوم، چه تر اوسه ندي انتخاب شوي.

زما ملګري.

رابرټ اوکلي، سابقه سفیر په پاکستان کښې، د جورج بوش فامیلي ملګری

او د ده خانم فیلس اوکلي، سابقه اول معین.

دان وډورډ Don Woodward سابقه رئیس د سفارت مشاور په کابل کښې

او رئیس د ډیپلوماسۍ نو به خارجه وزارت کښې.

AGREEMENT

THIS AGREEMENT, dated as of the 10th day of August, 2000, by and between GLOBAL PETROLEUM AND MINING CORPORATION (herinafter called"G.P.M.C."), and the ISLAMIC EMIRATE OF AFGHANISTAN (herinafter called"IEA").

Preamble

WHEREAS, the IEA has extensive raw material deposits and mineral resources at its disposal, particularly, but not exclusively, in the form of oil, gas and other minerals; and

WHEREAS, G.P.M.C. is a company that will be incorporated by the signatories to this agreement in Switzerland in the form of a stock company; and

WHEREAS, G.P.M.C. has relations with the raw material and oil and gas producing industry in the European and American regions; and

WHEREAS, in consideration of the foregoing and the mutual promises of the parties hereto, the parties to this agreement have agreed as follows:

Commission

1. The IEA by and through its duly authorized Minister of Mining and Industries commissions G.P.M.C. exclusively to transport to the northern territory of IEA a refinery with refining capacity of at least 10000 barrels a day; however, it is agreed that G.P.M.C. may increase its production capacity to whatever limit can produce without harming the eco system of the land and the enviroment.
2. IEA agrees to guarantee the delivery the refinery of G.P.M.C. a minimum of 10000 barrels a day.

Processing Fee

It is agreed that IEA shall pay to G.P.M.C. a processing fee of six USD (6.00) per barrel payable by IEA to G.P.M.C. on the end of each calendar month, up to 20000 barrels production per day.
It is also agreed, that in case of higher production the processing fee shall be four USD (4.00) per barrel with no limit of increased of production per refinery.

Anticipated Products

4. The approximate anticipated products based on assay sample (20,000 Bbls

Product	Percentage	BPD
Unleaded Gasoline	10	2,000
Diesel Fuel	23	4,600
Kerosene	22	4,400
VGO (Cat Feed)	24	4,800
Residual Fuel (Bunker Fuel)	21	4,200

Term

5. These profits and the rights and obligations of G.P.M.C. specified in paragraph 1. hereof shall exist for a period of twenty (20) years from the date of this Agreement. IEA shall have the ownership of the refinery at the end of the Twenty year Agreement.

Taxes

6. The IEA agrees to exempt G.P.M.C. from any and all taxes including but not limited to custom, state, local and excise taxes for the first five years. It is also agreed that G.P.M.C. will pay federal income tax for the remaining period of this Agreement.

Commissioning of Third Parties

7. The IEA agrees that G.P.M.C. may commission third parties to carry out planning work and measures in order to achieve the goal set out in paragraph 1 hereof.

Performance

8. It is our estimation that:
   i. The preliminary engineering work will be completed within (6) months from the date of signing this Agreement.
   ii. The delivery of the refinery equipment shall be completed within (6) months from the date of signing this Agreement
   iii. The anticipated production shall start no later than six (8) months from the date of delivery.

If for uncontrollable events, these dates may be extended or shortened. IEA will be notified of such changes.

Right of First Refusal

9. It is further agreed that G.P.M.C. shall have the right of first refusal to explore for mineral resources and raw materials in the States of Sari Paul, Sheberghant and Mazar-I-sharif for a period of (20) years from the date of this Agreement.

Requirement of Approval

10. G.P.M.C. recognizes that approval of its activities may be necessary through the ministry of mining and industries, but it is agreed that such approval will not be unreasonably withheld to prevent the objectives of this Agreement being realized.

11. Where the subject matter of the Agreement is concerned, it is restricted to fields of activity that are approvable and are not forbidden under the national regulations of the Ministry for the G.P.M.C.

12. Should national authorities prohibit those acting or G.P.M.C. from engaging in their activity or prohibit the giving of the required approval for carrying out the activity, G.P.M.C. is not obligated to effect performance as set out in this Agreement. In this event G.P.M.C. shall not be liable for damages.

13. If only a part of G.P.M.C.'s activity should be refused, this Agreement shall continue to apply to that part of G.P.M.C.'s tasks which is approvable and is approved.

Security

14. The IEA undertakes to guarantee G.P.M.C. and the persons it employs in performing its obligations under this Agreement full protection and safety. The IEA shall take all the steps that are necessary in order to rule out any danger to protect the property and possessions of G.P.M.C. and of the firms commissioned by G.P.M.C., particularly, but not exclusively, all means of production such as refineries for example. Where G.P.M.C. or persons commissioned by G.P.M.C. are concerned, the IEA undertakes the obligation to compensate to the full extent for any damage to property.

Applicable Law

15. This Agreement shall be governed by and construed and enforced in accordance with the laws of Islamic Sharia and Islamic court and or judiciary system in the State of Afghanistan.

Severability

16. If any term, provision, covenant or restriction of this Agreement is held by a court of competent jurisdiction to be invalid, void or unenforceable, the remainder of the terms, provisions, covenants and restrictions shall remain in full force and effect and shall in no way be effected, impaired or invalid. It is herby stipulated and declared to be the intention of the parties that they would have executed the remaining terms, provisions, covenants and restrictions without including any of such which may be hereafter declared invalid, void or unenforceable.

Successors and Assigns

17. This Agreement shall be binding upon and shall inure to the benefit of the parties hereto and their respective successors and assigns.

Captions

18. The captions contained in this Agreement are solely for convenience of reference only and shall not be deemed to effect the meaning or interpretation of any paragraph hereof.

Minister of Mining and Industries
Of the Islamic Emirate of Afghanistan

Date [illegible]

President, Global Petroleum And Mining Corporation

Date Aug-10-00

Frankfurt Savoy Hotel

Wiesenhüttenstraße 42
60329 Frankfurt/Main
Telefon (0 69) 2 73 96-0
Telefax (0 69) 2 73 96-7 95

Mr. Mohammad Kabir Mohabbat
12142 South Meadow
Houston Texas,
USA

Frankfurt Savoy Hotel, 10.08.00

Room No. : 107
Arrival : 07.08.00
Departure : 10.08.00
Time : 10:27
Cashier : 10 RM
Page : 1
CL Number :
UST-IDNR : DE 114209092

INFORMATION

Description	Date	Debit	Credit
Room Rate -3519 Herrn Mohammad Kabir	07.08.	175.00	
Room Rate 502 Mr. Mohabbat	07.08.	199.00	
Room Rate 502 Mr. Mohabbat	07.08.	199.00	
Room Rate 502 Mr. Mohabbat	07.08.	175.00	
[illegible] 3519 Herrn Mohammad Kabir	07.08.	22.50	
PayTV 502 Mr. Mohabbat	07.08.	22.50	
Cash 3519 Herrn Mohammad Kabir	07.08.		175.00
Cash 502 Mr. Mohabbat	07.08.		366.90
Cash 502 Mr. Mohabbat	07.08.		43.10
Cash 502 Mr. Mohabbat	07.08.		163.00
Telephone	08.08.	174.00	
[illegible] Bar	08.08.	137.50	
Room Rate	08.08.	199.00	
Room Rate -3519 Herrn Mohammad Kabir	08.08.	175.00	
Room Rate 507 Mr. Mohabbat	08.08.	199.00	
Room Rate 502 Mr. Mohabbat	08.08.	199.00	
[illegible] 3519 Herrn Mohammad Kabi	08.08.	22.50	
PayTV 507 Mr. Mohabbat	08.08.	22.50	
PayTV 507 Mr. Mohabbat	08.08.	22.50	
Cash 502 Mr. Mohabbat	08.08.		500.00
Telephone	09.08.	329.25	
Minibar	09.08.	69.50	
Room Rate	09.08.	199.00	
Room Rate -3519 Herrn Mohammad Kabir	09.08.	175.00	

Savoy Hotelbetriebs GmbH · Sitz Frankfurt/Main · Geschäftsführer: Bernhard Dröer · [illegible] HRB 18 287 · [illegible] 114209092
Commerzbank AG · Frankfurt · BLZ 500 400 00 · Konto 68 12 224

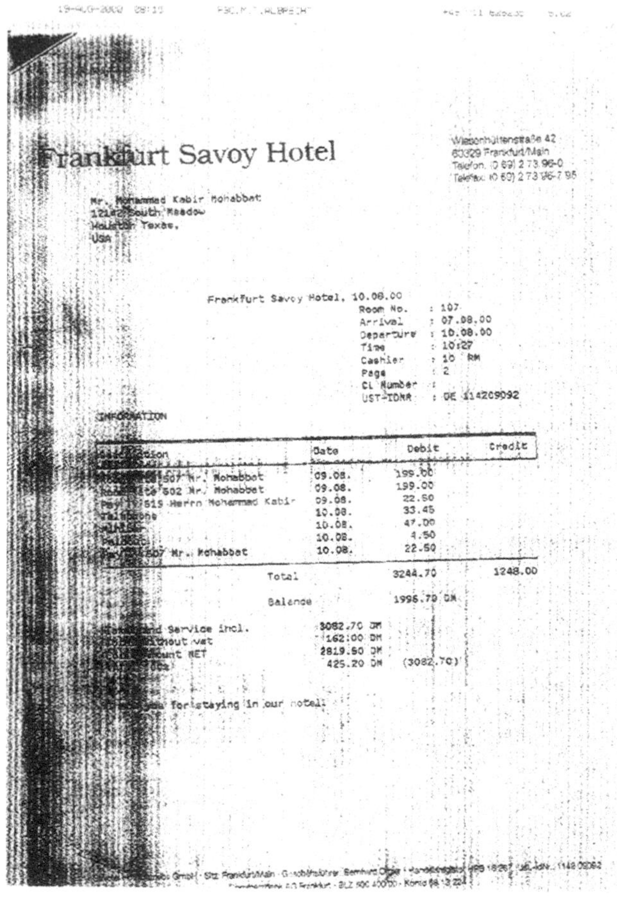

Frankfurt Savoy Hotel

Wiesenhüttenstraße 42
60329 Frankfurt/Main
Telefon (0 69) 2 73 96-0
Telefax (0 69) 2 73 96-7 95

Mr. Mohammad Kabir Mohabbat
12142 South Meadow
Houston Texas.
USA

Frankfurt Savoy Hotel, 10.08.00

Room No. : 107
Arrival : 07.08.00
Departure : 10.08.00
Time : 10:27
Cashier : 10 RM
Page : 2
CL Number :
UST-IDNR : DE 114209092

INFORMATION

Description	Date	Debit	Credit
[illegible] 507 Mr. Mohabbat	09.08.	199.00	
Room rate 502 Mr. Mohabbat	09.08.	199.00	
Pay [illegible] 515 Herrn Mohammad Kabir	09.08.	22.50	
Telephone	10.08.	33.45	
[illegible]	10.08.	47.00	
[illegible]	10.08.	4.50	
Pay [illegible] 507 Mr. Mohabbat	10.08.	22.50	
Total		3244.70	1248.00
Balance		1996.70 DM	

[illegible] and Service incl. 3082.70 DM
[illegible] without vat 162.00 DM
[illegible] amount NET 2819.50 DM
[illegible] 425.20 DM (3082.70)

[illegible] for staying in our hotel!

[illegible] GmbH · Sitz Frankfurt/Main · Geschäftsführer Bernhard [illegible] · Handelsregister HRB 18 267 · Ust.-IdNr. 114209092
[illegible] AG Frankfurt · BLZ 500 400 00 · Konto 98 13 224

From : US EMBASSY [illegible]

U.S. EMBASSY
ISLAMABAD, PAKISTAN
POLITICAL SECTION
TELEPHONE: [illegible]
FAX: [illegible]

FACSIMILE TRANSMITTAL SHEET

TO:	FROM:
Mr. Kabir Mohabbat	Paula S. Thiede, Political Officer
COMPANY:	DATE: 10/05/00
FAX NUMBER: 281-568-0340	TOTAL NO. OF PAGES INCLUDING COVER: 1
PHONE NUMBER: 281-568 9506	SENDER'S REFERENCE NUMBER:
RE:	YOUR REFERENCE NUMBER:

☐ URGENT ☐ FOR REVIEW ☐ PLEASE COMMENT ☐ PLEASE REPLY ☐ PLEASE RECYCLE

NOTES/COMMENTS:

Kabir,

Please accept my sympathy, and that of all of us here at the Embassy, for your mother's death. We only learned of it now, and the Ambassador is out of town but shares our regret.

Our thoughts and prayers are with you during this time.

Sincerely,

Paula

DIPLOMATIC ENCLAVE, RAMNA 5
ISLAMABAD, PAKISTAN

Chapter 7: President Clinton Passes the Buck

I was back in the U.S. for about a week when I received a call from the State Department. If memory serves me, calling was Stephen McCain, the Deputy Director for Southeast Asia. He invited me to visit the State Department. He wished to discuss an important issue but would rather not say what it was over the telephone. My response probably puzzled him, "I've been there too much. Is it really that important?"

"Yes." It appeared that the State Department now wished to establish a *secret* relationship with the current Afghan Government. To my astonishment, he wanted to know whether *my contacts were good enough to capture bin Laden!*

I had to sit and wonder what they thought I was working toward all this time? I politely assured him that they were. I made an appointment to travel to Washington, D.C. sometime in mid-October to meet with Stephen McCain and Jeff Lindstead, the State Department's Director of Afghanistan, Pakistan and Bangladesh Affairs (APB).

I arrived in Washington on October 11, 2000, the night before the bombing of the USS Cole while being refueled in Yemen. Early the next morning I turned on the TV in my Virginia hotel room to the breaking news on CNN. The press immediately blamed Al-Queda and bin Laden.

My knee jerk reaction was to call off the meeting with the State Department since I didn't know what their reaction would be now. But after talking to my brother, Omar, I realized that my government would probably need me more than ever.

I entered the State Department building at around 9:15 a.m. I was escorted into Jeff Lindstead's office. Also present for the meeting was the Assistant Director of the Afghanistan Desk and a few other people.

"I hope this is a wake-up call," I said. "I have been trying to work on the issue of bin Laden since Mrs. Oakley left this department and no one seemed interested. Now it's all over television." Jeff told me that they were preparing to bomb the heck out of Afghanistan because of the USS Cole. I told him that I could arrange a meeting with the Afghan decision makers.

"Great! If they won't meet, tell the Taliban we are ready to go to war!"

I described in detail the two meetings that I recently had with the CIA Station Chief in Islamabad. Lindstead had been informed of the meetings, but not about what was said. I gave him a streamlined rendition of what occurred. "The Taliban said they would deliver bin Laden."

"You mean to tell me that the mullahs are willing to talk to us?"

"Yes."

"We are preparing an attack on Afghanistan. If you can arrange something, we will talk to them whenever possible," Lindstead assured me.

I explained that I needed money to bring these people out of Afghanistan covertly. "I can't invite two or three people. I must invite more than that to cover those people willing to talk with us secretly. The rest wouldn't know what was happening."

The State Department reps declined to pay for the trip. I thought it was a funny time to go cheap on me, but I would try to arrange something. They also warned me that if they didn't meet with the Taliban shortly, they would begin the bombing operation on Afghanistan.

Someone added almost sarcastically, "We'll see what you can do." I began to wonder whether they saw me as an obstacle, too, and hoped that I would fail.

Once home in Texas, I immediately called Kandahar and reminded them of what I had said earlier. "This is not a joke! Unless you show up wherever I ask you to go, you will not be in power for more than a month." The moderate mullahs asked me to come to Kandahar as quickly as possible. They would get together a delegation to meet with the Americans in Europe under the guise of business.

I informed Jeff Lindstead of the request. He said, day or night if you have confirmation of a Taliban meeting in Europe, all you have to do is call him at home or at work and a U.S. official will show up within 24 hours to meet them. President Clinton stopped the order to bomb Afghanistan as I was en route to Kandahar.

I talked to my business friends and partners and told them that it would be hard to push a deal through now. The United States Government was after the Taliban because of the Cole bombing. I explained what had transpired at the State Department and that in order to establish an open dialogue between the U.S. and the Afghan Government. "We must meet with members of the Taliban leadership. Otherwise our oil deal is history."

My colleagues agreed to pay for the trip. I borrowed money from my brother to pay my share of the mullahs' expenses. He gave me $25,000; my colleagues pitched in over $60,000 plus volunteered to pay all the hotel bills.

October 2000, I flew out of Texas as Michael Albrecht flew from Germany. We met in Islamabad. We both had a lot to lose if the U.S. bombed Afghanistan. In quick succession I met with Paula Thiede and I believe John Schmidt, the Deputy Chief of Mission, and Ron the CIA Station Chief. I informed them why I was there, but they already knew.

I made tracks for Kandahar to convince certain members of the Taliban that unless they came to a meeting with U.S. officials in Frankfurt they would get a "strong reaction" from the U.S. Government (and that was saying the least of it).

I assured the Afghans that my business partners and I would pay their expenses. They quickly agreed.

I collected the Afghan passports and took the documents with me to Islamabad in order to procure visas into Europe. Michael was waiting for me in Islamabad to help with the process, but we ran into stonewalling officials who did not wish to issue visas to the folks who just blew up the USS Cole. I really couldn't blame them.

Becoming frantic, I went back to the U.S. Embassy and asked for help getting the Taliban into Europe. They, too, declined to help. They didn't want to interfere with another country's right to issue its own visas.

I finally lost it with the U.S. Embassy officials in Islamabad, "Look, you asked me to arrange a meeting with the mullahs and I did. Now the Germans are scared. They don't understand why the mullahs want to come back to their country. Do you really want me to confide in them that an American delegation is coming onto their soil?"

"If you do that, then we can't meet at all," came the reply.

The U.S. Embassy officials were giving me no help to reach our mutually beneficial goals, so I asked my partner to do whatever he could to remedy the situation. "Call anyone you know in Europe. Get hold of the consulate in Germany and Islamabad." Michael Albrecht called Elmar Brok's office and Brok approached the Foreign Minister of Germany. Within twenty-four hours the intrepid Foreign Minister gave the order to issue visas for six members of the Taliban. I arranged to meet the mullahs in Pakistan.

The Taliban arrived in Islamabad on Halloween (October 31, 2000) and we spent the night at the Marriott Hotel and then flew to Germany the next day. Mullah Abdul Jalil (Deputy Minister of Foreign Affairs), Mullah Abdul Razaq (Minister of Commerce), the Governor of Central Bank of Afghanistan (whose name I still cannot remember), Mullah Mohammad Esa (who at that time was in Mazar-e-Sharif when ordered to Islamabad within 15 hours, an almost impossible task to accomplish), and Mullah Ahmed Jan traveled with us out of Pakistan.

Esa confided to me on the flight to Germany that Mullah Omar had called him and asked why Mr. Mohabbat was taking one-third of his cabinet out of the country. He expressed concern that there could be a conspiracy afoot – perhaps someone was going to shoot down the plane.

"When we arrive in Frankfurt," I said to Esa, "you can inform Mullah Omar that I am on the same plane as you."

"Are you going back with us on the same plane?" Esa asked.

"I will go back and make sure you are safely tucked into your beds in Afghanistan."

It surprised me to learn that Mullah Omar had no knowledge of the meeting. I wondered if he had a clue that airplanes from the strongest country in the world were probably lurking in the skies over his head poised to drop bombs.

We arranged to meet with U.S. authorities on November 2, 2000. Besides the U.S. officials, joining us in Frankfort were four U.S. business men and my brother, Dr. Omar Mohabbat. We rented a few suites and a number of rooms at the Arabella Sheridan in Frankfurt. Almost 20 individuals gathered at the hotel.

The morning of the 2nd, Mullah Abdul Jalil, who would be meeting covertly with U.S. officials, asked to talk with my brother and me privately. We discussed the issues that would come up that afternoon with the U.S. officials. Omar explained to Jalil that unless they were willing to negotiate honestly with the U.S. reps it would cost them their leadership. "There will no longer be a Taliban!" Omar emphatically declared.

"You know, Dr. Mohabbat, we are mullahs. If we died in this process, we will go to heaven. That's our belief."

My brother said, "In 1978, when the Soviets overthrew the government of President Daoud, I was a member of his Cabinet. He surrendered to the communists because he feared that they would hurt his family. He told them that whatever he had done wrong, his family had nothing to do with it," Omar paused to let this sink in. "If there is a revolution or a takeover of the Taliban government, I have no doubt that you will all go to heaven as martyrs. But have you given any thought to your children and wife, your sisters and mother? What will happen to them? You know they will be raped or killed. They will suffer dishonor. Think about those things!"

My brother's words visibly shook the Foreign Minister. He decided to meet with the U.S. officials that afternoon. I asked my old friend Abdulah Mangal to take us to the Airport Sheridan Hotel in Frankfurt. The U.S. officials were waiting for us on the fifth floor.

The covert meeting between the Taliban Minister and U.S. reps was set to begin at 3:00 p.m. Those representing the U.S. were Alan Eastem, Jeff Lindstead, Frank (the Assistant Director of Anti-Terrorism, State Department), Big Gary (Director of the CIA for Middle Eastern Affairs in Washington and well over six foot and 200 pounds), and Gary's deputy, also named Gary (who we came to call Small Gary simply because he was shorter and skinnier than Big Gary). I introduced the formal representative of the Afghan Government, Mullah Abdul Jalil, to the group.

First out of the proverbial gate was an angry Alan Eastem. He threatened the Taliban representative. He told Jalil that they would be destroyed and killed unless they handed over bin Laden. After what seemed like an hour of abuse, my brother Omar finally cut off Eastem's tantrum. "We have not brought Mullah Jalil here to be yelled at. The man before you is an honorable man. He is a cleric – he is a mullah. Perhaps he is simple, but he has honor and dignity. He has been sitting quietly while my brother, Kabir, translated everything you said word for word, even the words that aren't proper. I want you to calm down and drop your tone or I will call off this meeting right now. He did not come here to be insulted."

Eastem quickly changed tactics and began to attack me. He said that the U.S. reps had their own translator and this was the last meeting that I would be attending.

"Why?" I asked.

"It has to do with national security. We want to talk to the Taliban through our own translator, our own people. We won't need you after today. Thank you for bringing Jalil over," Estem said dismissing me in a perfunctory manner.

I patiently let him finish and then said, "I think he may understand about fifty percent of what you are saying, but his English isn't good enough to speak back to you. I am very embarrassed. I bragged about how American I am and how many good friends I have at the State Department and the first thing you do is try to get rid of me. I hope he didn't understand what you said, because I don't know how he will react."

I couldn't believe it, after I had done so much to bring these contentious groups together. I had even paid for the trip. "I am suspicious of your reasons for trying to get rid of me. I am here to act as mediator because you two are fighting. If I leave you with each other and you use words that are not proper then he has no way to talk back to you. This meeting will collapse and you will both be sorry." I was not going to take a chance on a misunderstanding unless the Taliban representative agreed that he didn't need me either. I suggested that we leave this issue and return to it later in the day.

Finally, the U.S. side quieted down and the Taliban official started talking. Jalil expressed hope that the meeting would not continue in the previous tone. He didn't understand what had gone on, but the tones were very angry.

Calmly he said, "Let's have our meeting start on good terms." He began by thanking the U.S. Government and the American public for sticking by them in the 1980's during the Afghan war with the Soviets. He gave thanks to the U.S. on behalf of the mujahidin members of the Taliban who now sat on the Council of Ministers. The meeting calmed down for a moment. Then Eastem began spewing threats again.

At this point, the representative of the Afghan Government asked for the documents that the U.S. promised to provide to take back to Kandahar so they could put bin Laden on trial themselves. You see, they had been promised proof that Osama bin Laden was involved in the USS Cole bombings by me. At the time, I thought this would be an easy task for my government. I had passed this information on and was expecting hard proof that would convince them to put the Cockroach on trial.

Frank, the Deputy Director for Anti-Terrorism Affairs at the State Department, stood up and handed the Taliban rep a clipping from the *New York Times*. If the situation wasn't so serious this act of passing a clipping off as proof would have been laughable.

"What is that," I asked.

"Yesterday's *New York Times*." The article was about an officer in the U.S. Army who confessed that he belonged to Al-Queda and that he was part of the conspiracy surrounding the Cole bombing.

After I translated what was said, Jalil said, "This is what you call evidence!" How many articles do you want me to have published in the Afghan newspapers accusing you of being a terrorist? This is not fair nor is it according to diplomatic principles. You are giving me an article from your newspaper and you want me to believe you?"

Frank started yelling so hard I thought the veins on the side of his throat would burst. He accused the Taliban of being involved in the Cole, suggested that Al-Queda was involved, and said that the Afghan rep had all the proof in the world that he needed and he knew it. Frank was so loud everyone else in his delegation became uneasy.

Trying to bring calm to the meeting, I jumped in and told Frank he needed to see a dentist because of his ugly front teeth. Everyone laughed. It cut the tension.

"Seriously," I said, "you need to slow down. I'm speaking two languages here and it's becoming hard to concentrate. Besides, this is embarrassing. I thought you came here for reasons of diplomacy; I thought you were diplomats. You are putting me in a very awkward position. We still don't know what the Taliban want. He thinks I am on your side and you think I am on their side. This is childish! Let's have a fair, diplomatic meeting. I refuse to translate any more language that is abusive or that directly insults this man. He has no idea what you're talking about. He told me he doesn't know what happened to the USS Cole nor does he know anything about the Khobar Towers bombing. Stop this bullshit!!" I used the word because the U.S. diplomats had been smearing it around the room quite handily.

The meeting wasn't going well. The U.S. delegation didn't seem to care about the U.N. Resolution that called for the Cockroach to be turned over to a third country. All they cared about was getting bin Laden into their hands, NOW! Oddly enough that was why the member of the Afghan Government was present, to arrange bin Laden's delivery to the U.S. The meeting broke up after hours of shouting back and forth between U.S. authorities and me with little else being accomplished.

We returned to our hotel. Then my brother and I met and talked about what had happened. I felt ashamed to have participated in it, but Omar encouraged me not to give up. He suggested that I arrange another meeting between us and Jalil for about nine or ten o'clock that night.

The other members of the Afghan delegation began looking for their colleague after he had been missing for hours. My brother and I made up the excuse that we had to take Jalil to the doctor. They bought it since my brother Omar was a doctor.

That night my brother and I met with Jalil again. Omar wanted to go over everything one more time. Jalil complained that the U.S. delegation had treated him poorly. Omar and I agreed, but there was nothing that anybody could do about it. My brother was very persistent that the talks should continue.

"There is a time when you must face reality. The United States is the most powerful country in the world. Whatever pleases them, they will do. I can't stop them and you can't stop them. It is much better to be on their good side."

The representative of the Afghan Government said that the U.S. was not really interested in negotiations; they were interested in war. My brother convinced him to return to the meeting the next day. Jalil tentatively agreed to meet again with the U.S. delegation at 11:00 a.m.

Early the next morning, I received a call from Mullah Jalil. Resigned to giving diplomacy another try, he agreed to weather another meeting. So we went back to the Sheridan Hotel at the Frankfurt Airport. This time we were met at the elevator doors by Big Gary and Jeff Lindstead. Gary asked Jalil to go up with him while Jeff asked me and my brother to follow him. This surprised the Taliban rep. He didn't quite understand what was happening and neither did I. They stopped in their tracks and stated firmly that they wanted me to go with them.

I explained that I would wait for them in the lobby, but Jeff said that I must attend a private meeting with him. Jalil and I stood there looking perplexed. Then Jalil asked what kind of meeting was he being invited to attend that did not include Dr. and Kabir Mohabbat?

The U.S. authorities explained that they wanted their own translator because they were going to talk about high level secret things. They wanted only the people from the National Security Agency there.

This frightened Jalil. The Taliban official said that he was there at the request of the Mohabbat family, especially the honorable Dr. Omar Mohabbat, an elder in the Afghan community. "I have a lot of respect for him, and Kabir Mohabbat has done nothing but convince me that you people are good. If you take me away that means it is a secret meeting and that means that you can fabricate things or say things that I never said."

It suddenly crossed my mind that the U.S. delegation may intend for the talks to collapse, so I spoke up, "What the hell are you trying to do? Are you trying to corner the Minister? Without us, he will not attend any meeting!"

"Don't provoke them," Jalil warned me.

I spoke to him in Pashto, "These delegates want to meet with you alone. You have noticed that from day one they have tried to get you alone. I don't know what they fear. They're holding all the weapons."

The Taliban representative said to the U.S. officials standing in the hotel lobby, "Okay, let's meet some other time. If you are really interested in meeting, then you come to Kandahar." This statement visibly upset Big Gary and Jeff Lindstead.

My brother asked me in English so the U.S. reps could understand what was being said, "Where'd you get these peasants? I thought they were diplomats. How could they ask for Jalil to meet alone with the CIA? If the Taliban thought this was a set up, they could kill you and our family." Finally the U.S. officials acquiesced. It was a bad start to a grueling morning.

When we finally entered the meeting room, the U.S. delegation was already at the table. Omar told them that this was the most horrifying thing he had ever heard of, asking a person you don't know and wasn't even very willing to talk with you, to meet privately with the CIA.

"Mullah Abdul Jalil is a diplomat; he is a member of the Ministers' Cabinet. He is not a spy here to meet with spies and he is not here to be sold to you. He doesn't need your money. He never asked for money. This is an international issue. It must be solved diplomatically. Whatever you want, we will try to convince him. Are you trying to do something like this because we didn't let yesterday's meetings collapse?" my brother Omar asked them bluntly while I translated everything he said to the member of the Afghan Government.

"You want to take him to a different room so in an hour you can say we don't agree on any issue and then you can announce to the world that the Taliban were not cooperating and then you can bomb the hell out of Afghanistan and its people. I could care less about the Taliban movement, but I am worried about our family members there. I have international obligations."

The U.S. delegation backed off. Big Gary and Small Gary asked if they could meet with me alone. I said, "No, not now dammit! How could you take me out of this meeting in front of Minister Jalil. He might think that I am in this with you. If this is not a trap, then you had better clarify that I had no idea that this was going to happen."

We found out later that Mullah Jalil began to trust my brother and me even more because of the tone we took with the U.S. authorities. He couldn't believe what he witnessed. The mini-conspiracy on the part of the U.S. officials gave us even more leverage with the member of the Afghan Government. Because we were Western educated, we had been marked as suspicious from the beginning – probable agents – until he saw the intensity of our reaction to the American officials.

Omar said, "If the subject is Osama, then let's talk. If the subject is politics, let's quit now." Everybody settled down and agreed to talk about our common enemy, Osama bin Laden.

The Taliban rep summarized what had occurred to date in their attempts to deliver the renegade Saudi: "You asked us first to hand him over to the Saudi government and the Saudis wouldn't take him. Then before this meeting we agreed in principal to take him to Europe. But now you won't agree to that and you want him handed over to the U.S. Government."

Then the Taliban rep offered something unbelievable to the U.S. representatives. Omar asked me not to translate it because I was still angry. He took over translation and I agreed to be quiet while they talked out the issue.

By the way, Jeff Lindstead told me these two meetings were audio taped. If anyone wants to hear what happened, they should use a freedom of information request to get the tapes from the U.S. State Department.

The Taliban's solution to the problem of Osama bin Laden: "*What if you send a cruise missile over to get bin Laden?*"

Astonished, the U.S. reps cried, "What!?!"

The mullah asked, "How long would it take you to prepare to hit bin Laden with a cruise?"

The response: "Probably two to three weeks with a presidential order. We'd have to get the president to sign it, but that's not hard to do."

"Why do we have to wait that long? Instead, you send your men – not more than two or three – and we will take you to bin Laden and point him out," the spokesman pointed his index finger at a member of the U.S. delegation. "This is Osama bin Laden. Then you just wait ten seconds while we turn the other way and you shoot him on the spot. Then we will deal with the rest of Al-Qaeda one by one."

You should have seen the U.S. delegation. They started clapping and said, "You mean to tell us that you will let us come into your country and take care of this issue."

"Yes," he replied.

"Bingo," I thought. Bin Laden would soon be out of my life and the last road block to the Afghan oil would be removed. Life is good!

The atmosphere in the room changed. Everyone started laughing and celebrating. "Now we're talking," the U.S. delegation cried out. They now knew that the Afghan official was a man who could deliver for the Afghan Government.

The Taliban representative said, "You should have one or two persons come shoot the son of a bitch. We will take you that close to him. Or if you want to send a Cruise Missile, I promise we will have him pinned down, in the same spot, probably the same bedroom, for a month and he will not be allowed to leave his bedroom."

We all laughed, but then Jalil jokingly said, "Well Osama has four wives, he might be in a different bedroom."

Then someone added, "Maybe he'll be with all of them in the same room," everyone burst into laughter again at the thought.

Things began to improve.

Jalil explained to the U.S. delegation, "You shouldn't be surprised that there are terrorists in Afghanistan." He explained that there had been war for decades before they came to power, and that should not be forgotten. "There is a saying in Afghanistan, wherever there are dead bodies, stray dogs appear." In Afghanistan stray dog means a rabid or crazy dog, one whose bite spreads disease. He implied that Osama is nothing more than a stray dog feeding on the remains of Afghanistan.

Alan Eastem said, "We admire the way you have brought security to your country. We admire that you are doing something about drugs. We admire a lot of things that you are changing that would have cost the international community billions and billions of dollars to fix. Just to disarm the War Lords and the thugs left over from the communist era would have cost billions."

The U.S. authorities continued to shower the Taliban rep with compliments. They then announced that the road between the United States and Afghanistan was open. "Osama bin Laden was the one stumbling block and this block should soon be lifted," they assured the Afghan authority.

Then Jalil asked, "But what if the block is too heavy for us to carry alone? Would you give us a hand to get rid of this block and then we can start driving on a two-way street together?" We all shook hands in agreement. A member of the U.S. delegation said that the U.S. should extend hands of help. It was really a good way to start the process of removing bin Laden from Afghanistan.

The Afghan official was asked how long it would take to capture bin Laden. He assured them that it should take no more than a week or so to capture and hold him as soon as the U.S. signals it is ready to act.

Mullah Jalil then asked whether they could delay the new batch of international sanctions that were coming in mid-January 2001. He pointed out that the delay would give them more credibility in Kandahar now that they had the beginnings of a good dialog and relationship with the United States.

Eastem said, “Absolutely not!”

My brother and I tried to convince the mullah that there wasn’t much America could do because the international community had decided on this issue. We responded that if the Taliban ended the bin Laden problem, the sanctions would disappear shortly thereafter.

“Once we issue a decree for Osama’s surrender, if you decide to get him yourself, what would happen if you don’t get him? For example, what would happen if he was found dead somewhere in the mountains?”

No one on the American side was willing to respond to this comment. To this day I believe that Jalil was telling the U.S. officials that if they were not prepared to act immediately, what would happen if the Taliban acted for them. Would it prevent more sanctions from being dropped onto Afghanistan?

The Afghan official reassured the U.S. that if ultimately President Clinton decides to send a Cruise Missile, the Taliban would have to object publicly and criticize us for three to six months, but behind the scenes the two nations could begin acting as friends.

The American delegation asked Jalil not to do anything to bin Laden until the next meeting. Alan Eastem said that they had assigned William Milam, the Ambassador to Pakistan, to be the Taliban’s contact person. He was the highest ranking U.S. diplomat in the area.

The meeting ended on a good note. Both sides shook hands and promised to meet as soon as possible after the November Presidential election. The Americans explained that they couldn't do much now. If they started sending Cruise Missiles to Afghanistan, the extreme right in the U.S. would claim that Clinton and Gore had concocted a conspiracy to aid Gore's presidential election. "Action might take a while. We must see who is elected President of the United States."

After adjourning, members of the U.S. delegation asked me to meet with them once Mullah Jalil and my brother returned to the hotel. I agreed. When I got to the hotel I asked Omar his opinion about meeting with the U.S. delegation. He said that at this point there wasn't much difference between meeting with the State Department or the CIA or the FBI or anyone else who represented the U.S. He said that I had put myself in a situation where I must now deal with all of them.

I went back to the Airport Sheraton Hotel and met with both Gary's alone in their room. When I walked in one of them said, "Kabir there is time for diplomacy and there is time for covert operation."

"Okay!?!"

They explained that I must pull away from the Taliban once I introduce them to Ambassador William Milam and to the CIA's Station Chief in Pakistan. I would not be allowed to attend the next meeting.

I asked why they were in such a rush to get rid of me. I explained that the Taliban may not meet with them alone. "After what you pulled today, he is already paranoid. He finally got comfortable and made the best deal there ever was. I have done nothing but work hard and almost put my life on the line for you and here you are trying to get rid of me again."

The Gary's said that was the covert way of doing things and there weren't any diplomats in these kinds of deals, but I wasn't buying it.

I said, "I am American. I came to America when I was 18 years old. I have spent most of my adult years in the U.S., but I brought the Afghan culture with me. I am going to use the best of both cultures. I want to show Afghans how good America is."

With a voice laced with pessimism Big Gary replied, "There was never an Afghan that we couldn't buy." (Sometime back, my second wife Karen warned me that I was better off joining the mafia than joining the CIA. "At least the mob shows loyalty toward its members.")

Angry, I stormed out of their room and returned to my hotel. Thereafter I met with some businessmen and watched the Taliban begin the process of ordering new Afghan bank notes. I watched as the representatives of the Afghan Government signed a contract with the German printing firm.

I promised to escort the Taliban back to Islamabad. We caught a plane from Frankfurt and headed toward Dubai. This first leg of the flight was eight hours.

When we walked on the plane, the steward asked, "Who are the guys in the turbans?"

"Top officials of the Taliban."

Most of the plane crew came by and shook their hands. They had never met a member of the current Afghan Government before.

Once in Islamabad, I went straight to the American Embassy and talked with Paula Thiede. Without Jalil's knowledge, I made him an appointment with the American authorities. I wanted him to meet Ambassador Milam as soon as possible.

Jalil stayed with me at the Marriott Islamabad. Our appointment at the American Embassy was for 6:00 p.m. At about 5:30, I received a call from Paula Thiede stating that the embassy staff was installing listening and audio devices. She asked for a delay of an hour. I told Jalil that the Ambassador was busy and that we would go at 7:00.

I hired a private taxi. I asked the driver to stay at the hotel and let one of my bodyguards, Pir Murad, drive the car. He agreed. Pir was excited to drive the taxi because he had never been in the American Embassy before. Once we arrived, the gate opened and we drove directly into the residence of the American Ambassador, William Milam.

At the door, we were received by Paula and Ambassador Milam. I told Paula that they should be glad that Jalil came at all since we made him wait another hour and there were others who wanted to see him. Paula rolled her eyes and said that people had to install all kinds of things before our meeting could commence.

Just as she finished her statement, Ron the CIA Station Chief showed up. This surprised me because I didn't know he had been invited to the meeting. I winked at the Station Chief and we pretended not to know each other as we went through introductions all over again. I didn't want Jalil to feel uncomfortable and so we pretended that I had arranged for Ron to be at the meeting (which I had not). I explained who the Station Chief was. Without hesitation Jalil said that he expected someone from the Agency to be there.

Ambassador Milam warmly received Jalil. They exchanged good will, and Jalil again thanked the U.S. for the weapons and logistics provided during their war against the Soviets. He believed that they owed the U.S. their country and their God and that they would always be indebted to America. The Ambassador thanked the Afghan official for his kind words.

Mullah Jalil opened up a little and began talking directly to Ambassador Milam through me as translator. Ron sat and listened for about an hour as they talked. (I got the impression that Ron wasn't allowed to speak while the Ambassador was meeting with someone.) Jalil explained to the Ambassador that their positions in the Afghan Government were only temporary. "We are here only for a short period of time."

Then the Ambassador confirmed what was said in the October/November 2000 meeting in Frankfort where the Taliban rep had made the following proposals concerning bin Laden:

1) They would like to see Osama bin Laden tried by Afghans in an Afghan court. All the U.S. had to do was get one

person from each country who had a relative killed in the embassy bombings of Kenya and Tanzania to testify. He or she would come to Afghanistan and file a complaint against bin Laden for being the man behind the bombings. They even insinuated that the witnesses could be coached about what to say.

(Sometime after this proposal was made in Frankfurt, Alan Eastem informed Afghan authorities that he could not provide anybody from the two countries whose embassies had been bombed. Members of the Taliban would laugh at this and say, "If such a powerful country could get two people willing to file a complaint and let us do the rest, bin Laden would be hanging somewhere in a stadium within seventy-two hours.")

2) They could open up a diplomatic channel and bring him to justice in an Afghan court where the prosecutor was an American and the judges were from different countries, say three Christian and three Muslim judges.

3) Send in an assassin. They needed someone from outside the Taliban since they really didn't have the evidence to prove that he was a murderer themselves. That person would be taken within a meter of Osama bin Laden, the terrorist would be pointed out, and then everyone would look the other way while he was shot in the head.

4) Osama bin Laden and his men could be gathered together in one spot and the U.S. could send a Tomahawk Cruise Missile over to hit them. The Afghan Government would then complain to the world for three to six months that the United States wasn't fair and that the Taliban shouldn't be blamed for not giving up Osama. But after three to six months, after things had calmed down, we would come back to the table and start a new dialog and re-establish a working relationship between our two countries.

Ambassador Milam was excited to hear what Mullah Jalil had to say, but the Ambassador believed the diplomatic solution to the matter was to have bin Laden extradited to a third country. So they agreed, in principal, that was what would happen. Now to find a country.

Back to square one. Good luck, I thought. I had grave doubts that one could be found. I agreed with Milam that the diplomatic solution was probably good for the image of all parties concerned, but I wondered whether damning the P.R. and speeding to a swift military solution wouldn't be best.

Jalil said, "We gave you four options. Pick the easiest. We are here to help you."

Then Ambassador Milam amused everyone present by comparing bin Laden to a snake. "We need to take the snake by the head."

"Yes, if you want to kill a snake, you must crush the head," Jalil said.

The Ambassador retorted, "Once you crush the head of a snake, the rest will die by itself." Everyone laughed.

At about ten o'clock, we said good bye to the Ambassador and agreed to meet again right after the new U.S. President is sworn in – toward the end of January. I was having trouble understanding why something couldn't be done about it now, it was still November. The end of January was months away and shouldn't one strike while the iron is hot? After all we were talking about going after someone like bin Laden.

Within a week of returning to Texas I received a call from Small Gary. He said it was urgent for me to come to D.C. and asked if it was possible for me to meet with Big Gary.

I said, "Sure."

In the meantime, somebody would get in touch with me.

"Great."

He was going to introduce me to a local man. That way I wouldn't have to travel back and forth to Washington from Texas.

"Fine."

Then they asked me to bring copies of my old telephone bills.

I got on the plane to Washington on the 26th of November 2000. Once at the hotel, Small Gary showed up with someone whose name I have forgotten. I asked him where Big Gary was and he said he couldn't make it (he had to take his wife to dinner), so we went to a noisy restaurant close to the hotel and ate at the bar.

Small Gary said that they wanted to know who had attended the meeting at the U.S. Embassy in Islamabad and what had occurred. It surprised me that they had so little information. After all, the complete meeting had been taped. He asked to see my telephone bills. I agreed. There were a lot of numbers listed, even that of the Taliban's Minister of Defense. He confided in me that the British had taught them that the first thing to do in a covert operation is to tap the telephone. I asked him not to tap my phone because they don't need to, but "If you have to, you have to." For security reasons, he had to, but it didn't matter. I had nothing to hide.

We spent the whole evening talking about events in Afghanistan. Then we returned to my hotel room and Small Gary pulled out a yellow envelope. He had reimbursement money for me for the flight and hotel expenses that I and my business partners had incurred working on behalf of the U.S. Government.

"How much?" I said.

"$15,000."

"Wait a minute, our bill was $85,000. The airline tickets for the last minute flights alone were almost $40,000 and the hotel expenses were that much again, plus I had to shuttle back and forth to Islamabad. You keep the money."

"Take it and I'll see you get more. Unless you take it, then you won't be officially recognized by the U.S. Government."

I finally understood. I was just another foreign whore to my government. "I can't," I complained. "Then I would be letting my business act as a front." He insisted that I take the expense money.

I left Washington disappointed. I wondered what the hell I was getting myself into. I figured the negotiations between the Taliban and the U.S. Government would cost me almost $15,000 out of pocket per trip – money that I didn't have. But it did look like I would eventually get reimbursed for the money that my partners and I had spent. Things were defiantly looking up.

Back in Texas I got a call from a national security contact named Jack. He wanted to meet me at a restaurant on Post Oak Boulevard in Houston. The whole thing made me uncomfortable, but I met him.

A week later I got another call from him. I explained that meeting with him alone made me nervous and I would no longer do it. I wanted to ensure that my words got to the proper authorities and that nothing was misconstrued. In other words, I wanted a witness with security clearance at each meeting. We planned to meet at Bennigan's at the Southwest Freeway and Kirby Drive, but I told him I wouldn't unless someone from the FBI or Mario Gutierrez from the Houston Police Department was present. Jack insisted that there was no need for the FBI or Mario. But I insisted, "I would like to have him with me."

At the next meeting, Mario and Jack showed up together. Neither knew what happened in Islamabad or Frankfurt.

"Has anyone informed you about anything that I'm doing?"

"No." It was all news to them. While Mario took notes, I explained in detail about my last trip to Pakistan and the fact that the Taliban was ready to turn the Cockroach over to the U.S. Eventually we discussed how much expense money I should receive for each trip that I had already made or was about to make. I promised to help where I could if it didn't cost me anything anymore. Jack agreed that the costs of my efforts would be picked up by the government. (But we were never fully reimbursed for the expenses of the October/ November 2000 trip to Frankfurt.)

In the middle of December 2000, Jack called and wanted to meet. He explained that he needed to wait for the new administration to take over before we could plan contingencies to settle our Cockroach problem. (I had hoped that Bush Jr. would be the winner of the American election. As the former governor of Texas, I knew what a good man he was. To my surprise, Bush barely eked out a win on Election Day, but I cheered him on nonetheless.)

"You would be willing to go back and talk to the Taliban about the change of government?"

"Sure, and they will understand, too, about the change of government."

Thereafter Jack, Mario and I met weekly. We discussed the fact that the Afghan Government was ready to hand over bin Laden and the four options for action given by that government's representative to the U.S. Jack complained that he wanted to retire, but decided to wait awhile to see what happened with bin Laden.

On January 1, 2001, George W. Bush was sworn in as President of the United States.

[The Arabella Sheraton Grand Hotel Frankfurt statements begin on the next page. They are organized by room number under Mr. Alameel's name. Kabir did not provide me with full copies of all of David Alameel's bills in Germany. Most likely, all the pages were not in his possession. Kabir may only have received copies of the pages showing the total of each room as proof for reimbursement by Kabir to Alameel. L.M.]

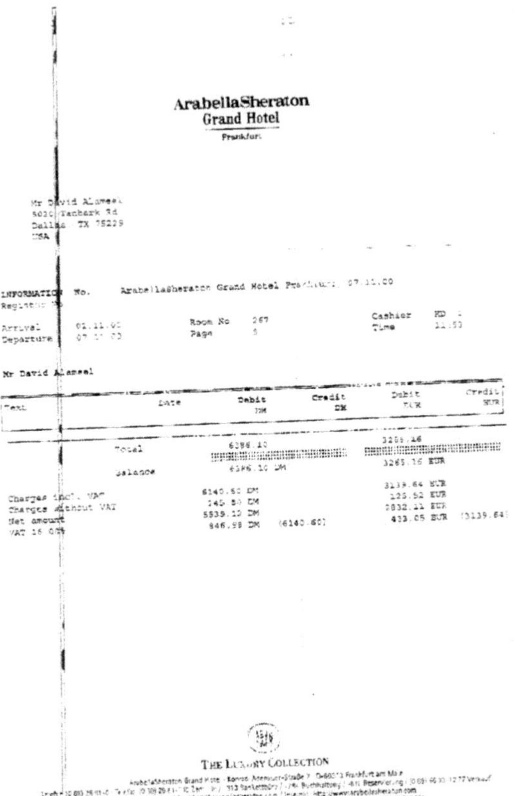

ArabellaSheraton
Grand Hotel
Frankfurt

Mr David Alameel
5020 Tanbark Rd
Dallas TX 75229
USA

INFORMATION No. ArabellaSheraton Grand Hotel Frankfurt 07.11.00
Registr[illegible]

Arrival 01.11.00 Room No 267 Cashier [illegible]
Departure 07.[illegible] Page 5 Time 11:50

Mr David Alameel

Text	Date	Debit DM	Credit DM	Debit EUR	Credit EUR
Total		6386.10		3265.16	
Balance		6386.10 DM		3265.16 EUR	
Charges incl. VAT		6140.50 DM		3139.64 EUR	
Charges without VAT		245.50 DM		125.52 EUR	
Net amount		5539.12 DM		2832.11 EUR	
VAT 16.00%		846.98 DM	(6140.60)	433.05 EUR	(3139.64)

THE LUXURY COLLECTION

ArabellaSheraton
Grand Hotel
Frankfurt

Mr David Alameel
5020 Tanbark Rd
Dallas, TX 75229
USA

INFORMATION No. ArabellaSheraton Grand Hotel Frankfurt 07.11.00
Register No.

Arrival	01.11.00	Room No	267	Cashier	HD 1
Departure	07.11.00	Page	8	Time	11:53

Mr David Alameel

Text	Date	Debit DM	Credit DM	Debit EUR	Credit EUR
Total		6386.10		3265.16	
Balance		6386.10 DM		3265.16 EUR	
Charges incl. VAT		6140.60 DM		3139.64 EUR	
Charges without VAT		245.50 DM		125.52 EUR	
Net amount		5539.12 DM		2832.11 EUR	
VAT 16.00%		846.98 DM	(6140.60)	433.05 EUR	(3139.64)

THE LUXURY COLLECTION

ArabellaSheraton Grand Hotel · Konrad-Adenauer-Straße 7 · D-60313 Frankfurt am Main
Telefon (069) 29 81-0 · Telefax (069) 29 81-810 Zentrale / -813 Bankettbüro / -784 Buchhaltung / -811 Reservierung / (069) 29 13-12 77 Verkauf
E-mail: grandhotel.frankfurt@arabellasheraton.com / Internet: http://www.arabellasheraton.com
Arabella Hotel GmbH & Co. Betriebs KG, Sitz: München, Amtsgericht München HRA 57 806 · VAT-ID-Nr. DE 129 723 586
Komplementär: Arabella Hotelgesellschaft mbH, Sitz München, Amtsgericht München HRB 40 441 · Geschäftsführer: Uwe Kraus
Bankverbindungen: Deutsche Bank AG Frankfurt, Konto-Nr. 2 129 815, BLZ 500 700 10, IBAN DE50 5007 0010 0212 9815 00
HypoVereinsbank Frankfurt, Konto-Nr. 4 270 275 884, BLZ 503 201 91

12/03/2000 22:00 6192264770 SAN DIEGO CAA INC PAGE 01

ArabellaSheraton
Grand Hotel
Frankfurt

Mr David Alameel
5020 Tanbark Rd
Dallas, TX 75229
USA

INFORMATION No. ArabellaSheraton Grand Hotel Frankfurt, 07.11.00
Register No.

Arrival	01.11.00	Room No	484	Cashier	HD 1
Departure	07.11.00	Page	5	Time	11:53

Mr David Alameel

Text	Date	Debit DM	Credit DM	Debit EUR	Credit EUR
->#2184 : Apollinaris 0,5					
Minibar #2484 : Vittel	06.11.	9.50		4.86	
Minibar	06.11.	13.00		6.65	
->#2484 : Granini Orangensa					
Minibar	06.11.	6.50		3.32	
->#2484 : Granini Apfelsaft					
Minibar	06.11.	6.50		3.32	
->#2484 : Granini Multivita					
Minibar	06.11.	6.50		3.32	
->#2484 : Schweppes Ginger					
Minibar #2484 : Coca Cola	06.11.	6.50		3.32	
Minibar	06.11.	6.50		3.32	
->#2484 : Coca Cola Light					
Minibar	06.11.	19.00		9.71	
->#2484 : Apollinaris 0.5					
Minibar Snacks	06.11.	6.50		3.32	
->#2484 : Macadamia Nüsse					
Minibar Snacks	06.11.	8.00		4.09	
->#2484 : Gouda Käsekräcker					
Minibar Snacks	06.11.	8.00		4.09	
->#2484 : Gouda Käsekräcker					
Paid outs	06.11.	6.00		3.07	
->#484 : CHECK #5335					
Telephone	07.11.	9.75		4.99	
Telephone	07.11.	36.75		18.79	
Telephone	07.11.	31.50		16.11	
Breakfast Brasserie	07.11.	38.00		19.43	
Breakfast Brasserie	07.11.	3[illegible]0		19.43	
Total				3452.24	

ArabellaSheraton Grand Hotel [illegible] Frankfurt am Main
Telefon (069) 2981-0 · Telefax (069) 29 81-810 Zentrale / -813 Bankettbüro / -784 Buchhaltung / -811 Reservierung / (069) 6633-12 77 Verkauf
E-mail: grandhotel.frankfurt@arabellasheraton.com / Internet: http:// [illegible]
[illegible] München HRA 57 938 · VAT-ID-Nr. DE [illegible]
Komplementär: [illegible] München HRB [illegible] · Geschäftsführer: [illegible]
Bankverbindungen: Deutsche Bank AG [illegible] IBAN [illegible]
HypoVereinsbank Frankfurt [illegible]

[illegible] SAN DIEGO [illegible] PAGE [illegible]

ArabellaSheraton
Grand Hotel
Frankfurt

Mr David Alameel
[illegible] Vanpark Rd
Dallas, TX 75229
USA

INFORMATION No. ArabellaSheraton Grand Hotel Frankfurt, 0?.11.00
Register No.

Arrival 01.11.00
Departure 0?.11.00
Room No 484
Page 5
Time 11:53

Mr David Alameel

Text	Date	Debit DM	Credit DM	Debit EUR	Credit EUR
Balance		6752.00 DM		3452.24 EUR	
Charges incl. VAT		6746.00 DM		3449.18 EUR	
Charges without VAT		6.00 DM		[illegible] EUR	
Net amount		5821.52 DM		2975.50 EUR	
VAT 16.00%		[illegible] DM	([illegible])	47[illegible] EUR	([illegible])

THE LUXURY COLLECTION

ArabellaSheraton Grand Hotel · Konrad-Adenauer-Straße 7 · D-60313 Frankfurt am Main
Telefon (0 69) 29 81-0 · Telefax (0 69) 29 81 [illegible] · Reservierung [illegible]
E-mail [illegible] · Internet: http://www.arabellasheraton.com
Arabella Hotel GmbH & Co. Betriebs KG, Sitz: München, Amtsgericht München HRA [illegible] · VAT-ID-No. DE 129 723 586
Komplementär: Arabella Hotelgesellschaft mbH, Sitz München, Amtsgericht München HRB 40441 · Geschäftsführer: Uwe Kaus
Bankverbindungen: Deutsche Bank AG Frankfurt, Konto-Nr. 2 129 815, BLZ 500 700 10, IBAN DE50 5007 0010 0212 9815 00
HypoVereinsbank Frankfurt, Konto-Nr. [illegible]

ArabellaSheraton
Grand Hotel
Frankfurt

Mr David Alameel
5020 Tanbark Rd
Dallas, TX 75229
USA

INFORMATION No. ArabellaSheraton Grand Hotel Frankfurt, 07.11.00
Register No.

Arrival 01.11.00 Room No 485 Cashier HD 1
Departure 07.11.00 Page 4 Time 11:53

Mr David Alameel

Text	Date	Debit DM	Credit DM	Debit EUR	Credit EUR
-s#2485 : Granini Orangensa Minibar	06.11.	9.50		4.86	
-s#2485 : Apollinaris 0.5					
Telephone	07.11.	57.75		29.53	
Telephone	07.11.	9.00		4.60	
Telephone	07.11.	150.00		76.69	
Telephone	07.11.	50.25		25.69	
Telephone	07.11.	1.50		0.77	
Telephone	07.11.	8.25		4.22	
Telephone	07.11.	4.50		2.30	
Breakfast Brasserie	07.11.	38.00		19.43	
Total		4560.00		2331.49	
Balance		4560.00 DM		2331.49 EUR	

Charges incl. VAT	4560.00 DM		2331.49 EUR
Net amount	3931.03 DM		2009.90 EUR
VAT 16.00%	628.97 DM	(4560.00)	321.59 EUR (2331.49)

THE LUXURY COLLECTION

ArabellaSheraton Grand Hotel · Konrad-Adenauer-Straße 7 · D-60313 Frankfurt am Main
Telefon (0 69) 29 81-0 · Telefax (0 69) 29 81-810 Zentrale / -813 Bankettbüro / -784 Buchhaltung / -811 Reservierung / (0 69) 66 33-12 72 Verkauf
E-mail: grandhotel.frankfurt@arabellasheraton.com / Internet: http://www.arabellasheraton.com
Bankverbindungen: Deutsche Bank AG Frankfurt, Konto Nr. 2 129 816, BLZ 500 700 10, IBAN DE50 5007 0010 0212 9816 00
HypoVereinsbank Frankfurt, Konto Nr. 4 270 275 864, BLZ 503 201 91

12/03/2000 22:00 6192264770 SAN DIEGO CAA INC PAGE 06

ArabellaSheraton
Grand Hotel
Frankfurt

Mr David Alameel
5020 Tanbark Rd
Dallas, TX 75229
USA

INFORMATION No. ArabellaSheraton Grand Hotel Frankfurt, 07.11.00
Register No

Arrival	01.11.00	Room No	492	Cashier	HD 1
Departure	07.11.00	Page	8	Time	11:54

Mr David Alameel

Text	Date	Debit DM	Credit DM	Debit EUR	Credit EUR
Balance		9882.00 DM		5062.59 EUR	
Charges incl. VAT		9848.00 DM		5035.20 EUR	
Charges without VAT		34.00 DM		17.38 EUR	
Net amount		8523.66 DM		4358.08 EUR	
VAT 16.00%		1358.34 DM	(9848.00)	694.51 EUR	(5035.20)

THE LUXURY COLLECTION

ArabellaSheraton Grand Hotel · Konrad-Adenauer-Straße 7 · D-60313 Frankfurt am Main
Telefon (0 69) 29 81-0 · Telefax (0 69) 29 81-810 Zentrale / -813 Bankettbüro / -784 Buchhaltung / -811 Reservierung / (0 69) 66 33-12 77 Verkauf
E-mail: grandhotel.frankfurt@arabellasheraton.com / Internet: http://www.arabellasheraton.com
Arabella Hotel GmbH & Co. Betriebs KG, Sitz: München, Amtsgericht München HRA 57 336 · VAT-ID-No. DE 129 723 886
Komplementär: Arabella Hotelgesellschaft mbH, Sitz München, Amtsgericht München HRB 40 447 · Geschäftsführer: Uwe Kaas
Bankverbindungen: Deutsche Bank AG Frankfurt, Konto-Nr. 2 129 815, BLZ 500 700 10, IBAN DE50 5007 0010 0212 9815 00
HypoVereinsbank Frankfurt, Konto-Nr. [illegible]

12/03/2000 22:08 6192254770 SAN DIEGO CAA INC PAGE 05

ArabellaSheraton
Grand Hotel
Frankfurt

Mr David Alameel
3020 Tanbark Rd
Dallas, TX 75229
USA

INFORMATION No. ArabellaSheraton Grand Hotel Frankfurt, 07.11.00
Register No.

Arrival	05.11.00	Room No	9978	Cashier	HD 1
Departure	08.11.00	Page	1	Time	11:54

Mr David Alameel

Text	Date	Debit DM	Credit DM	Debit EUR	Credit EUR
Dank[illegible] ->#9978 : CHECK #7446	06.11.	789.40		403.61	
Total		789.40		403.61	
Balance		789.40 DM		403.61 EUR	

Charges incl. VAT	789.40 DM		403.61 EUR	
Net amount	680.52 DM		347.94 EUR	
VAT 16.00%	[illegible].88 DM	(789.40)	55.67 EUR	(403.61)

THE LUXURY COLLECTION

ArabellaSheraton Grand Hotel [illegible]

Bankverbindungen: Deutsche Bank AG Frankfurt, Konto-Nr 2 129 815, BLZ 500 700 10, IBAN DE50 [illegible]
HypoVereinsbank Frankfurt, Konto-Nr [illegible]

FROM : PHONE NO. : 824504 824505 824506 Dec. 14 2000 01:13PM P1

EMBASSY OF THE ISLAMIC EMIRATE OF AFGHANISTAN
ISLAMABAD

دافغانستان داسلامی إمارت لوی سفارت
اسلام آباد

No :
Date :

گنه :
نیټه :

Dear Governor and PRESIDENT ELECT George W. Bush Jr.,

On behalf of the people, and the government of the Islamic Emirate of Afghanistan, I would like to take this opportunity to congratulate you as elected president of the great nation, the United State of America.

As you may well know, two great men, Ronald Reagan and George Bush Sr. stayed by our side in the fight against the communists for twelve years. It was the determination of the people of Afghanistan and these two great leaders that made the world see peace and communism obsolete. This struggle left 2 million Afghans martyred in combat and 1.5 million wounded. We will never forget what the Americans have done for us during our Jihad against the Red Army.

We assure you, all our differences can be solved through talks and mutual respect. We also assure we are not revolutionaries here to discomfort our neighbors or the region. We want to live in peace, with the world's community. We hope that at your earliest convenience you will take the time to come and visit our war-torn country and see what the Russians have done. We also believe you should know that they are our defeated enemy. They will do or say anything to discredit Afghans. The Russians through initiating draft resolutions of sanctions against Afghanistan wants to create distance between the people of Afghanistan and America.

At this time we would like to ask you to please stop the free flow of money to them, that we the people of Afghanistan deserve. We would like to again convey our thanks and gratefulness to President Bush Sr. for his dreams of rebuilding the great nation of Afghanistan. I am sure you are the most qualified American to be elected president. Please be fair, and hear our side of the story too. May God always lead you in the right direction.

Sincerely,

Mullah Abdul Salam Zaeef,
Ambassador of the Islamic Emirate of Afghanistan,
Islamabad

House No 8, Street No. 90, G-6/3, Islamabad Tel : 051-824505-6 Fax : 051-824504

Chapter 8: President Bush Dances the Texas Sidestep

Sometime before I left for Afghanistan in January 2001, Jack told me that I had an enemy in the Bush administration. That fact surprised me. "I have no idea who that could be," I told Jack. I tried my best to help George Bush get elected. I even asked my wife Karen to vote for Bush when she didn't want to." (At that time I had not yet become a U.S. citizen, so I couldn't vote.)

Jack explained that he had a hell of a time getting approval for my trip. For a reason that he couldn't determine, someone resented me on the Bush team, but for the time being, I would be allowed to continue working on the problem of bin Laden.

Toward the middle of January 2001, Jack, Mario and I met at Houston's Restaurant near Kirby Drive and the Southwest Freeway in Houston, Texas. Jack had good news! Higher ups had agreed to pay me $25,000 per trip to Afghanistan. Jack's news came just in time. I had no other property to mortgage. Since the payments exceeded my travel expenses, I assumed the overage was to help defray the costs of my last trip.

Jack asked me to apologize to the Afghan Government for the U.S. Government.

"Why?"

"The January meeting has to be delayed for a month or so."

"I will be more than happy to take the message." I really didn't want to smuggle any member of the Taliban into the Embassy in Pakistan alone while international sanctions were being enforced, so I encouraged Jack to go with me and to meet Jalil himself. "They are simple people. You will like him." But he didn't want to go. He requested that I make sure that the Taliban were still willing to "pick up the obstacle so we can both drive on the freeway."

"I'll be happy to go. Just let me know when."

"Toward the end of the month," he said.

Mid-January 19, 2001, more sanctions went into effect against Afghanistan. This time a ban on the members of the Taliban traveling outside their country was imposed. From that point forward, I had to work from inside of Afghanistan to keep the Taliban's Council Members in my camp.

Before leaving for Afghanistan, I asked Jack for a statement in writing. Its purpose was to explain to the Afghan Government that the U.S. was not ready to act and that our apology had the approval of the highest person in national security. Later he handed me a plain sheet of paper with the following typed in all capital letters:

A) THE QUESTIONS RAISED AT YOUR LAST MEETING WITH OUR REPRESENTATIVES HAVE GENERATED MUCH DISCUSSION. YOUR REQUEST FOR SPECIFICS IS UNDER CONSIDERATION, BUT THERE IS NO ANSWER FOR YOU AT THIS TIME. IT IS THEREFORE BEST TO POSTPONE THE PLANNED MEETING UNTIL THERE IS A DETAILED RESPONSE.

B) YOUR INTEREST IN A MEETING IN WASHINGTON HAS BEEN NOTED AND IS ALSO UNDER DISCUSSION, BUT A DECISION ON THIS HAS NOT BEEN MADE.

C) DO NOT CONSIDER THIS POSTPONEMENT TO INDICATE A LACK OF INTEREST IN FURTHER DISCUSSIONS, RATHER, UNDERSTAND IT TO MEAN THAT YOU HAVE RAISED IMPORTANT AND COMPLICATED

QUESTIONS WHICH ARE UNDER ACTIVE DISCUSSION WITH THE APPROPRIATE OFFICIALS.

Around the 30th of January 2001, I left the United States for Islamabad. When I reached Pakistan I tried to contact Paula, but she had been replaced by Angie Bryan. I met Angie in the Embassy cafeteria. We then met with Ambassador Milam and officials from the National Security Council. They requested that I go to Kandahar and apologize to the Taliban for the U.S. not being able to meet as planned. The National Security Council was interested in meeting with the Taliban, but it had to wait until the new administration took over. I asked for the new meeting date and they replied, "Mid-March."

"Okay."

From Islamabad I flew to Quetta, Pakistan which isn't that far from Kandahar. At the Pakistani border I was provided security by the Taliban and they picked me up and took me to Kandahar. Hours later I arrived at one of the Taliban's guesthouses which had been built by Unocal in 1998. I was exhausted from the grueling trip over deplorable roads. My clothes were caked in dust. At first glance, I could barely see my eyes because my face was covered in mud. I was desperate for a shower.

Members of the Afghan Government sent a welcoming message stating that they would visit later in the evening and we would have dinner. I rested for a few hours then someone kindly surprised me in my Spartan room with a pot of tea.

That evening four members of the Taliban's ruling Council of Ministers showed up at the door. A clean large square cloth called a *desterkhan* was promptly spread on the carpet. Upon it was placed an abundance of food. The five of us sat down to eat. The smell of the food drew me back to my childhood.

Being a *foreigner*, they provided me with a fork, spoon and knife. I apologized to them, "I know you are used to eating only with a spoon." But no one seemed to mind my lack of manners.

Everyone working in the guesthouse, including the chef, soon joined us for dinner. There were about twenty men sitting around the desterkhan. The Governor of Kandahar suddenly realized that one person was missing. He called out and asked, "Where is so-and-so's bodyguard?" The man came running and joined us. I noticed that one of the members of the Council was sitting next to another's bodyguard. The higher ranking one said, "Would you pass the chicken *qurma*. I think you guys are eating too much and I want chicken."

Seeing two men of such different ranks sitting and eating together carried me again to my childhood and visits with my relatives of the Jaji tribe. Everyone sat together with no distinction between the powerful and the poor. After dinner, tea was served and then everyone stood to leave.

I chose that awkward moment to say, "I have been appointed by the U.S. Government to come here to apologize to you for the meeting that was scheduled to occur sometime in January 2001. Because of the new President a few things have changed." I reassured everyone that they had reappointed me. I explained that it had not yet been made clear what my mission is, but they did say I was an envoy. (Earlier Jack told me how happy he was for me to have the title, but it was never mentioned again, so I assumed that I still owned it even with the change of administrations.) "You must understand that there was a recent change of government, but I was told by the Ambassador and people from National Security that everything on the table is a 'go,' but it will take a *Presidential Order.*"

I told them that because of the election, President Clinton decided not to take the initiative to act because it would have looked bad, like he was scared of complicating the Monica Lewinsky scandal (like the tail was wagging the dog again). Also Clinton's acting could possibly backfire on Mr. Gore. It could look like an election ploy.

"So they waited until the election was over and handed the whole thing to the new administration which promised that it would be one of their immediate goals and an important issue." With great confidence I reassured those present, "They will take action in no time."

Little did I know!

At dinner in Kandahar, I explained to some members of the ruling Council of Ministers of the Afghan Government, that I had learned from the media over the years that Republicans were serious about communism and terrorism, especially Mr. Bush Sr., the new president's father. I opened with a note of warning, "I don't know the Bushes personally, but I know about most of the new President's cabinet, especially Dick Cheney and Don Rumsfeld. There should be no lies to these people. They would love to have you removed. It's not a joke."

Someone at the dinner at the Kandahar guesthouse said that they knew of them, too. "We will do everything possible to help the U.S. We gave our word in Frankfurt to the U.S. delegation and we gave our word at the U.S. embassy to its top official in Islamabad, Pakistan. All people should have to do is shake hands and give their word to each other."

They understood perfectly that things like this could not be in writing. They accepted me with grace as a U.S. envoy and reaffirmed the Afghan Government's agreement to negotiate with me. They asked me to write a response to the new administration.

I said that a letter was not necessary. "I will tell them myself and I will make sure that the President, George W. Bush, gets the message through his people."

"We will negotiate and talk and we will help the new administration," one of them said. They reassured me that whenever the U.S. Government was ready to do something about bin Laden, the Taliban were ready to act. They would restrict Osama bin Laden's movements in Afghanistan and keep him close by. They promised that bin Laden would not move without permission from a top ranking Taliban member.

They then asked a second time for a listening device with which to spy on bin Laden while they held him under house arrest. Earlier I had asked my contacts in the U.S. for such a device, but they explained that it was too early for something like that. I promised representatives of the Afghan Government that on my next trip, or when they next came to visit the U.S. Ambassador in Islamabad, they would receive a device.

Again someone suggested planting it in bin Laden's bedroom, "That way he wouldn't be able to talk without the U.S. and Afghan Governments listening in." Someone again joked, "Which bedroom? Which wife?" I managed to laugh as if the joke was being told for the first time. I hoped that the joke would soon be at bin Laden's expense.

"It is a great opportunity to gather information from bin Laden's own lips. The U.S. will give me a device. They trust me," I assured them.

The members of the Council of Ministers were uneasy at first about the apology that I delivered, but I reassured them that it takes time for a large and diverse organization such as the government of the U.S. to make a decision. Since it was Bush Jr.'s first few weeks in the office, it would not look good for him to act aggressively so quickly.

The meeting ended at 3 a.m. We were happy that we had an opportunity to talk openly with each other. The demands of the U.S. were the same as those stated in Frankfurt. The offers made by the Afghans were also the same. They said again that they would gather all the top Al-Queda leaders in one spot near Kandahar and that the U.S. could either come in and kill them or send a Cruise Missile to wipe them out. Having experienced an American missile attack after the African embassy bombings, the Afghans assumed we would prefer the alternative.

Since I really didn't want to raise suspicions, I didn't ask where they would corral the Cockroach. There was no need for me to ask. That was knowledge for the intelligence community. My job was just to arrange meetings. Plus, I didn't want them to think I was a spy. They were comfortable with me not asking questions about his whereabouts. They understood I was only doing what was asked of me.

We called it a night. They were very happy about the new administration because they believed George W. Bush to be a man of experience and courage – a man of his word.

The next day I was asked if I wished to see Kandahar. They provided me with security and jeeps. I visited several sites in the city including one of Mullah Omar's pet building projects, a shopping mall. I also went outside Kandahar and visited with some of the local people. It was a pleasant trip. I hung around the city for two days.

As I left, the Taliban extended an invitation to U.S. officials to come and visit them. They reiterated, "They are always welcome in Kandahar." I promised I would deliver that message to the new administration in Washington. They reassured me that in spite of the sanctions, they could sneak anyone into the country and they promised to protect them with their blood and their honor. Of course I made it clear that any American breaking U.S. and U.N. sanctions would have to have special permission from President Bush.

I reported back to U.S. Ambassador Milam and Ron the CIA Station Chief in Islamabad. They were very glad to hear that I was back in one piece and that nothing had happened. I showed photos of my trip and told them that, as requested, the Taliban would meet with U.S. officials in mid-March.

I left Islamabad on February 9, 2001, and spent a few days with my business partners in Frankfurt. I left Kandahar proud of what I had accomplished for the U.S. Government.

A few days after returning to Texas, I met Jack and Mario at the Denny's located at the Southwest Freeway near Weslayan in Houston. I told Jack about everything that had occurred during my trip. He had not been informed about my progress while I was away.

He expressed dismay over the fact that he had tried to get in touch with officials in Islamabad, but they would not give him any information about my trip. I told Jack that the American Ambassador to Pakistan had agreed to meet with the Taliban in March 2001, even though U.S. and U.N. law prevented their representative from leaving the country.

At a later meeting, I explained to Jack that I had trouble with the people at the embassy in Islamabad. In Kandahar, members of the Taliban and I discussed the issue of drugs which had seemed important to the people in the State Department. At the embassy, I explained that the Taliban had agreed to eradicate every poppy they could find. The Taliban's Director of their drug enforcement agency even visited with me and expressed his government's willingness to act.

"What did he look like," Jack asked.

"About 6'3", cross-eyed, and 220 lbs. He told me what I already knew, that a decree had been issued by Mullah Omar for the eradication of poppies. They had eradicated as much as they could in the last month and a half of the growing season. I had been very impressed with what they had done in so short a time. I promised that when I took this news back to the U.S., they would be very glad to hear it and would be delighted to help. Then the Taliban's drug officer asked me, 'Will this make the Americans happy?"

"That's really too much for me to answer," I said. It was important back in 1998 and I was sure that it was still true; no one had told me any different. I explained to the Taliban's drug officer that the step they were taking was a giant step for humanity. Being tied to drugs was not in the interest of Afghanistan, it wasn't in the interest of the Taliban, and it sure wasn't in the interest of religious men.

I told Jack that the Afghan drug officer then asked to meet with someone from the U.S. Drug Enforcement Agency. "Jack, I told the Afghan drug officer that I would be delighted to arrange that. It only goes to show you how naive I am. I assumed that when I returned to the embassy everyone would be excited and would immediately respond and help eradicate the poppies. But when I got to the embassy and talked to Ambassador Milam, he got upset with me and said, 'This is not what we asked you to do. You are not assigned to get involved in the drug issue.' "

"Mr. Ambassador, I can do quite a few things simultaneously," I told him. "You have to trust me."

"No! We don't want you to touch that issue."

"I won't let go of it. I have already asked a Taliban official to meet with someone here at the embassy from our Drug Enforcement Agency. I'm sure we must have someone here. Milam said there would be no meeting between the Afghan Drug Enforcement Director and anybody from our Drug Enforcement Agency." I told Jack that I was really disgusted with the response I got.

"Let me clarify a few things for you, Kabir. I have been going through hell for you since we last met. Everything was fine when Clinton was in office, but now – Kabir, I don't know who you know at the National Security Council, but there is animosity towards you; it's unbelievable. I'm using everything I've got and I'm barely able to keep you inside the loop."

"Excuse me, why are you doing that? If they don't want me – Wait a minute, are you telling me now that I have enemies at the national security level?" The whole concept of having highly placed enemies was ludicrous.

Then I remembered that Ambassador Milam had told me that Zalmay Khalilzad, an Afghan who had joined the U.S. Government as an interpreter and who had worked in some capacity for Unocal, was now an assistant to President Bush's National Security Council and an advisor to the Pentagon. Could he be the problem? I hadn't seen him since he checked out my translation skills in the early 1980's, but I knew he knew me.

Jack said, "Nevertheless, again, let me clarify things. You are currently involved in the drug issue which we were working on in early 2000. We don't want you to have anything to do with that issue now. It can be resolved later."

"No, it is already resolved. The Taliban stopped it and Mullah Omar issued a decree."

"No, they have a lot of drugs. They just want to hike up the price," Jack said in a cynical tone.

"That isn't the truth," I argued. "The Taliban government has burned the drugs and they have closed down the heroin factories. They are eradicating the poppies. They are beating the people who are trying to manufacture heroin. They put sellers on the backs of donkeys, made them face the beast's tail and ride them through town. Sometimes they covered their faces with tar and the houses of landowners caught with drugs are burned down."

"This is not what we want you to do. You have a mission to complete," Jack said.

"Okay, Jack, then do me a favor. In March when we have the appointment between the Ambassador in Islamabad and the Afghans, please have somebody from the DEA there. Or can I meet with someone in Houston?"

"No way," Jack said. "You are already meeting and talking to too many people. But let me ask you another question, Khabir. I read in the national security report of your last trip that Ambassador Milam is fussing and asking a lot of questions about you."

"What do you mean?"

"Did you tell Ambassador Milam who you are?"

"No, I didn't tell him much, but I did let him know that I was there on behalf of the U.S. Government to meet with the Taliban."

"Does anyone else know?"

"Yes. Zaeef, the Afghan Ambassador to Pakistan. He is a friend of mine. I saw him after I returned from Kandahar because he provided me with transportation from Quetta to Kandahar. He came and visited with me and I thanked him on behalf of the U.S. Government. I explained to him that

I had been appointed Envoy to the Taliban and I wanted to thank him for the help that he provided."

"Oh my God, did you tell Zaeef that?"

"Yes."

Jack said, "Zaeef and Ambassador Milam met sometime in February 2001. That is when Zaeef told him who you were and the ambassador went nuts. He asked how come he was not informed about your appointment as an envoy."

"That is not really my problem. That is your problem. You should have informed him," I replied.

"No, we want to keep this covert."

"Why covert? He is our ambassador."

"You keep putting me on the spot," Jack said.

"Well, this is the only way I am willing to operate. If the right hand doesn't know what the left hand is doing, it creates problems."

"There aren't going to be any more meetings between so many governmental agencies." Jack said emphatically. "This is a covert operation and those are my orders. I will see what I can do to keep you involved."

"Try to. If you can't, don't worry about it. This is my duty. You need me for the delivery of the Cockroach. It isn't going to happen without me. You know it and everyone in the U.S. Government knows it. I am putting my life on the line for you guys to make this thing with bin Laden happen."

Jack warned me one last time to stay away from the drug issue. "I will try, but I think the issue will come up big time when the Afghan officials and the U.S. Ambassador meet." Jack said fine, but warned me again to stay away from the drug issue.

When the meeting ended I didn't really know where I stood with representatives of my government. I assumed that the part about having an enemy in the National Security Council was just talk by Jack to get me to bend to his will. Later, I found out that Jack did go through a lot to get me back into the process. I was about to be kicked out because they thought I had a big mouth and talked too much.

But I warned everyone up front that I did; it's part of my personality. If I operated the way they wanted me to, I would mess up and get into a lot of trouble. There is a saying in Afghanistan that a big mouth can be walls to protect you or it can be a force of destruction. I always saw my talkativeness as a protective wall and I was too old to change. This old dog didn't want to learn any new tricks, especially tricks that called for me to sit down and stop barking.

Jack warned me that because of government policy, the March meeting was the last one that I'd ever attend. "We want you to step back, but we will keep you informed."

Toward the first week of March 2001, I again met Mario and Jack, and again Jack told me that he had a hellacious time getting me approved for the meeting between the Taliban and the U.S. Ambassador in Islamabad. He warned me again and again that this was the last meeting that I would attend because from that point forward it was going to be a covert operation. I asked him what was going on, but he didn't know. All he knew was some guy in power hated me.

"Zalmay Khalilzad?"

"Yes." Jack hung his head as if he didn't wish to discuss it.

"Is there any way you can make an appointment for me so I can meet the people in Washington, look them in the face and talk eye to eye?" I asked.

"You should be thankful that you are still here and that I'm meeting with you. Those guys don't want to see you. They just want to be rid of you as fast as possible."

"Okay," I laughed, "more power to them. They don't need me, I don't need them," I said sounding like a childish brat, but I almost meant it. I would have had my fill long ago if it weren't for the business possibilities hanging over Afghanistan like ripe fruit begging to be picked from the trees. Then the thought crossed my mind, "Maybe they want to pluck the opportunities first." I smiled. I knew they couldn't do that without me – not without a war.

With my Government's begrudging permission, Jack, Mario and I soon met again. At this time, I was getting calls from Kandahar almost daily. I was sure that my phone was tapped, but I didn't care. I wanted U.S. officials to know that nothing untoward was occurring on my part.

One of the calls I received was from the Mullah Esa, the Afghan Minister of Mining and Industry. He congratulated me. My oil contracts were finally official. Without my knowledge, Mullah Omar had issued an order which said that I did not have to go through the full approval process. The oil fields in the north of Afghanistan were mine.

"Are you kidding me? You were giving me such a hard time at the ministry."

"It was an order from Mullah Omar. I can no longer give you a hard time as Minister of Oil and Industry," Esa said.

"I guess I did it, didn't I?"

"Oh yes! How did you get Mullah Omar to sign an order?" he asked. "No one in the Council of Ministers – no one in authority believes what has happened. Everyone thinks you have a very close tie to Mullah Omar that you don't wish to divulge."

"No, I promise you I have not met the man. But someday, when I really do explore the oil and gas fields of Afghanistan, I will be more than happy to meet with him since he is the Amir of Afghanistan."

I met Jack and Mario and shared my good fortune. "You must inform the proper officials because I don't want to do any kind of business without the U.S. Government's knowledge."

"Kabir, I want to assure you that once you go to Islamabad and bring the Taliban back to the table, all the big companies like Unocal and Halliburton will come to you. You don't have to go anywhere."

I said, "I have contacted some small businessmen here in Texas and they are willing to invest in a refinery, but I can't do any business because of the Cockroach. I am counting on you to do something about him. Let's go get him! Let's finish the whole thing once and for all!"

This became my mantra. The Taliban and I both had every reason to want bin Laden out of Afghanistan. Once he was out, we both would be bathing in oil. Jack was very happy for me. Life is good!

Sometime thereafter, I received a call from Kandahar telling me that from now on I needed to talk in code. From that date forward, the Cockroach would be known as the *Snake* to the ranking members of the Taliban with whom I communicated. I had to smile. Bin Laden had been promoted from Cockroach to Snake by the Taliban.

The caller explained that close to the first week in March 2001, the Snake had been placed under house arrest. The Afghans had taken all of his communication equipment away from him and had ordered him and his men to stick around the immediate area. I figured that my government probably knew exactly where he was in Kandahar because of our satellites.

"He is here with us. We are keeping a close eye on him," I was informed by a ranking member of the Afghan Government. Again they requested listening devices so they could track what bin Laden said to those around him.

I apologized and said that the people in the embassy were probably working on it now.

Later I explained to Jack and Mario that I had told U.S. authorities at the Embassy in February about the Taliban's request for bugs. "For God's sake, they are asking for listening devices, Jack. Please don't send me away empty handed." Then I asked, "Do you know where bin Laden is?"

Jack smiled, laughed and said, "Yeah, it's true. He's under house arrest." Then he pleaded with me, "I've put my career on the line because nobody in Washington believes that you can bring the Taliban to the U.S. Embassy because of all the sanctions and because the Taliban officials coming to the embassy are wanted men. How the hell are you going to sneak them into Pakistan? Everyone at the border of Pakistan and Afghanistan knows them by sight."

"Don't worry about it. You do your job, I'll do mine." Jack called me later and said that he had secured approval for me to go to Afghanistan "for once and for all."

Jack and I met at the La Madeleine coffee shop on Kirby in Houston's Rice Village. This time Jack had Steve Gentry, the director of Houston's FBI in tow. Gentry was the one who had given me the name and address of his friend, Mike Morris, the FBI's Legal Attaché at the Embassy in Islamabad, back when all this began. I thanked Gentry for introducing me to Mr. Morris and told him that I hadn't let him down. We talked about all that had happened since we first met.

Worried about my wellbeing, Gentry kindly reminded me that there was a sanction on any type of traveling by the Taliban outside their own borders. They could not travel unless it was a human emergency or with the approval of the U.N. Security Council. I explained to him that the Taliban had good connections with the Pakistan authorities. I was told that they traveled almost freely with U.N. sanctions or without them. Then I raised the issue of drugs with Steve. "The Taliban are waiting for an answer about the drug issue."

Gentry said that there is no way that he could really get someone from the DEA office to meet with me on such short notice before my trip back to Afghanistan, but he would arrange a meeting between the Afghan director of their drug enforcement agency and someone from the American Embassy in Pakistan who was working on the same issues. He then fell into lockstep with government policy and said, "This is not what we asked you to do."

"I am stuck with the drug issue now whether you like it or not."

"Okay, we will see what we can do."

Jack looked pale that day. We decided to meet in a few days and he would bring $25,000 to cover my and the

Taliban's travel expenses and the costs of smuggling leading members of the Taliban into Islamabad.

We met a few days later. Jack looked forlorn – clearly not the Jack I had dealt with in the past. I asked him if he had gone through a lot for my sake.

"You're fucking right!" He handed me a brown bag with twenty five thousand dollars, and said, "Please, Kabir. If it's not possible for the Taliban to get to the embassy, don't go."

"Jack, these people are anxious to go to Islamabad. I will go straight to Kandahar and see them on their way. I will arrange everything. Everybody in the area has a beard, everybody has a turban. They'll blend in. I will sneak them into Pakistan."

"Do you have some kind of arrangement?"

"They don't even consider Pakistani authorities a threat or a challenge. They will go through the border without any hesitation – without any problem."

Jack admitted that there was another problem: if anybody found out that the Taliban crossed the border, both Pakistan and the United States would be in trouble. It would be particularly bad for the U.S. since we put the first sanctions on the Taliban and were the ones requesting the international sanctions.

"We really are the ones breaking the law."

"Don't worry. I am not going to mention this to the Taliban."

"I hope nobody else will."

"Please don't think the Pakistanis are stupid enough to say anything about it," I said. It would be a liability to Pakistan and to Afghanistan. You gave me this chance. Don't worry, I won't let you down. How about, I promise to pay the twenty five thousand back if I fail to bring the Afghan officials to the embassy. Does that make you feel better?"

"Yes, even if you can only pay back half of it. I am getting all kinds of crap because I believe in you, but people in Washington are telling me that you are just bullshitting."

"You didn't tell them about my last trip to Frankfurt? How the Taliban came to negotiate bin Laden's delivery? And how you sent me back as a messenger to apologize for not acting on their offer?"

"Yeah, but you know how people can be," Jack replied.

"Of course, I understand that. But don't worry, let me go." As we parted Jack wished me good luck. He even offered to take me to the airport, but I turned him down. I asked one last time if he had put in a request for listening devices.

"Yes, you go to Islamabad. You meet with the people there and they will arrange everything."

I left Houston for Pakistan on the 15th or 16th of March 2001, I forget which. I called in at the American Embassy. My contact was Angie Bryan. She escorted me into the Ambassador's office. People from the National Security Agency were present.

I explained that I was leaving the next day for Kandahar and going straight to the Taliban. It would take about 24 hours to get there, and once there, after completing my business, I would turn around and come straight back. We made an appointment at the American Embassy for the 21st of March, a day I will never forget because it was the first day of the Afghan New Year.

My two bodyguards and I left for Kandahar. I was taken by the Afghan Government's diplomatic car to the Afghan-Pakistan border where I met its government's reps. Two jeeps waited to whisk me straight to Kandahar.

My escort on these trips to Kandahar was always the Taliban Military Attaché Mullah Qadir. Prominent in the Afghan Government, the Pakistan authorities allowed him to travel freely in and out of their country. It was his responsibility to make sure that my travel to and from Kandahar was safe. Once finally there, I needed to rest from my journey, but Taliban officials kept coming by to see me. They wanted to talk to me and I needed to talk to them.

During my last trip I had met Akhtar Mohammad Osmani, Deputy Amir and Commander of the Kandahar Corps. While getting ready for this trip, he slipped my mind. I had bought each of the people I was about to meet a small gift, but I forgot about Osmani.

I had a pen in my pocket that had been given to my brother Omar. I gave it to him. He was very grateful for my small gift from a pharmaceutical company. But I was ashamed to hand it to him. Prominently displayed on the pen was a company logo and a word signifying a prominent brand of medication for erectile dysfunction emblazoned down its length which caused my embarrassment. Luckily he wasn't familiar with English lettering.

After everyone left, Osmani and I talked at length. At one point I asked him about the *loya jerga* that elected Mullah Omar Amir. He said that clerics, elders, mullah's and tribal chiefs, rich and poor, came by donkeys, horses, bicycles, air, bus, cars and on foot, probably over fifteen hundred in all, to Kandahar to approve Mullah Omar as the Amir of Afghanistan."

"Who will be in charge if something happens to him?" I asked.

"Me," Osmani replied.

"I didn't know."

"Well, I am Mullah Omar's deputy." Apparently Omar had appointed him deputy the year before. "If anything happens to Mullah Omar, God forbid!, I will be the next Amir."

Osmani was younger than me – probably somewhere between 32 and 34 in age. A charismatic man, he usually wore a smile prominently displayed on his tan face. He flashed it and said, "Would you like to meet him?"

"Not yet. But thank you for the offer. I am sure you could arrange it."

"Yes, very easily." He glanced down at his Walkie Talkie. "He is only a call away."

I was amused at the thought of chatting with Mullah Omar. Talking with him was nothing that I was really interested in doing, no matter what my government would have wanted. I asked Osmani how the Taliban came into power.

He explained that during the civil wars, somewhere in Kandahar, Mullah Omar, Mullah Jalil, and Mullah Hassan were in a mosque when a group of people came yelling and screaming for help from the mullahs staying there. They said, "What kind of mullahs are you? People are being raped, boys and girls have been kidnaped and you guys don't do anything but eat and enjoy your life inside the mosque."

Mullah Omar asked him what was wrong. The man told him that his daughter and a neighbor's daughter had been kidnaped. They were taken to one of the members of the War Lord Rabbani's faction where they had been raped. The man plead with the mullahs that nothing was being done.

Mullah Omar looked at Jalil and Hassan. He asked if they were ready to do something about it and they said they were. Jalil asked about ten younger mullahs to join them. Osmani was among the ten, as was Zaeef. They borrowed guns from local tribesmen and were soon joined by the local people.

After the mullahs screamed "*Allah Akbar!*" (God is great!), they started shooting War Lord Rabanni's men. They shot three or four men at the gate of the compound. Others nearby began to panic and run. Everybody started screaming, "The mullahs are coming!" Within an hour, nothing was left in the camp except a bunch of dead bodies and several dozen guns lying around. I marveled at the thought of religious men carrying guns and killing people.

Then Osamni said, of this group of fighting mullahs, Omar was the only one who knew how to drive. During their attempt to escape the charging mullahs, Rabanni's men left a tank behind. Mullah Omar got into the tank and managed somehow to turn it on. Since it sat in a big empty field, there was really nothing for him to run over by accident, so he drove the tank back and forth across the field getting the feel of it.

In the meantime, the religious men took the guns abandoned by the retreating men and called upon other mosques to send their mullahs and taliban out to help. Eventually they became a force of about a hundred men who chased War Lord Rabanni's men to the next town while Omar drove the tank there. There they found the commander who had ordered the kidnappings and hung him from the barrel of the tank. He hung there for four or five days.

At some point, the mullahs decided to go to the next town to find other thugs that were committing similar crimes and atrocities. Each time they entered a city, the thugs were gone and arms and ammunition lay about, so they took them. Men from every mosque and school, and others, down to the mothers in their homes, soon joined them because the band of armed mullahs were preferable to the greedy, corrupt War Lords.

"They were vigilantes like in old Western movies," I thought and then asked, "Did you have any kind of logistical problems?"

Osamni said, "Everywhere we went in the rural areas, people greeted us with open arms. We really didn't need to carry food because the people fed us. That is how the movement started.

Then suddenly we had volunteers, too many of them, coming to help us from everywhere. We didn't have enough weapons; we didn't have enough ammunition; we didn't have enough food. We asked the Pakistani government for help, but they hesitated to help us. We contacted the U.S. Government. An official came and talked to some of the Taliban. He said they would offer help if we did something about the drug trafficking between the cities of Quetta and Kandahar. We agreed."

"The U.S. helped a little through its Pakistani friends and we took over the road from Kandahar all the way to the border of Pakistan. Within a month, there was no trafficking of any kind. This gained us the trust of the United States and Pakistan. People started taking us seriously. Then we took over the city of Kandahar."

"We hardly fought. All we did was go into a town and say, 'Surrender and drop your weapons!' We gave everyone forty-eight hours to turn in their weapons at the mosque nearest their home. If we found any guns after forty-eight hours, the punishment was twenty hard lashes in public. You wouldn't believe how many people turned over their weapons. We had so many there weren't enough volunteer soldiers to carry them off. We didn't have any trucks to haul them, so we started renting trucks from private people or people would volunteer to help move them. We tried to store them in different areas around Kandahar. We decided to make an example of Kandahar by making it the most peaceful city in Afghanistan. Then, we hoped, others would follow our example."

"For two years that's what we did – do our best to make sure that nobody was robbed, killed, tortured, or raped in Kandahar. That's when people started trusting us. Within two to three years we gained the trust of the locals and the tribal people."

It was interesting to hear the story of the Taliban's beginnings from their point of view. I had heard other's guesses, but this was the first time it came from someone who was there. I was left with questions. I wondered about the contribution of Pakistan's ISI (intelligence service) to the movement, and I noticed that Osamni left out the bit about the Taliban led blood bath in Mazar-e-Sharif. That explanation would have to wait for another day, when we trusted each other more.

Before leaving at 12:30 a.m., Osmani joked that Mullah Torabi was coming to see me in the morning. "Isn't he supposed to be in Kabul? Why is he coming to visit me?" I whined. At the high, nasal tone of my voice, we both started laughing. Torabi was the Minister of Vice and Virtue. I had hoped that I hadn't been in the country long enough to draw Torabi's attention. But – there was my refusal to grow a beard!

Osmani leaned over and grinned at my look of distress, "We took your complaint, that he was personally lashing people on the streets, very seriously. We went to Mullah Omar and told him that the Vice and Virtue Police were too forceful; people are starting to hate us because of them." Osmani smiled at me, but I wasn't sure what that smile meant.

"Last December Mullah Omar warned the ministry to stop beating people on the spot. He warned them, one more complaint and the minister would be summoned to Kandahar. Sometime in February 2001, Mullah Omar called Torabi to Kandahar, gave him a tongue lashing and ordered him to sit at home for the next three months."

Apparently Torabi had been ordered to relax his zealous distribution of the law (a true understatement) and to stop hitting people in public. Of course Islam calls for public punishment, but that should be rendered by a judge. Mullah Omar told Torabi, "The job of the Ministry of Vice and Virtue is to implement the law and take offenders to the nearest police station so they can be put before a judge. If the judge decides that they require public punishment, then so be it."

It was a start. Hitting people in the streets, for whatever reason, had to stop. I nodded my approval, but realized that it would take years of public relations work to change the negative worldwide images that the Taliban had created.

"I hope this man never makes an issue out of my not having a beard."

"Mr. Mohabbat, trust me, you will be the last person that he will ever say anything to about not having a beard. You do whatever you want. You are our guest."

I asked my bodyguard to wake me at seven o'clock. "I need time to shower and shave, but mostly I need time to get my pants on before Mr. Torabi arrived for breakfast." I could tell by the narrowing of my bodyguard's eyes that he didn't like Torabi all that much either.

The next morning, Land Cruisers and pickup trucks suddenly appeared in front of the guesthouse. I invited everyone inside. After being seated, I explained that the American government had asked me to come and talk to them.

First, I thanked everyone there for the eradication of the poppies. "This will have a big effect in Europe and in America. It will affect the whole world and people will begin acknowledging the fact that you are doing something positive. But you have work yet to do. You need to work to understand the rest of the world."

They agreed that after more time passed, they would learn these things, but they were still too young a country. Their prime concern was security inside their war-torn borders.

"But no one will come to visit or do business with this country because it has a bad reputation with foreigners," I explained.

Surprisingly enough, foreigners were one of their main concerns. People like bin Laden, people who they couldn't control, were coming into the country. They wanted to go back to square one and control everything within their own borders. As the Afghan Government gradually regained control of all aspects of the nation's life then they would allow other influences to creep back in, but right then their country was still in a state of war. Mostly they weren't able to control their northeastern border which was under the control of the Northern Alliance.

I barely touched on the subject of Osama bin Laden. I was told by my contacts in the Taliban that I should not talk too much about him, to let them bring up the issue of bin Laden naturally. Eventually they did. When they brought it up, I agreed that he was a big problem.

"Let's find him a third country to go to. Let's talk to some of the Arab nations about him. He was in Afghanistan for many years and you welcomed him, now it is time for him to go somewhere else." They laughed at my statement.

One of them said, "We have asked him many times to leave, but all he does is ask us, 'Where do you want me to go?' He has no place in the world that will take him. We heard it on the radio. Even the voice of America says that no country in the world was going to accept this man."

I avoided appearing too interested in bin Laden by saying, "That really is not my concern. You do what you have to do."

At that moment, the cook came in and told us that breakfast was ready. We moved to the next room. On the floor was spread a desterkhan and on it was a wonderful breakfast. My mouth watered at the sight of so much food. While traveling, meals were becoming few and far between. We sat cross legged on the floor and began eating.

I explained to the men that soon I must return to Pakistan. "I am leaving for Quetta today. Tomorrow I have a flight to catch." They were surprised.

"Why don't you stay a little longer?"

"I have other things to do. Hopefully next time I come back to Kandahar, I can spend more time with you." We lingered over breakfast talking about the pipeline and the drug issue.

We established a date and time for them to show up in Islamabad to meet with officials at the American Embassy. I apologized for the inconvenience of having to smuggle them into Pakistan. I understood that the whole process was a lot of trouble, but it was for the best. "You have to take chances to make peace in the world," was the only remark one of them made.

I left Kandahar walking on air. I felt proud of what I had accomplished. I was trusted by the new leaders of my old country and by the new leaders of my new country, well, partially trusted, anyway. The Snake would soon be delivered. My partners and I would soon be rich. Afghanistan would soon have all the oil it needed. Life is good!

The flight from Quetta, Pakistan to Islamabad takes about an hour and a half. After landing, I went directly to the American Embassy and met again with Angie Bryan. I told her that the Taliban would be here on the 20th and available for a meeting on the evening of the 21st. She was very happy. "We expect you at about 7:00 p.m. Should we give them dinner?"

"No, they are just coming for tea. They have issues they want to discuss."

On the March 20, 2001, at about 7:00 a.m., I received a call from Quetta. The Afghan delegation had arrived in Pakistan. Mullah Abdul Jalil, Deputy Minister of Foreign Affairs, was at the airport awaiting a flight to Islamabad and should be in town around ten. So much for international sanctions!

Because flight schedules are unpredictable in that part of the world, I rushed to the airport at about 9:00 a.m. in case he arrived early. My bodyguard, several Taliban officials, and I waited anxiously for his arrival. Eventually we saw Jalil disembark from an airplane. We swooped him away to the Marriott Hotel.

He looked very tired. He had ridden all night from Kandahar to the small border town of Spin Boldak in Afghanistan. There he got out of the car and on a side road walked a mile around the border checkpoints. Once inside Pakistan, a waiting car swept him away to the airport where he caught the flight to Islamabad.

At the Marriott, he checked into his room and went straight to sleep. I woke him at 5:00 p.m. and by 7:00 we were on the road to the U.S. Embassy. As soon as we arrived at the embassy's heavy gates, they swung open and we slowly drove towards the Ambassador's residence.

Angie Bryan and the Ambassador were waiting on the doorsteps. We were received with hospitality. Jalil asked me what happened to the lady who had been there before, and I said Paula Thiede had been sent back to the United States. Her duty assignment had changed. He asked why women were always assigned to their discussions. "Are they sent as a provocation?" he asked in hushed tones. "You know we are shy around women? Are they trying to slow down our talks?"

I asked him to be tolerant.

He replied, "Of course."

And so began the talks between the U.S. and the Taliban on March 21, 2001. The Ambassador's butler entered and served tea. Then the ambassador excused himself saying that he needed to talk to me in private for just for a minute. We went into the next room. "Kabir, I have some bad news."

"What is that Mr. Ambassador?"

"I have orders that everything must be delayed. We are not ready to act."

"Mr. Ambassador, are you kidding me? If you had told me that before I left for Kandahar, I wouldn't have gone."

"Kabir. That is the message that I received from D.C. *today*."

"For god's sake, what are you going to tell Jalil?" I asked.

The Ambassador responded, "Everything is a go, all we need is another month."

I had gone through enormous obstacles, broken U.S. and international laws to bring an important representative of the Afghan Government to the embassy. The Taliban had bin Laden in Kandahar under house arrest and my government couldn't make the decision to either pick him up – or shoot him – or hit him with a missile – or serve him tea. What was I supposed to tell the representative of the Afghan Government waiting in the next room?

While in Kandahar, they asked me whether the Americans were sincere and wanted action. I assured them they we were and did, but I was beginning to have doubts. Embarrassment consumed me. I returned to the room. Everyone was sitting around chatting and drinking tea. I sat there trying to pretend that the delivery of bin Laden wasn't a hideous monster that the U.S. Government was trying to ignore.

Jalil asked me to mention the electronic devices that they needed to plant in bin Laden's residence. "Do we have anything ready for them to take back so they can monitor his movement – what he is saying – what he is doing?" I asked, my voice a little too high pitched. I was afraid to hear the answer.

Then Ron, the CIA's Station Chief, apologized and said that they weren't ready. "We are working on it, but we need approval from a top official of the U.S. Government."

The Taliban's rep asked, "Are you not here with the full authority needed to negotiate with us? I am here on full authority to negotiate with you. What is the use of the meeting that we are having right now if you are not in charge of what you are doing? Are we here to get this man or are you playing a game with us? Be straight forward!"

As I understood my responsibility, it was getting the U.S. and the Taliban to talk to each other. Any opinion that I might hold wasn't important. It was plain to see that the Afghan was agitated. He asked the American officials, "Why all the procrastination? We asked you for a listening device and now you won't deliver."

Jalil knew the American officials mistrusted their word and their judgment. With bugs in bin Laden's house, the Taliban wouldn't have to report to the Americans. Everyone could hear for themselves everything that bin Laden said. It would give everyone involved direct access to intelligence information about al-Qaida and its leader.

I finally disclosed to the Taliban that the U.S. wasn't ready to pick up bin Laden and they were asking for more time.

"What kind of time do you need? Could we just agree on a date? Just give us some idea! What is your plan? You must have a plan!?! Are *you* going to capture the man alive? Or, are *we* going to fight him for you? Or, are *you* going to hit him with a Cruise Missile? We have given you his hand, sir, what are you going to do with it?"

Under the circumstances, the Ambassador acted as professionally as he could. He asked the Taliban rep for a few minutes to discuss this with his colleagues. The mullah agreed to wait.

After the private meeting, Ambassador Milam explained to those gathered at the embassy that if he was in charge – or if he had been allowed any kind of discretionary power – he would have gotten to the bottom of this issue and they would have a date. But he wasn't in charge. I wondered whether his admission was a barb aimed at those listening to and recording our conversation.

I explained to Jalil that for an issue of this magnitude, the decision couldn't be made by one man. "They have to call for a national security meeting and national security consists of many departments of the U.S. Government. Not unlike the Afghan Government, there are people who may oppose either bin Laden's assassination or his surrender. Each department has its own opinion and sometimes it takes weeks or months to reach a decision."

Eventually the meeting ended. Jalil was smuggled back into Afghanistan with the understanding that he would be contacted soon. How long they could hold bin Laden under house arrest near Kandahar was anyone's guess.

ABS.: AM PROJEKT CONSULTING; 497119979456; 27-FEB-01 15:53; SEITE 2/
05/01/2001 14:59 +49-711-8091311 RA.THEUMER U.KOL. 01/03

Theumer, Wieland & Weisenburger
Anwaltskanzlei

Anwaltskanzlei · Dornierstraße 17 · 70469 Stuttgart

strictly confidential
Mr Michael Albrecht
c/o AM-Project Consulting GmbH
Talstr. 41
70176 Stuttgart

Rechtsanwälte
Frank Theumer
Rainer Wieland, MdEP
Christof Weisenburger
Steffen Konstantinow
Markus Ch. Nohring
Achim Wichtermann
Michael Maier
Michael Speiser

Dornierstraße 17
70469 Stuttgart

Tel. 0711/809131-0
Fax 0711/809131-21

05.01.2001 / CW
Az.: 09895/01 5 / 1
Durchw. 0711/809131-11
Sek. Fr. Hahn

AM-Projekt ./. consultation

Dear Mr Albrecht,

we refer to our meetings dated the 22nd of December 2000 and the 03rd of January 2001.

You provided us with a copy of the contractual agreement between the Ministry of Electrical Energy (MEE), Kabul/Afghanistan and BBC Brown Boveri and Co. Ltd. (BBC), Baden/Switzerland from the 23rd of May 1985 and annex documents.

Concerning this contract you informed us that your mandator, the MEE considers that the mutual obligations based on the contract are not completly fulfilled.

In accordance to our first meeting we started a brief

In ständiger
Kooperation mit
Anwaltskanzlei:
Kruger, Schmidt & Doderer
Wilhelmstraße 23
74072 Heilbronn
Tel. 07131/6797-20
Fax 07131/6797-25

Rechtsanwälte
Dr. jur. Martin Kruger
Felix Schmidt
Tamara Doderer
Simone Seethaler
Silke Hohenstein

Bankverbindung: Gerlinger Bank eG, Kto.-Nr. 53 000 035, BLZ 600 695 56
Bankverbindung: Baden-Württembergische Bank AG, Kto.-Nr. 2101988000, BLZ 600 200 30

ABS.: AW PROJEKT CONSULTING; 497119979456; 27-FEB-01 15:54; SEITE 4/
05/01/2001 14:59 +49-711-80913171 RA.THEUMER U.KOL. S. 02/03

- 2 -

Theumer, Wieland & Weisenburger
Anwaltskanzlei

check of the legal situation. This brief check which is now completed can, of course, not substitute a detailed examination of the whole matter, both on the legal side and on the real state of the facility which is to be delivered by SBC.

Such an examination is necessary as well to prepare a meeting with SBC for a first exchange of opinions and possible concrete negociations how the parties intend to finish that project properly.

We understand that MEE is not interested to bring that case to the court or to another deciding body. But even an agreement offside any court which includes posibly further common projects needs the mentioned examination.

We are ready to prepare the legal base in detail and the resulting alternatives to act. We are ready as well to accompany your mandator in the negotiations and contribute with the best of our knowledge to a succesful result.

We allow us to mention that the three necessary steps (examination, negotiations and formulating an agreement) need extensive expenditures of knowledge and time.

Granted for now that the legal interest which corresponds with the amount of money which is argued by the parties is SFR 10.000.000,00 the German remuneration law for legal advisers entitles remunerations as shown in the following:

- examination **USD** 42.000,00
- negotiations **USD** 42.000,00
- contribution to and/or formulating an agreement **USD** 63.000,00

These fees doesn't include taxes and expenses for travelling, translation, communication and similar expenditures.

ABS.: AM PROJEKT CONSULTING; 05/01/2002 14:59 +49-711-80913121 RA.THEUMER U.KOL.

- 3 -

Theumer, Wieland & Weisenburger
Anwaltskanzlei

Please understand that we ask to meet some conditions to which we are
either legally obliged or which we consider as highly appropriate and
crucial for the success in that case.

In order to continue our activities we need a power of attorney either
direct from your mandator or by you which needs a legitimation by your
mandator.

It is unalterable for us handling the case that all further informations demanded are delivered to us fully, without delay and to the best
of ability, particularly concerning the progress of the project in the
past, the stop of the works at the facilities, your efforts in the
past to urge BSC to continue, data base about times and amounts of
paying and the exchange of letters concerning the progress and possibly written expressed intentions to end the project.

Concerning the payment we are obliged to request informations which
meet all requirements of German and European laws to fight money laun
dering. This means mainly that we must be able in the given case to
prove to the authorities that all money descends from legal sources.

As soon as we receive power of attorney and order to enter into the
first of the abovementioned steps we will begin the detailed examination, demand you if necessary for further informations and present yo
on a short term base the alternatives to act and our suggestions.

In addition to that it would be useful if you communicate with your
respond your ideas of a payment schedule.

If you have any further questions don't hesitate to contact us.

Yours sincerely
Rechtsanwalt

Christof Weisenburger

FROM : Ministry Of Water and Power FAX NO. : 92 91 287953 Jan. 14 2001 11:10AM P1

Planning department

No:

Date: January 13, 2001

To : BBC –Brown –Boveri & Co. Ltd.
Zurich – Oerliken Works
Affolterntrasses
Ch-Zurich –Oerliken –Switzerland
Attn : TGK-1 Mr. Naef

Subject: completing and commissioning of the extension of existing BBC Gas turbine Power Plant at Kabul North West into Combined cycle Power Plant. Contract agreement singed 23.5.85.

Dear Sir,

This letter is to information and certify that Mr. Michael Albrecht is authorized to discuss and negotiate the matters of commissioning and completing the erection works of combined cycle on behalf of the Ministry of Water and Power I.E.A with BBC company now called ABB company.

Thanks for your kind co-operations.

Sincerely yours,

Alhaj Moulavi Ahmad Jan
Minister of Water & Power

Ministry of Water & Power
Badam bagh Kabul Afg
Local Tel.30304
InterTel. 092-91-287953
Fax: 092-91-287953

'AN-19-2001 01:07 AM MOHABBAT 2815680340 P.0

January 18, 2001

Embassy of El Salvador

Washington, D.C.

Phone 1-(202) 265-9671, fax 1(202) 234-3834

On the behalf of the people and government of I.E. Afghanistan I wish to convey our deepest sympathy concerning the recent earthquake that has devastated your Country. The peoples of Afghanistan can surly empathize with the tragic loss of life and property that this recent disaster has brought. At present, The Afghan people are suffering from the drought of unprecedented magnitude. Still we would like to offer our hearts and thoughts to your people and government. Please, do not hesitate to call on us for moral support, or human services we can provide.

Sincerely,

Mullah Abdul Jalil Akhund
Deputy Foreign Minister of I.E.
Afghanistan

ABS.: AM PROJEKT CONSULTING; 49711997945б; 28-FEB-01 16:05; SEITE 3/3

interna

Herrn
Michael T. Albrecht
Leuschnerstrasse 52
D-70176 Stuttgart

CH-8006 Zürich, 20. Februar 2001 BE/kb

Global Petroleum and Mining Ltd, Stans

Sehr geehrter Herr Albrecht

Ich hoffe Sie haben das neue Jahr gut gestartet. Wir haben einige Zeit nichts mehr voneinander gehört und ich bitte Sie, mich über den Stand der Geschäftstätigkeiten zu informieren.

In der Zwischenzeit sind einige kleinere Rechnungen für die Firma angefallen, so die Steuerrechnung für das Jahr 2000, die Rechnung für die Domizilhaltung in Stans sowie die Rechnungen für Handelsregister- und Notariatsgebühren, sowie für unsere Aufwendungen. Damit wir diese Verpflichtungen und auch die später eintreffenden Rechnungen bezahlen können, schlagen wir Ihnen der Einfachheit halber vor, uns einen Betrag von Fr. 10'000.00 zu überweisen. Wir werden mit diesem Betrag ein Konto auf den Namen der Global bei der Bank einrichten und die Rechnungen ab diesem Konto bezahlen. Bitte überweisen Sie uns den Betrag in den nächsten Tagen auf das Konto der interna Treuhand + Informatik AG Zürich, Credit Suisse, BLZ 0558, Kto. 949448-61.

Für eine prompte Erledigung danke ich Ihnen bestens und erwarte gerne Ihren baldigen Bericht über den Stand der Aktivitäten der Global Petroleum and Mining Ltd.

interna
TREUHAND+INFORMATIK AG

W. Benz

Adresse Zürich

.88.: AM PROJEKT CONSULTING; 497119979456; 5-MAR-01 18:51;

ALSTOM

Power
Gas Turbines

Mr. Michael Albrecht
AM PROJEKT-CONSULTING GmbH
Talstrasse 41
D70188 Stuttgart
Germany

Contact person:
Dieter Buck
Tel:
+41-56-2056106
Fax:
+41-56-2057530
E-mail:
Dieter.buck@power.alstom.com

Date:
21 February 2001

Subject: **Contract for Extension of Kabul North West to Combined Cycle Power Plant dated May 23, 1985**
"Anfrage Status Quo 2001" dated Jan. 17,2001

Dear Mr. Albrecht
Above mentioned Contract was signed on May 23, 1985 but in September 23, 1988 the Contract was suspended due to prolonged force majeure events leading to termination of the Contract.
Accordingly each party to the Contract is discharged of any further obligation to perform and of any liability.
Due to the organisational changes 1988, we in Baden are not longer responsible for the smaller size Combined Cycle Plants and smaller Turbines (limit 50 MW) as well as for any "add on" or "modification" for this type of plants.
You should direct your inquiry to our Industrial Power Plant Segment, with the following representatives who may assist you.
Mr. J. Vinkenfluegel +33-1-41493078 (Paris)
Mr. L. Wenebrink +49-911-4130795 (Nürnberg)

If you need further information or additional assistance please let me know

Sincerely Yours

Fritz Megerle
Sales Director

Dieter Buck
Executive Sales Manager

ALSTOM Power (Switzerland) Ltd
[illegible] 15
CH-5401 Baden/Switzerland

Tel.: +41 (0)56 205 77 33
Fax: +41 (0)56 205 71 71
www.alstom.ch

1 / 1

85.: AM PROJEKT CONSULTING; 49711 9979456; 5-MAR-01 18:51; [illegible]

AM PROJEKT- CONSULTING GmbH
Talstraße 41
70188 Stuttgart
Tel 0711 - 997 94 55
Fax 0711 - 997 94 56
Mobil 0170 834 74 33
ampgmbh@web.de

AM PROJEKT-CONSULTING GmbH

To the
Ministry Water & Power
Mister Waheed
Badam bagh Kabul
Afghanistan

Stuttgart, 27 February 2001

Power Plant Project in Kabul/Alstom Company Switzerland

Dear Mister Waheed,

refering to our telephone conversation I am sending you the fax, containing the answer of the Alstom-company, Switzerland
Right now, they are in the believe, that their duty according to the contract signed in 1985, is over.
Of course we know better, the Alstom company in switzerland is only playing a game. You know how long it took, till they respond Your and our requests. Right now they are in a very bad position.
There are two questions left:

1. Was the last amount of the project paid before or after the 23.September 1988 ?
2. Who confirmed that the Alstom-company was able to take the money from the UBS-Bank account in Switzerland at that time ?

Please send me an answer to the above mentioned questions as soon as possible, my lawyers will put the Alstom-company under big pressure. They are not acting in a propper way.
We send You also the 'master plan' together with the cost of the first steps of the project, which has been worked out by me and the lawyers.
To remind You: Mr. Wieland is partner in the lawyer-agency and, at the same time, member of the European Parliament. He is also representing, as the vice chairman, the justice department in the European Parliament.
So we will be successfull, on behave of the country Afghanistan and their people, who are deeply in need of electricity.
As soon I will recieve Your fax, our work will continue.
Please send my regards to his excellency, Mullah Ahmad Jan. I will show up in Islamabad by the middle of next mounth to discuss the next steps.

Yours faithfully,

Michael T. Albrecht
AM-Projekt Consulting GmbH
Germany

Fax to: KABIR MOHABBAT - 3 Pages -
0012814949621

Good Morning, Sir,

This is, what I received from Nick Anton. Do You have any background-information ??? Is this document agreeable for You ??
I also received Your fax from yesterday, please send it to every shareholder and send me the "delivery-confirmation", that they received it. Sad, that it has to go that way. But I guess there is no other choice.

About the private loan You took from me, please send me the amount of USD 5000.- to Marions bank-account. The tax people hooked me a second time, this is the emergency I told You about, so please stick to Your promise and take care for this immediately. Thank You.
Here are the dates of Marion's bank-account in Germany:
Marion Junginger,
Kreissparkasse Esslingen, Germany SWIFT-NO.: ESSL DE 66,
BLZ 611 500 20,
Account-No. 1 000 39 70 .

I also informed You about the cash which is needed for the company G.P.M. Ltd. In Switzerland. I send You the letter of the trustee, Mr. Benz, Zurich. Of course every shareholder of G.P.M. Ltd. is responsible for the amount of 10.000.- Swiss Francs, equivalent to his shares. I understand Your letter from yesterday only for "no activities in the future", but You are also responsible for what happened in the past. Like the other major-shareholder, Dr. David Alameel And every minor-shareholder. Also me, for example.
How should we handle that case? Please give me some information. Thank You.

Enough for now, please send our greetings to Your family.

Michael T. Albrecht

Stuttgart, 28. February 2001

.85.: AM PROJEKT CONSULTING; +4971199879456; 28-FEB-01 16:04; SEITE 2/

Global Management and Development SAL
Richard Jereissati
Address : 812 Tabaris , Achrafich
Beirut, Lebanon.

Fax #: 011 961 1 200 258 VIA FAX & Express Mail courier

Dear Mr. Jereissati

This letter will serve as a confirmation of our agreement that stipulates that your company will handle the currency deal with Afghanistan exclusively since it represents the security printing company. After your company receives its agent's fees (hereafter called the commission) which will equal 10% (ten percent) of the total cost of the printing as charged by the printing company to the Afghani Government, it (Global Management and Development) will be responsible for the distribution of said commission. The ten percent commission on the total amount (estimated at approximately 40 Million US dollars) will be divided as follows:

Global Management and Development SAL	40%
Nick Anton	15%
Kabir Mohabbat & group	45%

Also please confirm to us by return fax, that your company will wire the money to both of us within a period that will not exceed one month after the involved amounts are paid by the Afghani Government to the printing company.

In case the amounts are paid by the Afghani Government to the printing company in phases, the said commission will be paid on a pro rata basis in relation to the amount paid in each phase and the same percentages would be applied. The same rules will apply to any subsequent security printing.

Nick Anton **Kabir Mohabbat on behalf of his whole group**

________________ ________________

P.S. Please wire the owed amount to each member separately as follows:

Nick Anton:

Bank ________________
Routing number: ________________
Account number: ________________

Kabir Mohabbat&Group:

Bank ________________
Routing number: ________________
Account number: ________________

ABS.: AMP; 00497119979456; 30-MAR-01 13:14;

AM PROJEKT- CONSULTING GmbH
Talstraße 41
70188 Stuttgart
Tel 0711 - 997 94 55
Fax 0711 - 997 94 56
Mobil 0170 - 834 74 33
ampgmbh@web.de

MVS-IMCI

AM PROJEKT-CONSULTING GmbH

MVS – IMCI
Mr. Jeuther
Jahnstrasse 22

74252 Massenbachhausen

Gerhard Jeuther

Project Currency – Reprint for the country Afghanistan, Our Meeting in Frankfurt / M. 2001.03.29

Dear Mr. Jeuther

This letter will serve as a confirmation of our agreement that stipulates that your company will handle the currency deal with Afghanistan exclusively since it represents the security printing company. After your company receives its agent's fees (hereafter called the commission) which will equal 10% (ten percent) of the total cost of the printing as charged by Your company to the Afghani Government. AM Projekt Consulting GmbH, Mr. Michael T. Albrecht, will be responsible for the distribution of said commission.

Please confirm to us by co-signing this document, that your company will wire the money to us within a period that will not exceed one month after the involved amounts are paid by the Afghani Government to You.

In case the amounts are paid by the Afghani Government to the printing company in phases, the said commission will be paid on a pro rata basis in relation to the amount paid in each phase and the same percentages would be applied. The same rules will apply to any subsequent security printing.

This letter was signed in Frankfurt / M. on the 29. March 2001.

AM-Projekt Consulting GmbH
Michael T. Albrecht
Stuttgart

MVS-IMCI
~~Giesecke + Devrient GmbH~~
~~Herr Knörle (Sales – Representative)~~
~~Munich~~ Herr Jeuther
Massenbachhausen

ABS.: AVP; 004971199873466; 30-MAR-01 13:18; [illegible]

FAX TO:
MR. KABIR MOHABBAT
HOUSTON / TX

2 PAGES

Good Morning, Sir,

I hope, You arrived save and relaxed back in the U.S.. Lufthansa is on strike, that's why the plane did not leave Amsterdam . The pilots want more cash…… ……
Anyway, shortly I want to inform You about the meetings from yesterday:

1. The agreement with the company MVS – IMCI, Mr. Jeuther (General Manager) is signed. Mr. Jeuther is able to deliver different parts of the whole project, including the first steps.

2. The agreement with the other company, G – D, Munich is not signed yet. Both, Mr. Knörle and Dr. Gasteiger informed me about the legitimation, which is urgently needed before planning the next steps. The legitimation has to be addressed to Mr. Knörle, and it has to be in original form, no copy will be acceptet. Very important: This document has to be signed and sealed by the President of the National Bank or "The very big guy, the in fact president of the country", not by the ministry of foreign affairs. I informed Mr. Knörle, that they will receive a fax in the first step, the original document will be handled afterwards shortly. Otherwise we will loose a lot of time. They will tell me within the next 3 days, whether this method is practicable or not.

Background information: Company G + D is printing about 120 currencies, stock papers, Passports etc.. Approximately 6000 employees are working, it is the leading printing Company in Europe
Somehow they knew about the meeting in Frankfurt, they also told me that a few people was showing up in the past, according that issue. Guess who tried to secure interests ?? but probably also some people from down there?

So, please look for the necessary documents, don't forget to check the issue "power Plant".

Good news so far, call me as soon as possible.

And say hello to Your family, also from Marion,

Michael T. Albrecht
Stuttgart, 2001-03-30

Dr. Anton Gasteiger
Vice President
Sales & Marketing

Giesecke & Devrient

Banknote and Security Printing
Giesecke & Devrient GmbH
Prinzregentenstrasse 159
P.O. Box 80 07 29
D-81607 Munich
Telephone +49 89 41 19-19 89
Fax +49 89 41 19-23 19
Mobile +49 171 5 53 24 31
anton.gasteiger@gdm.de

Wolfgang Knörle
Executive Vice President
General Manager
Banknote and Security Printing

Giesecke & Devrient GmbH
Prinzregentenstrasse 159
P.O. Box 80 07 29
81607 Munich

Giesecke & Devrient

Chapter 9: September 11, 2001

Mid-March 2001, I left Pakistan and quickly returned to Texas. Soon after arriving, I met with Jack and Mario. To my surprise, Jack had no idea what had just occurred in Islamabad. "The bastards wouldn't let me know what happened. All they would say is that you *did* bring the Taliban to the embassy."

Jack expressed concern that I could suffer international sanctions for my actions, but he also agreed to check with his superiors to see whether we could provide the electronic supplies the Afghan Government requested. The three of us agreed to meet again toward the end of April.

Then Jack called and asked for another meeting. Once face to face, he explained that I should not talk to anyone in the State Department any more. From now on, the Ambassador was in charge and he would tell those he wanted to know about the Taliban. He added, "I'm trying to keep you with us. If you refuse to shut your mouth, I don't know how much more I can do. There are people at the National Security Council who cannot wait to get rid of you."

"Do me a favor. Tell the people at the National Security Council to take this job and shove it. I don't need this shit. I go into Afghanistan. The roads are bad. I could die there and you're telling me the same old shit. If I hear it one more time, I swear to God I'll quit. Then don't even bother coming back to see me. I had to mortgage my house. I can barely make car payments. My oil deal is in limbo because of those D.C. turds. This is all fucking bullshit!"

When I finished my tantrum, I realized how childish I must have sounded to the seasoned professional. I knew (and he knew) that D.C. had me by the balls. Without the Turds in Washington, there was no getting rid of the Snake in Afghanistan. If there's no getting rid of bin Laden, then there's no oil for me. I was literally over a barrel and they knew it.

Jack plead, “Please, I am begging you.”

“I want to keep people informed,” I admitted sheepishly that I had called Mr. and Mrs. Oakley to tell them what was going on – and that I was about to get the Saudi terrorist. I felt that I had a moral obligation to them, especially toward Mrs. Oakley. I didn't want to keep any secrets from her and I knew she wasn't going to tell anyone because she was a Deputy Secretary of State for Intelligence Affairs. I was pretty damn sure she could keep a secret.

Jack warned me that my phone may be tapped by those outside the U.S. Government.

“Okay, I understand. Someone else could hear and it would be damaging. But I don't talk about important issues. Let's work toward getting bin Laden. Have the national security people get ready to give me orders by the end of April. Our main concern should be getting this guy.”

Time passed quickly while Jack and I were trying to get the National Security folks off their collective asses, but for weeks nothing happened. I kept getting calls from Afghanistan – Kabul and Kandahar – asking when the U.S. was coming. During this period, the people in Washington were worried about a U.S. Air Force spy plane that had been shot down over China. I used this incident to explain to the Taliban that the U.S. Government was busy solving the problem with the Chinese and to please be patient.

Jack and I kept pushing from the inside, but we were left smoldering on the back burner. It was frustrating. We discussed whether I should go back and tell the Taliban that we were not ready and apologize again. But I wasn't interested in returning unless Jack could assure me that orders to capture the Snake had been issued.

"I cannot assure you of that." I could tell that Jack was getting nowhere in D.C.

Jack called and left a message on my answering machine that Ambassador Milam was refusing to see or talk to anybody from Afghanistan until he had clear orders from Bush's National Security team. "I don't know what the fuck is wrong with Milam. I don't know what his reasons are for not meeting with them," he fumed.

I did. I immediately called Jack back and suggested that we meet. At length we talked about Milam's reaction.

"Jack, Ambassador Milam is a diplomat. He knows he can make excuses. He doesn't want to meet with the Taliban because he wants to be clear on national policy before seeing them. He was embarrassed earlier. I saw it; you didn't. He doesn't want it to happen again."

Milam, too, had been left hanging by President Bush's people. If he was getting no instructions from Washington, then any action he took would be held against him. And rumor was that he was rapidly approaching retirement. Controversy at this late date may be something he wanted to avoid. In his place, I would act the same way.

By mid-May 2001, things screeched to a halt. The issue of the U.S. spy plane had been settled. I was receiving a constant stream of calls from Afghanistan which I am sure my government knew about. Jack and I were meeting weekly in order to solve our problems, but the poor man really couldn't get any kind of commitment out of the indecisive bastards over him.

All this inaction made me begin to worry about my reputation. I reminded Jack again that I would not travel back to Afghanistan unless the U.S. Government was finally ready to act.

It was in this period that I began getting calls from Afghan officials warning that bin Laden was up to something, but they weren't sure what. Because months had passed since putting him under house arrest near the beginning of March, the Taliban eventually had to release him. He then moved from Kandahar to a location within thirty kilometers of Kabul.

I didn't ask too many questions; they volunteered the information. They added that he had about 250 top men with him. I asked Jack if he knew where bin Laden was now.

Jack said, "He's in Daronta."

"Exactly right," I confirmed. Thus from the end of March, both I and the U.S. Government knew where bin Laden was located. He stayed in the same location until immediately after September 11th.

I explained to Jack that it was getting dangerous for our contacts in Afghanistan. "Can we please do something right now – right away!?!"

The next week I got a constant stream of bad news over the telephone, I finally asked Jack for another meeting. I discussed with the Taliban the fact that, if the Americans weren't going to do anything about this man, then perhaps they should. I asked Jack whether U.S. authorities would allow me and the Taliban to take out bin Laden.

Jack checked with Washington. A few days later he came back and said that any action taken by me would be against the law. I would be prosecuted. He warned me, "Don't take the law into your own hands. We are going to do something about this."

"Listen, they are saying that something may happen and we didn't even supply those people with electronics so they could hear what the Snake was up to. You know this would help Washington, too. I know we have the technology. Please do something about this. They need some kind of electronic listening device. You could give it to someone I know, a confidant in Islamabad. He would smuggle them into

Afghanistan and give them to the Taliban so we could at least monitor what bin Laden is doing."

"It's out of my hands." I was then told that when I do finally go back, I will probably take the listening devices with me or they will be given to me in Islamabad.

"You know this is bullshit. I don't trust Bush's people any more. This is nothing but a delaying tactic. They're just delaying me – pacifying me – pacifying you. It's nonsense."

Jack agreed, but he didn't really know what else to do. He had pulled all the strings he could in D.C. Here it was the end of May and nothing was being done about bin Laden. At one point Jack even told me that he was thinking about resigning. I kept wondering why the President's staff refused to take out the Snake.

Finally, I asked Jack to go to Washington and talk to the people in charge of this issue. At the beginning of June, Jack left for D.C. When he returned he said that he now believed we were ready to go. All we had to do was mobilize everything. "You should be in Afghanistan by the end of the month." We began planning my trip.

I had been receiving and placing calls to the Taliban on a weekly basis. I was in contact with the highest levels of that government. Even their telephone operators began to recognize my voice. I was put through even when the Taliban were in important meetings. From the tap on my telephone line, the U.S. Government knew about these calls and they knew how easy it was for me to get a response from the Afghan Government within minutes.

While Jack was in Washington, I received a call from the Taliban. For the first time they said, "We don't know what it is, but something big is about to happen somewhere in the United States. We can't decode the messages, but please tell the Americans that something big could happen. It is something so great that no one will be able to repair the damage. There will be no repairing our negotiations."

They asked me to inform the U.S. Government immediately. I taped the conversation. When I met with Jack I gave him a copy of the tape. He immediately informed Washington.

Around the 10th of June 2001, Jack called and asked for a meeting at Houston's Restaurant on Kirby Drive. I could tell that something was bothering him. "I can't eat unless you tell me what's going on."

"I have good news and bad news," he said.

Irritated at being forced to play his game I said, "Give me the bad news first."

"I have been removed from this job. There's another man named Dan who has been appointed to work with you. He is a very nice man, very informed. He worked in the American Consulate General's office in Peshawar, Pakistan at the time of the mujahidin. The government thinks that this person is more qualified than me to make this happen. Plus, he knows the culture and he knows the people."

I listened crestfallen. He was trying in vain to reassure me that the change was for the best.

"So what is the good news?" I asked. Jack had been promoted to a job that he could not pass up. He had been given the highest job that he could attain. He would be making more money and he would be in a better position for retirement.

I had a hard time seeing how any of this was good news for me. I assumed without proof that this all meant that while in Washington, Jack had threatened to retire, so they promoted him.

Since they had another very experienced person representing my government's national security interests who would work out the details with me, I didn't mind too much. I would miss Jack, though, but I understood why he was leaving.

I congratulated Jack on his promotion. "But we're running out of time. Every day I am getting the same message out of Afghanistan that something big is going to happen.

I don't know the new man. I'm sure he is very professional, but I can't take the time to educate him."

I again begged Jack to stay with me until this issue was resolved. He said he would see what he could do to help before I left for Pakistan. Jack suggested that I meet my new contact.

"I have no problem with him, but I do have a problem with you leaving."

The new man, Dan, was to be in charge of the issue of bin Laden from then on. He may even want to talk directly to the Taliban or to their security people and work out all the details himself. It sounded reassuring, but was he really ready to act? Was Bush's government finally moving forward?

Two days later Jack, Dan, Mario and I met. Dan was okay, but he was no Jack. Jack told Dan how hard I had been working and that we were almost finished with the plan for my trip in two weeks to arrange another meeting between Afghan and U.S. officials so they could work out the details of how best to handle the issue of bin Laden.

Everyone there kept explaining how complicated the issue was, but I didn't see it. The U.S. wanted bin Laden out; the Taliban wanted bin Laden out; the Taliban was willing to let the U.S. choose the method to get him out. How complicated is that!?!

Perhaps I had watched too many movies over the years. In a movie, when a person is wanted by authorities, someone turns him in to the heavily armed people in charge, and they take him out. In my mind it was a simple problem with a simple solution. Take him out at the first opportunity!

"I don't see any complications," I said. "All we have to do is send over a missile. The Taliban invited us to do that very thing. All we really need is one or two. Are we so poor a country that we're running out of fuel for our missiles? How much fuel could it take? How about if I pay for the fuel? It can't be that much – forty, fifty gallons?"

They laughed, but it was no laughing matter to me. I wanted the Saudi Snake out of Afghanistan and lately the one obstacle I kept running into again and again was my own government.

I was finally set to travel on the 3rd week of June 2001. Everything was ready. All I had to do was show up in Islamabad and talk to the Station Chief. From there I was to go to Kandahar and bring the Taliban back to the embassy. There were details that had to be worked out on each side, like who was going to do what, and with whom, but I was hopeful that this was minimal stuff and that this trip was finally it.

I called Jalil and asked him if there was any possibility they could meet with U.S. officials toward the end of June. He said, "It's not a problem," but he reminded me that they were still on the U.N. sanctioned list and couldn't travel.

"Why can't they come to us?" he asked.

"Please, this is not the time for me to make these people come to you. Just one more trip, I promise. Next trip you won't have to come, they will come." So, on that condition he said, "Great!" I told Dan and Jack.

The Sunday before leaving the U.S., I got a call from the Taliban. They were worried that Osama was trying to move from where he was holed up near Kabul. They said to rush – before he moved. They wanted me to ask the U.S. Government if it had intelligence about why Osama was moving because they could not determine what was happening. They wondered whether he knew something of our plans.

Jack had always told me that since we were working on issues of national security, I could call him 24/7. So I assumed my relationship with Dan was the same. I immediately called Dan. I thought my news important enough to share, but Dan must have been in the middle of something. Angry, he said that this was not the day to call him. It was Sunday and he didn't work on Sundays.

Until that moment I hadn't realized that in the U.S. issues of national security could only happen Monday through Saturday, between the hours of eight and five. He said whatever it was, it could wait until tomorrow. I didn't think that it could, so I telephoned Jack.

Jack suggested that we meet. I met Dan and Jack for lunch the next day and I explained what had been said by Dan and by the Taliban. Dan apologized. He said that from now on I could call him at any time. I got the distinct impression that Jack had subjected Dan to a fearsome verbal lashing.

Around June 19, 2001, I took off for Pakistan. About two or three in the morning, I reached Lahore. The non-stop flight had taken about twenty hours. From Lahore I flew to Islamabad and arrived at 9:00 the next morning.

I called the American Embassy from the airport and asked them to give me enough time to shower and change and then I would come in and meet with my contract. My contact this time was Deputy Ambassador Black. He wanted me to come over as soon as possible. We made an appointment for eleven o'clock.

I was astounded to learn that Black had no idea why I was there. I brought him up to speed as fast as I could. He was surprised and happy to learn what was going on and wished me, "Good luck!"

They then took me to a secure room. Ron, the CIA's mission chief showed up. He appeared glad to see me. "Are we ready to go?" I asked.

Ron sat silent for a moment and then said, "Yeah, we are almost ready, but we need to talk to the Taliban."

"Let me ask you again, are we ready?"

"Yes, we are ready, but I can't discuss that with you now without them present. We will discuss it in detail once they are here."

"Great! Is the Ambassador going to be here?"

"Yeah, that's no problem."

"Okay, then I will go to Kandahar. Once there, let me relax for a day or two and get over my jet lag and then I'll be back. What about the equipment that we promised the Taliban that we would give them? The people back home said you would have electronic bugs for me to take to Kandahar so we can all listen to bin Laden."

Ron brought out a suitcase with a satellite telephone in it.

"Excuse me, what am I going to do with a telephone? I asked for bugs!"

"This will show our good will. That we want to have direct contact with the Taliban."

"What do you mean – direct contact? They have said over and over that they will not talk to you unless I am present."

"We understand that, but in case something comes up that we want to know or they want to know, they can call us directly."

"They don't speak English! You know that?"

"Well, we have our own translator."

"I will take the phone, sure. Am I allowed to use it?"

"Well, not really."

"I can't even call home and tell my wife that I'm okay." He shook his head, no.

"But if it's an important emergency, then I can call you?"

"Yes, that's true," Ron said.

"Okay, fine. But when they're here, please get authorization from Washington to give them bugs."

I was angry. It was unconscionable that the representatives of the Taliban government still didn't have the listening devices that they had been pleading for. It's not like they could go down the street to Radio Shack and get what they needed. But Ron knew that I wasn't about to remove myself from the situation, so he took advantage of me.

As instructed, I took the telephone to Kandahar. I flew to Quetta and traveled to Kandahar by road as I had done in the past. With me were two bodyguards because I was no longer sure what bin Laden knew and what he was up to.

I reached Kandahar and stayed at the Taliban's guesthouse. I was greeted by a large number of Taliban officials. We talked politics and business. I thanked them for trusting me with the oil deal in the north of Afghanistan and for giving me authority to negotiate business deals for them.

Minister Esa was there. He reminded me that we signed the oil Agreement in August of 2000, and that so far nothing had been done. I apologized to him and said that he would be made happy shortly. I reassured them that the contract was still valid and alive.

Then I explained that I was there to solve a bigger issue. One of the officials there confirmed my statement and suggested to Esa that he be patient. There were the U.S. and international sanctions that had to be dealt with first.

Because of my exhaustion, they allowed me to leave dinner early. In order to reach Kandahar, I had been traveling for two straight nights and days. I was beginning to have trouble focusing my eyes. I won't even bother discussing my mental state – or lack thereof. By eleven p.m. I was sound asleep.

At three, I was awakened when my bodyguard jumped on top of me. We lay there a moment like an uneasy short stack of pancakes before I pushed him off.

"What the hell is going on?"

"I think somebody tried to throw a hand grenade through the window," said my bodyguard, Mohammad Shah, who was an experienced mujahid who didn't know the meaning of deep sleep. He had fought against the Soviets. I trusted his judgment in all things warlike.

"There was somebody by the window," he panted.

"How could anyone throw a hand grenade through screened windows?"

"Somebody made a mistake. Whatever was thrown hit the screen and bounced back. I guess it didn't go off. I got scared and thought it might explode, so I jumped on you."

We turned on the lights and then Shah ran out of the room and awakened the other bodyguard and the cooks sleeping nearby. Someone heard the commotion and the Taliban's security forces began appearing. Everyone was frightened and jumpy.

Shah asked someone on the security force, "Who is in this compound?"

There was an eleven o'clock curfew in Kandahar. To be admitted to the compound that late, one would have to know the password. Apparently, one of the high ranking officials of the Afghan Government had been admitted into the compound. When the bodyguard found out who he was, he was shocked that someone so high up in the government would stoop so low as to throw a grenade into the quarters of a guest of the government.

But no one inside the guesthouse knew what actually had taken place. Everyone was scared and confused. I told them to go back to sleep and asked my bodyguards not to make a big issue out of what had happened. I don't want people of importance becoming scared of me being in the country. They may stop my visits to Afghanistan. We called for tea and I asked the Taliban security to have the official leave the compound immediately.

Rather than leaving, the high ranking Taliban official asked if he could meet with me, but I said, "No. Tell him to leave."

As expected, by morning the event of the night before had circled the rumor mill and was already common knowledge. The members of the Afghan Government who showed up for breakfast already knew what had happened. A powerful official asked to speak with me in my room in private.

"We are suspicious of what happened," he said.

Apparently the man caught in the compound the night before explained to authorities that as he drove by he saw lights, so he turned in and came into the compound.

The official asked me, "Are you suspicious of the man (he gave me a name)."

I hadn't been until that moment.

He said, "I give you my word, he has already been detained at his house. I am sending someone that I trust to question him. I can assure you, he will never be allowed to enter this compound again."

"That is up to you. I'm not here to cause any problems." I tried to play it cool. I had a lot riding on my ability to move back and forth across the border. "Things like this happen."

"Yes, we do know that things like this happen, but it shouldn't have happened to you because you are our guest. If anything happened to you, we would never forgive ourselves."

"I know your laws are very severe, but I'm not dead. Please don't kill anybody on my account. I'm still alive."

At that moment another angry government official walked into the room. "The man must be eliminated!" he swore. But I didn't feel it boded well for what I was trying to do if someone was killed for this incident.

I repeated, "No, sir. I am fine. I am alive. I'm here with you and we have work to do."

We all looked each other in the eye and ended our conversation. I felt a little sorry for the guy who tried to take me out because I could guess what his fate would be.

Jalil asked me about the electronic surveillance devices that I had promised.

I explained that they were in process. "When you come to Islamabad you will get them." Joking I added, "Perhaps the Americans don't trust me. They will probably give them to you themselves. But here is a phone – a satellite phone. If you need me or need to talk to the Americans, call."

I handed him the secure numbers that had been provided. "No one can hear your conversation. If there is any need, if I'm not around, or if I'm busy, you can always get in touch with U.S. officials."

"We don't speak English, but of course you're going to be there."

"No, it's for emergencies. It's a good will gift." He accepted it and thanked me. I suggested that we try it out and call the American Embassy to make a date for when we could all meet. He was delighted.

We called Ron in Islamabad. Again I acted as translator between the two groups. Ron asked me if I would hand the phone over to one of the Taliban, "just to say hello in Pashto," and I said sure.

Jalil spoke for a minute in Pashto and then began speaking in Farsi. He asked if the man on the other end spoke Pashto, but, of course, he didn't. Instead a man speaking an Iranian dialect of Farsi was on the phone. This worried the mullah because he didn't know who the voice on the other end of the line belonged to. He handed the phone back to me and I made an appointment for them to meet either June 30 or July 1, 2001, I forget which.

When Jalil got off the phone, he was upset. He had been asked some questions by the stranger on the other end, but he didn't want to supply the answers. He assured me that if it ever happened again, he would end the conversation and the relationship.

Officials from the Taliban came and went all day at the guesthouse. That night we had dinner and by the time it was over I must have met at least ninety percent of the Council of Ministers. I suppose they were trying to show their unity for what they were trying to do with the U.S. I was impressed and happy.

After my second night in Kandahar, I was awakened at six in the morning when my bodyguard patted me on the back and said, "Please wake up. Mr. Mutawakel, the Foreign Minister of the Taliban is outside."

I suddenly became aware of gravel crunching outside the windows. I looked up and saw Mutawakel pacing back and forth in front of the guesthouse. I guessed that the bodyguards had told him that I was asleep and had asked him not to disturb me.

I immediately jumped up, washed my face and went outside to greet him. We hugged each other and he introduced me to another representative of the Taliban, a Mr. Zadran who ranked second in the Afghan mission to the United Nations in New York. Mutawakel asked Zadran to wait for him because he had something important to discuss in private with me.

Mutawakel asked if we could have breakfast together. He had just found out the day before that I was in the Kandahar. It had taken him all night to drive the 120 miles between Kabul and Kandahar. After an exchange of pleasantries, I asked him not to question me about why I was there or why I had been traveling back and forth to Kandahar.

"If you ask me, I will have to tell you the truth and that means I must break promises that I have made to the Americans and to people you introduced me to."

"Then let me ask you this, are you being successful?"

"I am very successful, I assure you. But please don't ask any questions." Happy at my success, he laughed and then we sat down and talked.

Mutawakel came to see me because he was worried. Two American girls had been arrested by the Ministry of Vice and

Virtue a few days before I got to Kandahar for trying to convert Afghans to Christianity which was a capital crime.

"Mr. Mutawakel, what is going on?"

He said, "For God's sake, tell the Americans to stop it."

"You've arrested others?"

"Yes, four or five other people were arrested with religious leaflets which had been translated into Pashto, but not by the Ministry." He said that he immediately ordered the others to leave the country. "I don't want this kind of excitement in Afghanistan." If it hadn't been for him, they would still be under arrest.

"You mean you deported Americans."

"I deported the others immediately to Pakistan. If the people in the Ministry of Vice and Virtue had gotten hold of them like they had the two girls, they would not be able to leave. You know what the penalty is?"

"Execution."

"Of course, we are not going to execute any Americans or foreigners, but that is the penalty. I have enough headaches with the two girls already in detention. I don't want any more, so I deported everyone. I have ordered all religious foreigners to leave."

"Why?"

"Things look very bad for Afghanistan. Intelligence reports say something bad is going to happen and our relationship with the United States worsens by the day. The U.S. isn't cooperating with us." Apparently, he had been getting all kinds of hostile messages from the U.S. State Department.

"Don't worry about that. That may be just for show. I am working hard. I think we are almost at the end."

I reassured him that everything would be all right. We then took a few pictures of our dawn meeting. At this point, about eight Taliban officials showed up, so we had to end our conversation.

He patted me on the back and I returned the pat and said, "Just trust me and believe in me."

"I do. One hundred percent."

"Thank you." I went back to my room. More officials arrived and everyone sat with Mr. Mutawakel and we ate and talked.

I spent a couple more days in Kandahar resting and then left for Islamabad. On the appointed day, Mullah Jalil showed up in Islamabad. I took a room for us at a local guesthouse. I greeted him at the airport, got him into a private taxi and snuck him into the guesthouse. The next day we drove over to the American Embassy compound. Again, we went straight into the Ambassador's residence.

Ambassador Milam explained that his residence wasn't secure. Our intelligence services had told him that we had been overheard last time. So while exchanging pleasantries, we walked over to the embassy, a block's walk within the compound and went into the Ambassador's office on the second floor.

The Ambassador sat for a few minutes and then announced that he had to leave for another meeting. He said that Ron, the CIA Station Chief, was there representing our national security interests. He would work out all the details. The Ambassador suggested that perhaps we meet again afterwards. I walked with him to the door where I whispered, "Why are you leaving?"

"I have been ordered not to attend this meeting." He quickly walked out leaving me unable to respond to the news.

Jalil got to the point immediately. He asked, "Are you ready to act?"

Ron said, "Yes, we are ready to act, but our orders are on the way."

I said, "What the hell did you say?"

"Our orders are on the way. All we have to do is reaffirm the commitment of the Taliban again. Everything that we say is being immediately transmitted directly to the National Security Council, and people in Washington are listening to us now. They are going to make an assessment. Then there will be a team of professionals to lead a covert operation. They will come to Pakistan and work out the details. And from there go to Kabul and Kandahar."

Jalil said, "Have you decided how to do this or how to approach this?"

The Station Chief said, "No, we have not made that decision yet."

When Jalil saw hesitancy on the part of the U.S., he said, "Well, people die in Afghanistan every day from land mines. Would it simplify things for you, if he blew up on a mine, then everyone could feel sorry for poor Osama. Should that be an answer for us all?"

"No, that really is no answer. I need orders from D.C."

I thought everything was going well. At the time, I got the distinct impression that everything was being worked out and that there was a team of professionals coming. Jalil told me later in the guesthouse that he didn't believe the Americans would do anything about our mutual problem.

He warned me again, and he warned those at the embassy meeting again, that their intelligence lead them to believe that something big was going to happen and we should take note that we had been warned, but they had no idea what it was. The people in the embassy said that they knew about the warning and were concerned, but there was nothing they could do until their team arrived and they had orders from D.C.

Jalil went back to Kandahar. I reassured him that very, very shortly – perhaps within the month – they would get the go-ahead.

I would be back sometime in August, probably in two to three weeks. I had to return to the United States now and be sworn in as a U.S. citizen. It couldn't wait.

I arrived back in Texas on the 4th of July. Quickly thereafter I became a full-fledged, passport carrying Yankee Doodle Dandy.[2]

Back in Texas, I informed Dan about what had happened in Islamabad. I called Jack and asked him to come to Houston so we could resolve this issue immediately. Jack told me to get ready to fly by the first week of August.

On August 18, 2001, I landed in Islamabad and went to meet with U.S. officials. When I got to the Embassy, Ron handed me the same old tragic response, "Kabir, we are sorry. We don't have orders yet."

"The people in Washington told me to go – that they were ready to go," I pleaded.

"Yes, we did want you to come. Please just go one more time to Kabul or wherever you need to go and meet with the Taliban and tell them that we need another month."

Exasperated, I hung around Islamabad to get over an extreme case of jet lag before traveling to Afghanistan.

Before leaving, I called Jalil and he said to me, "Don't come back to Kandahar. You have raised a lot of suspicion. Go to Kabul. Minister Esa has been ordered to act as your

2 Kabir told me that the reps of the U.S. Government bypassed the usual citizenship process for him. He was in Afghanistan when they processed his paperwork. Because he was out of reach by phone, officials guessed at his birth year. The year that appeared on his U.S. Passport, 1954, is wrong. He was born in 1956.

host. That way, everyone will know that you came to Kabul to talk business. We will travel from Kandahar to meet with you in Kabul."

I flew out of Islamabad on September 2, 2001. Too exhausted to spend days in a car, I chartered a United Nations plane for my trip from Islamabad into Afghanistan.

Before leaving the U.S., I decided to take my business associate Michael and my nephew Aziz, with me so that I wouldn't raise too many suspicions. Hitching a ride on the airplane were reporters from various European papers. Of particular note was Wilhelm Dietl, a personable reporter who represented one of the German news agencies.

When we arrived in Kabul, the Taliban were excited to see me. I told them that I was really sorry but there were still no orders about what to do with bin Laden. The Americans needed another month.

Jalil started laughing and said, "Mr. Mohabbat, that's okay. However much time they want to take, they can take it. But we did warn them. We have warned them!"

"Yes, I understand. For the last eleven months it has been their move."

While in Kabul I asked the Taliban if I could see the parents of Dayna Curry and Heather Mercer, the girls who had been detained by the Ministry of Vice and Virtue for trying to convert Muslims to Christianity. They said, "Sure."

On September 3, 2001, I went to the compound of the United Nations building in Kabul where the girls' parents were staying. I got to the compound at about nine in the morning. David Donahue, the U.S. Consulate General of Islamabad, was there. He had been negotiating the girls' release for weeks. I introduced myself. He appeared glad to see me.

I asked Donahue if I could meet the parents of the American girls. I approached John Mercer and Nancy Cassell (Curry's mother). Mercer explained that his daughter had been working as a missionary trying to help the Afghan people.

I asked him if his daughter had been mistreated or dishonored in any way while in the custody of the Taliban.

Mercer said, "No." He did complain, however, that they were only allowed to see their children twice a week for one hour. "Could we see them every day?" They also asked if the girls could be moved from the prison to better housing.

"It will be done," I replied.

At the time, I don't think that they believed me. I hugged the stressed parents and asked them to trust me. "I am going to do something about your problem."

Later that same day, I asked the Afghan Government's Director of Protocol at the Ministry of Foreign Affairs to move the children from the prison to a better place – like a house – and he agreed.

The next day I saw the parents. They both started crying and said, "Thank you!" The Counsel General, too, was very happy with the change in the girls' living arrangements.

I gave the parents a telephone number so they could call their daughters anytime they wanted until the situation was settled. They both thanked me.

I told them that I would meet with them in Islamabad and explained that I had already arranged for the girls' release by mid-September – in about two weeks.

I don't think they believed me at the time, but they soon got their daughters on the telephone. The girls confirmed that they were being treated well and that they soon would be released. They explained to their fretful parents that the Taliban had not harmed them during their captivity.

I returned to Islamabad. I was due to leave for Texas the morning of September 12.

Around 1:00 a.m. in the morning of the day before my flight, I was at the guesthouse in Pakistan when a voice at the other end of the telephone said, "Please talk to Kandahar."

I picked up the phone. It was Osmani, Mullah Omar's deputy.

"Yes sir, it is late. I hope everything is okay."

"Have you seen the TV," he asked.

"No."

"The Twin Towers in New York have been hit by two airplanes and they are showing it on U.S. television."

He explained that an Afghan had called them from the U.S. because the reports on the television said that Osama bin Laden was responsible. They didn't have a TV so they called me and asked me to turn the TV in my room to CNN and tell them whether it was true.

Osami then said that I was on a speaker phone, "Mullah Omar and all the top officials of the Taliban are listening to what you are saying. Please stay on the phone and translate what the American news media is reporting."

When I turned on the television, the first of the Twin Towers was already down. I described in detail to the Taliban what was occurring on live television.

Osami asked me, "Who do you think did it?"

I answered, "Maybe those crazy right winged supremacists who blew up Oklahoma City."

He said, "You are probably right because we don't think Osama's capable of carrying off such a big act." I agreed with them. I honestly didn't think the Snake had it in him.

"If he did do it, we're praying that America doesn't blame us with Osama – as if we're all in the same boat," Osami said

I stayed up all night translating what occurred in New York for the shocked officials of the Taliban. I told them that the next morning I was going directly to the American Embassy.

At about nine o'clock on the morning of September 12th, I reached the Embassy and went in to see Ron, the CIA Station Chief. I was very angry and very upset. "You son of bitches!! You mother fuckers!!!" I cussed at them and then realized that I was screaming my lungs out. From their point of view, I must have sounded like a lunatic.

Then someone on the embassy staff spit at me, "Shit happens!!"

I realized he was right, shit did happen. Thousands were dead. Families fractured. Children – fatherless – motherless. It was all beyond belief. Shit happens!?! I wanted to hone those words into a weapon and kill all the unthinking, sightless bureaucrats of the Clinton and Bush administrations that I had been dealing with since November of 2000!!!

I sat in the Embassy watching my carefully crafted diplomacy fly out the window carrying my oil royalties in its beak. Back home I would be faced with thousands upon thousands of dollars of debt – not to mention one really furious wife.

Then in the time it takes a bullet to cross a room, I went from feeling pissed off to a state of complete depression at having lost the life that I had envisioned for myself, my family, and for the people of Afghanistan. Eventually a greater sadness overwhelmed me – we had not been able to prevent the murder of thousands of innocent Christians and Muslims in New York City.

"There's going to be a war isn't there?"

"Yeah," Ron said, "There will be a war if we don't do something very quickly."

"You're telling me that something must be done *quickly*!!!" I had to laugh. "Have you been asleep? I've been saying that for months."

"We'll do whatever it takes," the Station Chief pleaded, "Help us."

"Whatever it takes, I'll do!"

From Islamabad I flew to Quetta and then drove to Kandahar. Before I left Pakistan the Afghan officials explained to me that many of the simple minded Taliban did not believe that buildings as high as the Twin Towers actually existed – the whole story must have been made up by the Americans.

"Please bring as many pictures as you can." I went to a news stand and collected about fifty newspapers and news magazine showing the buildings standing and then destroyed.

At the Taliban's guesthouse, all of the Afghan national security members except Mullah Omar arrived to meet me. I showed them the pictures. To my disbelief, they really didn't know that buildings that tall existed. Curiosity and then dismay caused the magazines quickly to pass from hand to hand. The question on everyone's lips, "How could America build such tall buildings!"

Osami, Mullah Omar's deputy, stood there looking at a color photo and said, "What kind of shit would destroy such beautiful buildings?" Furious, he looked at the rest of the Taliban security officials gathered in the room and asked, "Who do you think did this?"

With a newspaper in hand, one of them said, "The Americans are implicating Osama."

Osami asked the group, "Does anyone here know where he is? I want to strangle him with my own hands."

Another official said, "That's why Mr. Mohabbat is here on behalf of the Americans. We will take this issue up with Mullah Omar."

I had to wonder whether they were putting on a show for me or whether they were really that simple.

From Kandahar, I arranged for the Taliban to meet with the Americans at a hotel in Quetta, Pakistan on September 16, 2001. Again the officials from Afghanistan smuggled themselves into the country. And, of course, during our meeting with them in Quetta, the National Security Council listened to every word said. Our meeting even made CBS news the next evening.

The meeting between U.S. authorities and the Taliban lasted nine hours. It was a long, excruciating rehash of everything that had been agreed upon beforehand. The reason for this was that all previous meetings between the U.S.

and the current Afghan Government had been covert. For the first time, Afghan officials sent an official delegate, Osmani, to meet with the U.S. delegation.

Since Mullah Omar must be directly involved in any decision of magnitude, Osmani asked for a week to travel back and forth, to get Mullah Omar's approval for any action taken against bin Laden.

I sat there wondering why this step had not been taken before they had set off for this meeting and why they couldn't just call him. I knew that the telephone I had given them earlier couldn't be used because then questions would be asked about why they had it.

Ron, the Station Chief who headed the U.S. delegation, said to the Afghan official, "Sir, I don't have a week. You must hand Osama over to me now! Once I leave Quetta, it's all over."

Osmani reduced their requirement from a week to three days: two for travel, one to capture Osama. Sounded reasonable to me, after all I had firsthand knowledge of the state of their roads.

Then the U.S. reps suddenly demanded that bin Laden be delivered, "*NOW!!! WITHIN 24 HOURS!*"

I guess because of their anger, no one on the U.S. side seemed interested in the logistics involved in delivering NOW!!! *A man who had yet to be captured and who was buried somewhere deep in mountainous Afghanistan with an army at his side.*

Again Osmani said it would take three days, but Ron would not give him that much time.

One of the Afghans turned to the Station Chief and said, "You don't really want Osama. You've had *eleven months* to get him. Your intention is to destroy the Taliban and I can assure you, if you drop one bomb on Afghanistan, you will never find Osama, and if you are thinking of invading Afghanistan, you will face the same results as the British and the Soviets."

Then, as an afterthought he added, "Things like this will not stay secret. We dealt with you in good faith!" The religious man then paused and said, "And thank you for coming," as if the statement would cleanse his soul of the anger he must have felt toward the incompetent U.S. officials who were poised to destroy his country.

A few days before the U.S. bombing started on October 7, 2001, I met with the American Consulate General in the Marriott Hotel in Islamabad. I explained that the Taliban had recently asked me to convey that they agreed to an unconditional surrender of bin Laden to U.S. officials.

The official retorted, "I will convey your message, but I am afraid that the train has already left the station."

I received no response to the Afghan's complete capitulation to U.S. terms. When the bombings of Afghanistan by U.S. planes began, I flew back to Texas.

I returned to the U.S. reeking of defeat. I called Dan and explained to him how the meeting in Quetta had gone. He showed no interest whatsoever. He even took a malevolent tone with me that had not been there before the trip, a malevolence that I would experience many times in the next few years as an Afghan-American.

In Texas, Taliban officials called me daily. They begged me to return one more time.

I did. I owed them that.

I flew back to Islamabad in December of 2001, hoping against hope to establish some type of contact between the U.S. and the Taliban. I still had fantasies about bringing home peace and Afghan oil and gas. While in Islamabad I called the U.S. Embassy many times, but no one there would talk to me.

All negotiations failed and so we went to war. The first to suffer were the Taliban officials who had tried so hard to establish a rapport with us. One of the first American missiles fired zeroed in on the satellite phone that I had given the mullahs sympathetic to the U.S., but they had abandoned it in a field long before the missile struck. Some of these same mullahs were rounded up and put in prison in Afghanistan. Zaeef, who had been promoted to Ambassador to Pakistan, was even transported to the prison in Guantanamo.

I told Mutawakel to surrender to the American forces in Kandahar. He was held in that city until Fall 2003, when he was released. Last I heard, he still lives in Kandahar.

As to Osmani, Esa, Jalil, Ahmad Jan, and some of the others who tried so hard to help me, last I heard they were still alive. I guess they disappeared into the mountains of Afghanistan or the teeming cities of Pakistan and waited for saner times.

After the bombing began in October 2001, I received a call from Dan. He demanded the phone number of a Taliban representative so U.S. officials could speak with him directly.

Irritated I told him, "I don't have to do anything for you anymore, but I will find you a phone number out of a sense of duty." I gave Dan a number. I never heard why he called or what happened.

Security is the problem in Afghanistan now. You can't have oil pipelines or refineries or oil wells or even do much business as long as you've got pissed off people willing to shoot other people and blow things up.

I understand from the media that President Karzai has little control of anything that happens outside of Kabul and that locals refer to him as the "Mayor of Kabul" rather than the President of Afghanistan. The countryside belongs to the War Lords again.

It's amazing how everything has come full circle.

Since September 11th, time hung heavy on my hands. I am up to my armpits in debt, thus giving you some of the motivation behind this book. The other motivation is to let everyone know what happened – or almost didn't happen.

I keep asking myself whether I was naive during it all. Was the whole thing about power all along? Or, oil? Or, was it about arrogance in office? A lack of initiative? An inability to go out on a limb? To make a decision?

I intend to leave answers to those questions to others. All that remains is for me to ponder – after all that I've seen and done – and had done to me – Is life still good?

Epilogue

For the most part, Kabir and I lost contact after finishing the book. I turned to other writing projects and he continued trying to inform people about what happened in the negotiations between the U.S. and the Taliban for Osama bin Laden. Although interviewed in other countries by television shows comparable to *60 Minutes*, few in the United States gave him more than passing attention. (We are at war!) Nor would anyone publish our book. (Much too controversial!)

In 2004, Kabir was invited by Motley Rice, the attorneys representing the families of the 9/11, victims to their office in Mount Pleasant, South Carolina. He and his attorney, Garland "Mack" McInnis, traveled as their guests. Kabir was interviewed by the plaintiffs' attorneys about the events that transpired between Afghanistan and the U.S. He gladly answered all of their questions.

Also present in the lawyers' conference room were quiet, steely-faced men with stacks of photographs who listened closely to everything he said. They then asked him to provide names and titles for the people in the photos. He did as requested. Later he answered all questions asked him by the 9/11 Commission's investigators.

A quick telephone call sometime after his visit to South Carolina was the last time I talked with him, but I knew from the sound of his voice that the once smiling, funny, personable, driven Kabir was now a broken man. In 2007, he died of a massive coronary. Months after his memorial service, I was told of his death. I never had a chance to say goodbye. This is my chance.

L.M.

My Travel Plans My Travel Plans My Travel Plans My Travel Plans My Travel Plans

AMERICAN EXPRESS

Corporate Services

Generated On : 1/07/04 @ 01:45 PM

Record Locator : M9JEZY
Agent ID : TQ
Page : 1

28 Bridgeside Blvd - Mount Pleasant, SC 29464
Phone: (843) 216-9288 / Fax: (843) 216-9631

Account Name
MOTLEY RICE LLC
28 BRIDGESIDE BLVD
MT. PLEASANT SC 29464
FONE 843-216-9000
DEL14JAN

"Itinerary Only"

Travel arrangements
prepared exclusively for :
Garland McInnis

January 15, 2004 **Thursday**

DELTA AIR LINES Flight: **4923** Class - COACH Canadair RegionalJet **Seat : 09C**
OPERATED BY ATLANTIC SOUTHEAST
From : **Houston Hobby, TX** **DEPARTING AT 3:10 PM** Meal service Flight time: 01:10
To : **Dallas Ft Worth, TX** **ARRIVING AT 4:20 PM** 247 Miles
Arrival Terminal: E

DELTA AIR LINES Flight: **4494** Class - COACH Canadair RegionalJet **Seat : 05A**
OPERATED BY ATLANTIC SOUTHEAST
From : **Dallas Ft Worth, TX** **DEPARTING AT 5:30 PM** Meal service Flight time: 02:27
To : **Charleston, SC** **ARRIVING AT 8:57 PM** 987 Miles
Departure Terminal: E

DOUBLETREE
DOUBLETREE SUITES CHARLESTON
DOUBLETREE SUITES CHARLESTON
181 CHURCH STREET
CHARLESTON SOUTH CAROLINA 2940

Room reserved for: MCINNIS/GARLAND
Check in: 1/15/04, Check out: 1/17/04, 2 Nights
Rate per night : 129.00 USD
Confirmation #: 85226975

Late Arrival Guarantee - Credit Card
Phone #: 843 577-2644
Fax #: 843 577-2697

GUARANTEED LATE ARRIVAL. CANCEL 48 HOURS PRIOR
TO ARRIVAL-LOCAL HOTEL TIME

January 17, 2004 **Saturday**

DELTA AIR LINES Flight: **1894** Class - COACH MD Super 80 **Seat : 20C**
S SKYTEAM-CARING MORE ABOUT YOU
From : **Charleston, SC** **DEPARTING AT 1:10 PM** Meal service Flight time: 01:13
To : **Atlanta, GA** **ARRIVING AT 2:23 PM** 259 Miles
Arrival Terminal: S

DELTA AIR LINES Flight: **4729** Class - COACH Canadair RegionalJet **Seat : 08B**
OPERATED BY ATLANTIC SOUTHEAST
From : **Atlanta, GA** **DEPARTING AT 3:50 PM** Meal service Flight time: 02:25
To : **Houston Hobby, TX** **ARRIVING AT 5:15 PM** 696 Miles
Departure Terminal: S

APR-14-2004 05:14 PM P.02
NO.139 P.2/2

VIA FAX & MAIL

April 14, 2004

Mr. Kabir Mohabbat
12142 South Meadow Drive
Stafford, TX 77477

Dear Mohabbat:

The National Commission on Terrorist Attacks Upon the United States is directed by statute to investigate the facts and circumstances surrounding the September 11, 2001 terrorist attacks, including the nation's preparedness for, and immediate response to, those attacks, as well as to evaluate the lessons learned from those attacks and to make recommendations for preventing future attacks. As part of its investigation, the Commission hereby requests to interview you, on issues relating to your meetings with both the Taliban and the U.S. Government on the Usama Bin Ladin topic.

Scott Allan, counsel to the Commission, will make the arrangements for your interview. The Commission would like to conduct your interview over the phone. Please call [redacted] as soon as possible to discuss the time of your interview, and to raise any other questions you may have.

Thank you very much in advance for your time and for your cooperation with the Commission and its staff in this important matter.

Sincerely,

Philip Zelikow

Philip Zelikow
Executive Director

Washington, DC 20407

26 Federal Plaza
Suite 13-100
New York, NY 10278

About the Authors

M. Kabir Mohabbat was born in Kabul, Afghanistan. He was reared in a politically active Pashtun family. At 18 his family sent him to the United States for higher education. Only days before the Soviet Union invaded Afghanistan, Kabir graduated from Southeastern Missouri State University with a degree in Political Science. Soon thereafter, he left the U.S. to fight for Afghanistan as a mujahid. Years later he became a businessman in Houston, Texas. In the 1990's, when the U.S. State Department needed a bridge to the new Afghan government – the Islamic Emirate of Afghanistan (the Taliban) – Kabir volunteered to help.

L. McInnis holds a LL.M. and a Ph.D., Law, from Lancaster University in Great Britain.

Other Books Published by First Draft Publishing

I am Akbar Agha: Memories of the Afghan Jihad and the Taliban
Sayyed Mohammad Akbar Agha

Following in the tradition of Mullah Zaeef's My Life With the Taliban, Akbar Agha's memoir tells a story of war, friendship and political intrigue. Starting in 1980s Kandahar, the difficulties and successes of the mujahedeen come through clearly as Akbar Agha struggles to administer a group of fighters. He details the different groups fighting in Kandahar, their cooperation and the scale of the Soviet Union's efforts to crush them. Not directly a participant in the Taliban government that ruled post-1994, Akbar Agha offers a sometimes-critical account of the administration built by many of his former fighters. After the fall of the Islamic Emirate in

2001, Akbar Agha was involved in the Jaish ul-Muslimeen opposition group and for the first time he has revealed his account of what happened in the kidnapping of UN aid workers. I Am Akbar Agha ends with an analysis of the problems afflicting Afghanistan and outlines a vision for the political future of the country post-elections and post-2015. Anand Gopal has written an introduction to the book.

"Mandatory reading"

— Graeme Smith, Senior Analyst for Afghanistan

Kandahar Assassins: Stories from the Afghan-Soviet War
Mohammad Tahir Aziz Gumnam

Assassinations are a near-daily occurrence in Afghanistan. Whether by rogue Afghan security forces or by lone individuals roaming the cities and districts, the threat of a target killing is very real. Kandahar Assassins offers an unparalleled view of this phenomenon from the perspective of the assassins. Published in 1986 in Pashto and a perennial classic in Kandahar's bookstores, Kandahar Assassins tells the story of two well-known assassins who operated in the southern city during the 1980s war. The stories of 'Lame Ghazi' and Commander Ghaffari involve ambitious raids and plots carried out within the Afghan-controlled city. This book offers a corrective to the idea that assassination is a new phenomenon in Afghanistan. Mohammad Tahir Aziz Gumnam was a doctor working in Pakistan at the time, allowing him access to a variety of figures within the Afghan mujahedeen. Originally from Kandahar, Gumnam offers insight as an Afghan who was close to both the events and the people he describes. Judging from this book, the style and manner of assassinations in southern Afghanistan doesn't appear to have changed much. Kandahar Assassins, therefore, offers a unique perspective on the world of these target killers and how they carry out their operations. It is an essential read for any soldier serving in Afghanistan as well as those seeking to understand the history behind the current conflict. Dr David Kilcullen wrote the introduction to this English translation of the book.

"a Thousand-and-One Nights of the Afghan jihad... a detailed and lyrical account of the war that he and his contemporaries fought against in Kandahar during the 1980s"
— Dr David Kilcullen (from his introduction), counterinsurgency expert and author

An Undesirable Element: An Afghan Memoir
Dr Sharif Fayez

This is the incredible story of a relentless educator named Sharif Fayez, born in 1946 in Herat, Afghanistan, who bore witness to the Communist invasion of 1979, the Iranian revolution of 1979, and who authored a ground breaking PhD dissertation that forever linked the best American poetry to Afghanistan by proving that Walt Whitman had read and been inspired by Rumi. It is the story of how Sharif pursues education above all else and becomes a professor at Kabul University only to flee illegally to Iran when the Soviets invade, where he becomes caught in the violent Islamic revolution as a professor at Mashad University. Surviving the Afghan and Iranian governments' ruthless campaign to silence academics and their students, as well as the Iran-Iraq War, he becomes a prominent voice of resistance against the Taliban and extremism in the 1990s, writing hundreds of articles, and ultimately returns to Afghanistan as a signatory to the 2001 Bonn Conference and as the Minister of Higher Education. He completely overhauls the Afghan education system, restores co-education to the country and establishes six new universities. He is almost single-handedly responsible for the incredible strides the Afghan education system has made since 2002.

"An Undesirable Element is a fascinating tour through the tumultuous years that helped create modern Afghanistan. Fayez survived Soviet Afghanistan and revolutionary Iran, only to find himself watching from exile as his country devoured itself. Improbably, he returns after 2001 to help resurrect Afghanistan's devastated higher education system, giving an insider account of the challenges of building education in a land dominated by warlords and fundamentalism. The result is a poignant reminder of how much Afghanistan has endured, and the flicker of hope that remains despite it all."

— Anand Gopal, author of *No Good Men Among The Living*

"A compelling read, An Undesirable Element recounts an Afghanistan many have forgotten. It serves as a rallying cry to once again imagine all that country might be. It's a tale as extraordinary as the land from which it comes."

— Elliot Ackerman, author of *Green On Blue*

"An Undesirable Element moves fast as flames and offers a luminous account of the last half century of Afghan conflicts and redevelopment. Trevithick's oral history of Sharif Fayez's story is a trove: from a kiss on the head by the Afghan former King Zahir Shah, Fayez's life intersected with the future leaders and quiet supporters of his country—both heroic and tyrannical—from Columbia University to a Post-revolutionary University in Mashad, Iran. Fayez is a modest but robust storyteller whose eventual position as Afghanistan's first Minister of Education after the Taliban is only one of the strange twists and turns his story offers. His deft handling in the rebuilding of Afghanistan should be read by anyone interested in how one can use patience and determination to bring hope to a country reduced to rubble."

— Adam Klein, editor, *The Gifts of The State: New Afghan Writing*

"The term visionary tends to be misapplied to those who are merely headstrong. But it is a perfectly apt description for Sharif Fayez, the most important figure in education in 21st-century Afghanistan, yet one that history may have neglected without his memoir. Such an omission would have deprived future generations of Afghans from understanding how Fayez, perhaps more than any single person, created hope for the country's young minds at the turn of the millennium and, in so doing, altered a nation's destiny."

— Martin Kuz, Freelance journalist

Obedience to the Amir: An early Text on the Afghan Taliban Movement
Mufti Rasheed Ludhianvi

In the last year of the Taliban's government in Afghanistan, visitors to Mullah Omar's office in Kandahar received a parting gift. As they left, the movement's supreme leader asked them to take a slim volume from a pile beside the door. He told them that if they wanted to know how the Taliban were meant to behave, they should read the book. The books which Mullah Omar handed out were Pashto and Farsi translation of *Eta't Amir*, or 'Obedience to the Leader'. Mufti Rasheed published the original in Urdu after having toured Taliban-run Afghanistan. Mullah Omar's endorsement indicates that he believed that Rasheed had captured the essence of the Taliban Movement. Michael Semple and Yameema Mitha have translated this important primary source and added a commentary and appraisal.

"In war, and especially guerrilla war, the best organised party is likely to win. While numbers of fighters and weapons count, organisation determines whether the leader can use them. This book is the guide the Afghan Taliban used to organise themselves differently from other Afghan groups. Anyone who wants

to defeat them or negotiate with them should understand the organisational principles that guide them."

— Barnett R. Rubin, Center on International Cooperation, New York University.

Taliban: A Critical History from Within
Abdul Hai Mutma'in

Taliban: A Critical History from Within by Abdul Hai Mutma'in offers an inside account of the Afghan movement and their government. In his preface, the author notes that his book will please neither supporters of the Taliban nor those who fight and condemn them. It is this trenchant quality that makes it unique among the memoirs of those who used to work for and with the Taliban. Mutma'in's account often feels like a corrective, critical of those outside the Taliban but also of the movement itself. Whereas most books of this kind stop with the invasion of the United States in October 2001, Mutma'in shares the story of how the Taliban fled, how resistance was organised and how they grew into a potent insurgency force. Mutma'in's book is essential reading for anyone seeking to understand the Taliban and recent Afghan history.

www.ingramcontent.com/pod-product-compliance
Ingram Content Group UK Ltd.
Pitfield, Milton Keynes, MK11 3LW, UK
UKHW021933190726
13853UKWH00004B/1410

9 783944 214313